RELENTLESS
PURSUIT

RELENTLESS PURSUIT

The DSS and the Manhunt
for the al-Qaeda Terrorists

Samuel M. Katz 1963-

A Tom Doherty Associates Book   New York

RELENTLESS PURSUIT: THE DSS AND THE MANHUNT FOR THE
AL-QAEDA TERRORISTS

Copyright © 2002 by Samuel M. Katz

This book is printed on acid-free paper.

All photographs are reprinted by permission.

Unless otherwise noted, all photographs are by Samuel M. Katz.

Book design by Jane Adele Regina

A Forge Book
Published by Tom Doherty Associates, LLC
175 Fifth Avenue
New York, NY 10010

www.tor.com

Forge® is a registered trademark of Tom Doherty Associates, LLC.

ISBN 0-765-30402-3

First Edition: June 2002

Printed in the United States of America

0 9 8 7 6 5 4 3 2 1

This book is dedicated to Nancy "The Viking Queen" Gallagher and DSS Special Agent Vincent O. Martinez III, better known to the world as "Termite."

This book is also dedicated to the honored memory of my friends from the New York City Police Department's Emergency Service Unit and the Port Authority of New York/New Jersey Police killed on September 11, 2001. They were true American heroes.

Contents

SPECIAL AGENTS

The U.S. Department of State's Diplomatic Security Service, or "DSS," isn't an organization originally designed for or tasked with spearheading America's law enforcement battle with international terrorism. It isn't an enforcement agency that receives a lot of publicity or many accolades. In fact, few outside the State Department knew that the agency even existed, and many inside it didn't know, either.

The DSS is the law enforcement and security arm of the U.S. Department of State. As a law enforcement agency, DSS is responsible for investigating violations of the passport and visa laws of the United States and protecting the secretary of state and foreign dignitaries who visit the United States. As the security arm of the U.S. Department of State, the DSS has the responsibility for ensuring the safety of Americans serving their government abroad in embassies and consulates around the world.

The DSS traces its history to 1916 and the First World War. The State Department had existed since the American Revolution and the diplomatic missions of its first emissary, Benjamin Franklin, though the need to create a security arm for America's diplomatic corps arose only in the twentieth century during a war called by some "the curtain of history." The Central Powers, led by Germany, had established a center of espionage activity in New York. U.S. identity papers, forged or stolen, were crucial for German and Austrian spies attempting to

secrete themselves into Britain. In order to combat this new phenomenon of "identity fraud," President Woodrow Wilson authorized the
State Department and Special Assistant Secretary of State Robert Lan-
sing to establish a security arm that could combat the operations of
hostile espionage forces within the United States. The new organization was called the Bureau of Secret Intelligence; it primarily investigated German espionage operatives and "IDI," or infant death identity,
cases involving sleeper agents applying for birth certificates of infants
who had died at birth. Investigators, often former "specialists" working
for the White House and the Secret Service, were called "chief special
agents."

When the Congress looked at passing a new espionage statute limiting espionage by foreign countries within the borders of the United
States, it was discovered that the law would affect both British and
German espionage. The intent of the Congress was to limit German
espionage and turn a blind eye on similar British activities and,
therefore, the espionage statutes were not passed until after the United
States entered the war in 1917. But the Germans had discovered weak-
nesses in the isolationist Americans. German Naval Intelligence realized that the largest immigrant population in the United States was
German, and that fraudulent U.S. passports could be used to circum-
navigate British authorities. A Passport Bureau was even created within
the German Naval Intelligence Group. British counterintelligence was
stymied. They could not arrest every American with a German name
or accent who entered Britain. As the Department of State issued passports, it was logical to Congress that the State Department be authorized to create a force to investigate and apprehend these passport
violators. Congress saw this as a means to respond to the problem
without passing legislation that would call for equal enforcement.
Three investigators were transferred from the U.S. Secret Service, and
a director was recruited from the U.S. Postal Inspection Service.
Agents were recruited from the Secret Service because they were experienced in counterfeit documents. The director was recruited from
the postal inspectors, since the Postal Service had the best document
lab. Four special agents were assigned to New York City.

Two years later Congress passed legislation requiring passports for Americans traveling abroad and visas for aliens wishing to enter the United States—documentation issued by the State Department. Soon, the chief special agents began to widen the focus of their investigations to include passport and visa fraud cases. State Department special agents also began protecting foreign dignitaries visiting the United States. By the early 1920s, however, the entire force consisted of only twenty-five badge-carrying special agents.

During the Second World War, the office of security inside the State Department used its passport and visa fraud mandate to go after Nazi and Communist agents operating inside the country—primarily inside the ports of New York City. Investigations into fraudulent passports uncovered Soviet espionage rings that quickly provided law enforcement with an insight into the activities of the American Communist party. In-depth investigations of German espionage rings, often spearheading counterespionage operations run by J. Edgar Hoover's FBI, unraveled numerous sleeper cells operating along the northeastern shore of the United States and exposed the activities of pro-Nazi groups inside the country.

Following the end of the Second World War, the State Department's security apparatus required a complete overhaul of tasks and capabilities. A cohesive—and highly effective—Soviet-led espionage effort was waged inside the United States and overseas. In 1948, the new Office of Security, or "SY," was established. SY established a program for regional security staffs inside the United States and, for the first time, security officers for missions overseas. These two security functions would merge, as would an intelligence-gathering service. Later that year, the Marine Security Guard program was initiated at U.S. embassies around the world and supervised by SY.

The late 1960s and early 1970s brought a new concern to the special agents assigned to SY: the threat of terrorism. Between 1968 and 1981, a U.S. diplomat was targeted by terrorists nearly 100 times a year. Terrorists, including Palestinians and Croatians, also operated inside the United States, making SY's dignitary protection mandate all the more precarious. SY instituted what became known as the "Eagleburger Plan," an ambitious attempt to meet the threats domestically and overseas by hiring new agents and purchasing new vehicles, radios, and other support equipment. Many Foreign Service veterans inside the endless corridors of the State Department did not look kindly upon the more hands-on role assigned to the agents in the field and those overseas. The State Department had always held its security agents at a disdainful distance. Diplomats, especially old-hand veterans who were in their thirtieth year of service, did not believe that security and diplomacy could exist together in the same sentence, let alone the same massive bureaucracy in the old War Department building in Foggy Bottom. SY constantly had to battle to maintain the small number of agents it possessed, and the programs it managed and safeguarded.

There was reason for the Foreign Service elite to be wary of the security officers. SY investigated security and other, sometimes far more personal, infractions both at home and overseas. SY agents, if the violation was serious enough, could ruin a diplomat's career, or even put him behind bars.

The State Department attempted to minimize much of what SY did in those early years, and it certainly wanted the organization kept out of the limelight and, in the words of one agent, "operating in the stone age." The passport and visa fraud program, carried out through a series of SY field offices located in the major cities inside the United States, was a perfect example. Special agents investigating passport forgers, even those involved in weapons and narcotics smuggling, investigated cases in their own automobiles without lights and sirens, without police radios, and, most ominously, without weapons. Weapons, including shotguns and machine guns, were to be deployed only on dignitary protection assignments, but even then the rule of thumb was "low profile."

Hearts fluttered inside many an office in Foggy Bottom on January 3, 1979, when an AP photo, featured on page one of most national newspapers, showed Special Agent Walt Deering, assigned to the Los Angeles field office, and protecting the home of Princess Sham, the Shah of Iran's sister, aiming his .357 revolver at a mob of protesters trying to storm her mansion. Months later, Walt Deering received numerous accolades for his role in protecting Britain's Princess Margaret during a trip to Los Angeles while an Irish Republican Army assassin was known to be in California. But still, for an SY agent, being seen in a national newspaper with your weapon drawn was tantamount to career-ending suicide. Miraculously, many in SY thought, Deering managed to remain on the job.

SY remained a relatively obscure arm of federal law enforcement until the early 1980s, when American embassies in the Middle East began to disappear in clouds of smoke and the fury of suicide bombers' trucks laden with a half ton of TNT. Between 1979 and 1984, there were nearly 100 terrorist attacks against Americans—American embassies were torched, blown up, and seized, and some 300 American citizens killed. In 1984, Secretary of State George Shultz formed an advisory panel to make recommendations on how to minimize the probability of terrorist attacks on U.S. citizens and facilities. This commission, headed by retired U.S. Navy Admiral Bobby Inman, would initiate sweeping reforms, starting with, on November 4, 1985, the creation of the Diplomatic Security Service.

By the mid-1990s, the DSS consisted of nearly 1,200 special agents working in twenty-two domestic field offices and some 152 embassies and consulates around the world. The special agents have traveled to Pakistan, Nigeria, Egypt, and the jungles of Colombia to bring to justice wanted terrorists, drug czars, organized crime kingpins, and serial murderers, although the U.S. Marshals Service and the FBI have often taken much of the credit and glory when high-profile criminals are brought off long-distance flights in shackles. Even though the DSS has thwarted an astounding twenty-two assassinations in progress, eighteen of them overseas, when most Americans think of bodyguards, the U.S. Secret Service comes to mind. The DSS has been the lead investigative agency in hundreds of organized crime prosecutions of narcotics smugglers, child pornographers, illegal alien and white slavery rings, and espionage agents, though credit for the arrests have often gone to the U.S. Customs Service, the Immigration and Naturalization Service, and the Drug Enforcement Administration. DSS special agents have been involved in wild shootouts overseas involving assassins, psychos, coups, and revolutions; they have evacuated embassies in nations on the verge of collapse, and pulled out the bodies of their comrades in embassies that have collapsed in the destructive wake of a suicide bomber. They've debriefed hostages released in the Middle East, and they've protected Princess Diana in the United States. They are America's cops overseas and, according to one supervisor in the New York City Police Department's Emergency Service Unit, "the best kept secret in American law enforcement."

The work is incredibly diverse—and demanding. According to one veteran special agent, in a lament written for a State Department publication,

> I've been around the world twice and spoke to everybody at least once. I've walked thousands of miles in the corridors of the State Department, rings of the Pentagon, and hallways of twenty-four embassies, seven consulate generals, nine consulates, four consular agencies, fifteen American centers, and five field offices—and only got lost once. I've shook hands with presidents, prime ministers, foreign ministers, congressmen, the Pope, a shah, guys wearing medals, guys wearing guns, guys carrying spears and Joe Montana. I've been to a three-sheet mezza, two high teas, and McDonald's on every continent in the world. I've walked among wild beasts in Africa, waded in four oceans, climbed pyramids in Mexico, Egypt and Iraq, and ripped my pants in Baltimore. I've flown on a DC-3 and Boeing 727 and Ugandan Airlines. I've been in two embassy bombings, three civil wars, a coups d'état, and some very wild embassy and State Department parties. Drank a thousand kinds of beer, some stuff from bottles with no labels, stuff from bottles with the wrong labels, and only got sick twice. I've heard country and western music sung by Bavarians, Koreans, Turks, Pakistanis, Iranians, Indians, Bolivians, Brazilians and some rednecks from Maryland. I've been shot at twice, investigated more terrorist and crime stuff than a TV hero, and even got to work as the second best secret agent in the whole world![1]

And, an agent can find himself in Osama bin Laden's backyard, in Tashkent, Uzbekistan, attempting to keep the secretary of state alive and the protective detail one step ahead and well out of range of the assassins.

BADGES WITHOUT BORDERS AGAINST AN ENEMY WITHOUT FRONTIERS

Backstop, Backstop. Fullback signal. . . . Fireball departure, en route fairground, advise advance."

"Backstop copies departure, will advise advance."

The voice barking news of the motorcade's departure was hoarse from the numerous journeys and the exhausting schedule. There had been the flight from Dulles to Frankfurt, the layover, and then the flight to Kiev, followed by forty-eight hours of nonstop protection work. And then, of course, there was the next stop—east—to the danger zone and the flight on Uzbekistan Air to Tashkent. A long journey suddenly seemed all that much longer. Washington, D.C., was so far away.

For Diplomatic Security Service Special Agent Tom Gallagher, wearing his signature dark Polo suit and clutching an M4 5.56mm carbine inside the GMC Suburban follow car shined to a shimmering black, giving in to exhaustion just couldn't be part of the equation on the sunny afternoon of April 17, 2000, on the tarmac of Tashkent International Airport. Secretary of State Madeleine Albright's U.S. Air Force 757 had just touched down in Uzbekistan's capital, and the motorcade for the four-mile haul north toward the city center would be a precarious one. Gallagher was the motorcade's shift leader.

For the last four years he had served in "SD," or Secretary's Detail, the force of agents assigned to the secretary of state's protective detail, first as a "hump agent," and then as a shift leader. Service in SD was not an easy assignment for a Diplomatic Security Service, or DSS, agent. Earlier in his career, while protecting Secretary of State Warren

Christopher during his trips to the Middle East, Europe, and South America, Gallagher was overseas approximately 50 percent of the year sitting inside planes, standing outside hotels, and carrying a gun outside palaces, foreign ministries, and a myriad of other venues. Service in SD meant that an agent could be in the darkest hole of Africa in the morning, sweating in a 110°F swelter, and then, by night, checking in to a hotel in Moscow, shivering from the cold and the fatigue, only to be ready the following morning to meet and greet the secretary of state's aircraft at Sheremetyevo International Airport after another night in a strange hotel, on cold sheets, in a country and time zone too far from home.

Life for a special agent assigned to SD protecting a secretary of state was hard. Protecting Madeleine Albright raised the challenge to a new level. Secretary of State Madeleine Albright believed that promoting American foreign policy required America's chief diplomat be on the move and accessible in the capital cities of the world. Secretary Albright was constantly on the go and so was her detail—traveling to hundreds of cities around the world.

Gallagher had been on virtually all of Albright's visits during her four years in the Clinton administration, and he had been to some of the world's most dangerous places. The agents assigned to a particular detail, especially those on a team working a shift together, managed the fear, the jet lag, the food poisoning, discomfort, homesickness, and fatigue by becoming a team. The agents lived with one another more than they did with their own families. Birthdays were often celebrated on a long-distance phone call, birth announcements came via e-mail, and anniversaries were remembered with gifts, sometimes bought in a flash at an airport duty-free counter, then shoved inside a FedEx envelope.

Up until a few years earlier, a U.S. secretary of state wouldn't even have visited Uzbekistan. The ancient cradle between the Amu-Darya and Syr-Darya rivers, Uzbekistan is the most historically fascinating of the Central Asian republics, and home of the famed Silk Road and Samarkand. It is a land of conquest and war. First it was conquered by Alexander the Great, then by Genghis Khan, and then by the Persians. The last of the modern invaders to stake a claim to the ancient Silk

Road was Russia, a growing empire that by the nineteenth century had conquered all of Central Asia. During the Soviet era, Moscow used Uzbekistan for its tremendous cotton-growing and natural-resource potential; Soviet inefficiency led to the shrinkage of the Aral Sea to half its former volume. Uzbekistan declared independence on September 1, 1991. Islam Karimov, former First Secretary of the Communist Party, was elected president three months later. As a buffer in Central Asia, Uzbekistan became one of the strategic countries most important to America's interests following the end of the Cold War. Its geographic position, bordering all the former Soviet republics, made it vital to U.S. foreign policy. Its geographic proximity to Afghanistan, just across the border to the south past the town of Termiz, was what made it volatile.

Nearly 90 percent of the population of Uzbekistan is Muslim. The Islamic Movement of Uzbekistan, or IMU, has used bombings, kidnappings, and assassinations to try and achieve a Talibanlike fundamentalist Islamic state not only in all of Uzbekistan, but in all of former Soviet Central Asia, including Kazakhstan, Kyrgyzstan, Tajikistan, Turkmenistan, and even in China's Xinjiang province. The group's early attacks focused solely on Uzbek targets, including a lethal bombing campaign in Tashkent in February 1999, though their scope has expanded and recent operations have been closer to the Uzbek-Kyrgyz border in order to widen the conflict.

What raised so much concern in the minds of Gallagher and the special agents on the detail was the fact that the IMU was a Central Asian arm of Osama bin Laden's pan-Islamic "al-Qaeda" terrorist network. The IMU had training camps in Afghanistan alongside bin Laden's forces, and the group was financed and supported by bin Laden's Arab, Chechen, Sudanese, and Filipino volunteers. For Osama bin Laden, based only several hundred miles to the south of Tashkent, a visiting secretary of state would make a tempting target. The State Department's Diplomatic Security Service had, in 1995, seized Ramzi Yousef, a trusted lieutenant of Osama bin Laden and mastermind of the 1993 World Trade Center bombing in New York, in the Pakistani capital. The State Department had placed a two-million-dollar reward on bin Laden's head, and bin Laden's suicidal soldiers in the field had destroyed two U.S. embassies in East Africa. Secretary of State Albright, true to her character as someone who did not mince words, had assailed bin Laden as the world's most insidious terrorist. Osama bin Laden's alliance with the IMU, and their brotherhood with the ruling Taliban in Afghanistan, meant trouble. The fabled Silk Road that had once been used to transport spices and emeralds to Europe had become the hub of bin Laden and his transnational terrorist army.

Was bin Laden's organization plotting to assassinate the American secretary of state inside Uzbekistan? Were the cells of IMU operatives, faithful proponents of the global jihad, hiding in safe houses in the ancient Eski Shakhar section of the city, in a *madrassa*, or religous school, in a cellar where young students were taught the Koran when it was outlawed by Soviet authorities? Were they going to try to hit the secretary's motorcade with small arms and RPGs, or would a suicide bomber disguised as an onlooker rush a venue where Albright was answering reporters' questions? DSS agents did not doubt the resolve of bin Laden to kill Mrs. Albright. They were adamant about not underestimating the means.

When Gallagher and his jump team landed in Uzbekistan, they were met by advance agents from the U.S. embassy in Tashkent to expedite them through passport control and customs. They rushed to a command post, ready to hear the latest intelligence reports, review the secretary's upcoming routes and sites, and meet and greet their counterparts in the Uzbek NSS, or National Security Service, the internal-security, intelligence-gathering secret police that had replaced the KGB inside the country. The local police might be corrupt and ineffective, but the NSS was quite the opposite. The Uzbeks were no-nonsense and, when necessary, brutal. "They were large, wearing cheap suits and carrying big Soviet-era handguns. They had gold teeth though they rarely smiled," remembered one agent assigned to the April 16, 2000, detail in Tashkent. "They took their mission seriously."[1] One of his liaison agents from the NSS was right out of Hollywood central casting. "His handshake was like gripping iron, and he smiled at you with a big gold tooth and he sized you down with a barrel chest that said 'don't fuck with me!' These guys meant business."[2] The DSS advance agents, and the jump team that crisscrossed the globe to be ready in time for the secretary's arrival, knew they would receive unlimited support from the NSS.

The Uzbeks wanted the fundamentalist operatives off the streets until the secretary of state had left the country, and many of the known IMU activists had been detained just prior to Albright's arrival. Gallagher was confident that the local authorities would do just that. But Tashkent was a big place, an ancient city of two million inhabitants with a reputation of maintaining its independence invader after invader. It was an easy city to hide in.

Before the secretary's motorcade was due to arrive, Gallagher checked in with the advance DSS team that had been preposted to Tashkent over a week before. The advance agents had gotten to know their local counterparts and had met frequently with the DSS RSO, or regional security officer, in the embassy. They had reviewed the security details for the sites, the venues, and the hotel in exhaustive detail. They knew where the exits were to any location the secretary would visit, and they knew where the restrooms were, too. The advance agents had mapped out motorcade routes and had charted the shortest possible course to hospitals or other locations should an attack on the motorcade injure the detail's principal. Most importantly, they had been in-country long enough to get a feel for the mood of the city and the competence of the local authorities. Already, in the days prior to Albright's arrival, police were restricting the movement of local residents in Tashkent, and were closing off roads to traffic, and conducting frequent document, vehicle, and personal identification checks at hastily set-up roadblocks throughout the town.

What bothered Gallagher and the rest of the team was Uzbekistan's porous and indefensible border with Afghanistan. Smugglers have, for centuries, wandered across invisible boundaries selling everything from sheep and blankets to heroin and Russian F-1 fragmentation grenades. It would not be difficult for the IMU or al-Qaeda to smuggle a hit team across the border and to position them somewhere near the city. To augment the detail's ability to fight off an attack, the secretary of state's motorcade would be supported by a Tactical Support Team from the DSS Mobile Security Division, a select group of commando-trained cops whose mission was to deflect any armed attack *away* from the motorcade. Wearing battle fatigues and Kevlar body armor, and trained in all aspects of special operations warfare, the MSD Tactical Support Team was a ballistic punch designed to eradicate any threat to the secretary with an unforgiving fusillade of gunfire. The heavily armed operators wearing body armor sporting American flags and Velcro patches that said POLICE: FEDERAL AGENT looked odd against the backdrop of the ancient Silk Road. But looks were irrelevant. Results were all that mattered when the enemy was Osama bin Laden and his legion of terrorists. The jump team and the detail in Tashkent knew that gunfire could erupt at any moment; an assassination attempt would be violent and bloody.

They had heard the tales from Africa when, in June 1995, a motorcade including U.S. ambassador to Burundi Robert Krueger was ambushed on an isolated stretch of road in Cibitoke, a lush mountain region in the northwest corner of the country, by gunmen firing AK-47 assault rifles. The ambush was at close range and unforgiving in its ferocity. The two DSS special agents assigned to the embassy, Chris Reilly and Larry Salmon, had managed to return fire and maneuver the targeted vehicles out of the kill zone. *Would what happened in Burundi happen here?* Gallagher thought as he reviewed motorcade plans and made final preparations with his counterparts in the NSS. *Would they be able to get the principal out of the kill zone in time?*

FOR THE MOTORCADE, A LONG STRETCH OF UZBEK POLICE CARS AND MOtorcycles, followed by an armored limousine, follow cars, MSD counter-assault vehicles, staff cars, and more police cars and motorcycles, fired up their engines the moment the secretary's aircraft taxied to the staging area on the tarmac. Gallagher was happy to see the secretary—as well as his friends on the detail—but this was showtime, and the four-mile route to the hotel was a minefield of possible threats, as the motorcade commenced its lights-and-sirens journey out of the airport and through the twisting mountain roads.

"*Motorcycle left,*" shouted one of the agents as she clutched her M4 carbine, ready to return fire in a flash. "*Motorcycle left, copy,*" replied the follow car's driver, transfixed on the road ahead in case there was an attack on the long convoy of speeding cars, and looking at the Uzbek police motorcycle cop racing ahead to close off an entry ramp to the main artery into Tashkent. *Where are they going to hit us?* one of the agents thought as he scanned the virgin terrain for any threats and monitored a flurry of radio activity.

Uzbek police and secret service agents had literally shut down Tashkent to safeguard Secretary of State Albright's arrival. All cars and pedestrians were banned from a zone established from the airport to the Intercontinental Hotel. The American embassy was also quarantined to prepare for the secretary of state's arrival, as was the Presidential Palace. As the motorcade progressed through the vacated streets of the city, agents sitting inside the follow car scanned rooftops, looking for snipers, and geared up for action at every junction, expecting a standoff attack to be initiated by improvised explosive devices.

The long motorcade, a long snake of black limousine and GMC Suburbans, pressed hard through the outskirts of Tashkent toward the hotel without incident. But the visit had only just begun.

The two days in Tashkent in April 2000 were but a brief forty-eight hours of nonstop feverish activity surrounding Madeleine Albright in a part of the world where ancient hatreds and transnational movements combined to form an alliance of violence. The special agents assigned to the Uzbekistan detail did not relent for their time in-country. Some of the special agents were native New Yorkers and had served in the DSS New York field office when the World Trade Center was bombed seven years earlier, in 1993. Others had previously been assigned to the U.S. embassies in Beirut, Cairo, Tel Aviv, Islamabad, and Mogadishu to respond to potential attacks. And some had conducted post-blast investigations in Saudi Arabia following two bombings that had targeted U.S. servicemen in the oil-rich kingdom in 1995 and 1996. Still others had been dispatched to East Africa following the twin suicide truck bombings of the U.S. embassies in Nairobi and Dar es Salaam. They had waded through the blood-soaked rubble to look for survivors and to secure those still alive. Some of the agents had donned body armor and grabbed MP5 submachine guns to kick in doorways, in both Nairobi and Pakistan, in order to seize those responsible for the bloody embassy attacks.

The sizable force of special agents* protecting the secretary of state in Uzbekistan had been briefed with the latest intelligence reports on the desires—and capabilities—of terrorists to target America's interests and dignitaries inside the United States and especially around the world. The latest intelligence data, most of it top secret, was a terse and daunting reminder of Osama bin Laden's lethal capabilities inside Uzbekistan. The service's Office of Intelligence and Threat Analysis sent agents to Tashkent to comb through the latest reports of Osama bin Laden's activities in Uzbekistan, as well as any word from Uzbek intelligence agents planted inside al-Qaeda. Special agents from DSS assigned to PII, or protective intelligence investigations, would don local garb and linger along motorcade routes, to provide that added edge from the inside.

DSS spared little expense or effort when preparing for international trips. Overseas was the DSS specialty, after all. The world was their precinct.

In the forty-eight hours that Madeleine Albright was in Tashkent, the agents assigned to her detail faced several gut-thumping moments where the DSS penchant for adaptation, improvisation, and doing a lot with little would come in handy. Besides visiting with the Uzbek president and foreign minister, Albright's visit to the contested hub of Central Asia was a goodwill mission—an expression of friendship and appreciation of Uzbekistan's worth as a land with enormous natural resources and as a nation caught on the minefield of history, trapped in an epic struggle against the forces of a fundamentalist religious underground.

In the Uzbek capital Albright visited the famed Kukeldash Medressa, a grand sixteenth-century academy of Islamic thought, and the fifteenth-century Jami mosque. Both the school and the mosque had, in the past, been used as pulpits for fundamentalist thought, and here,

---

*The exact number of special agents assigned to a specific detail is classified top secret.

on one sunny morning in April, America's chief diplomat was walking through classrooms and the imam's office. The madrassa and the mosque were across the street from one another. Agents, quickly grabbing their M4 carbines, were forced to improvise to create a safe corridor for Albright where she would be protected from sniper fire. Talking into the hand-triggered radios that were looped through their shirtsleeves into the smalls of their backs, the agents instructed the bulletproof vehicles in the convoy to swing back and block entrances and exits to the alleyways around the sites and instructed their team to cover the high ground and rooftops, where a sniper might be hiding.

The forty-eight hours were loaded with endless meetings, cocktail parties, and state dinners. DSS special agents assigned to the detail saw the trip through tired eyes and on aching feet. The secretary's trip to Tashkent concluded with a high-threat, no-nonsense motorcade to the airport. Nighttime moves were always precarious. Many of the IMU operatives were veterans of the Afghanistan wars, and night operations were an al-Qaeda specialty. Darkness bred cover, and cover created opportunity. In the former Soviet Republic of Georgia in August 1995, guerrillas had staged a coordinated assassination attempt on the life of President Eduard Shevardnadze by assaulting his motorcade at night with antitank rockets and small arms in the capital city of Tbilisi.

Albright's motorcade left the gray bleakness of Tashkent for the quick ride to her awaiting Air Force 757 and additional legs of the trip to Central Asia. The DSS jump team secured the aircraft up until the wheels lifted off the tarmac runway and the aircraft was airborne. Squads of uniformed Uzbek cops swarmed the shut-down airport in search of potential threats. The ceremony at the airport was brief. Albright boarded her aircraft and, in a matter of moments, it taxied toward its priority takeoff position. The MSD contingent, out of their Suburban and aiming their weapons at the countryside beyond the airport fence, gently caressed the triggers of their assault rifles, ready for, perhaps, an assassin's last chance to strike the U.S. secretary of state. "Wheels up," the moment when the principal's aircraft takes off and departs local airspace, was just before midnight.

Wheels up also means an end to the detail for most of the special agents assigned to the jump team. There are a few hours to drink in the hotel bar, grab a bite, and let off some pent-up anxiety. The agents bend their elbows and attempt to see which war story, the one about the firefight in Liberia or the bar girls in Beirut, is worse, and they exchange gossip and the other rudimentary bullshit that cops, no matter what their badges look like, and no matter which part of town they serve and protect, are such experts in. But the laughs and the beers are a temporary respite. The next morning the agents will be checking out of their hotel, rushing to an airport, and heading to the next destination on their itinerary. Some will travel elsewhere in Central Asia. Some will work an advance in the Middle East. Others will return home to Washington, D.C. Their job doesn't end.

America's war against terrorism hasn't ended either. Since 1985 DSS has been in the vanguard of America's bloody war against a never-ending litany of terrorist armies. It has been a global campaign waged with sacrifice and fortitude in a struggle where America's national security has been challenged. It is a challenge the agency accepted with pride and with vigor. After all, one DSS motto is, "All that is necessary for the triumph of evil is for good men to do nothing!"

Chapter 1

SIGNPOSTS ALONG THE ROAD

*"Fight in the cause of Allah those who fight you,
but commit no aggression; for Allah loves not transgressors."*
(THE KORAN: AL-BAQARAH 2:190)

Darkness hit the streets of Manila early that January evening. A cool Pacific breeze shuffled the plush green leaves of the acacia trees, creating a slow and sweeping sound of soothing splendor that was interrupted only by the eardrum-shattering honking of Manila traffic. Pedestrian traffic on Buendia Avenue was sparse on the night of Saturday, January 19, 1991, in front of the Thomas Jefferson Cultural Center, the U.S. government's library attached to the U.S. embassy. A good old-fashioned war was being waged in the desert wastelands of the Middle East, and American and British warplanes were lobbing some of the world's most sophisticated ordnance at Saddam Hussein's all-the-weapons-petrodollars-could-buy army. Operation Desert Storm was a TV war—one waged lived via satellite on CNN twenty-four hours a day. Evening in Manila was late morning in the Gulf, and the generals always had a rousing press conference before lunch in Saudi Arabia. Buendia Avenue was an American enclave. Most of the residents were home in front of their 21-inch Sony Trinitrons having a Budweiser and watching a war.

The two men walking slowly on the avenue toward the Thomas Jefferson Cultural Center that evening were also interested in the war, though they were participants in the conflict—not spectators. Built like linebackers—if the NFL had had a franchise in Baghdad, that is—both men sported olive complexions and nervous body language. They

25

looked out of place on the avenue, even taking great care to parallel park their small Japanese-made sedan, which was something few in the Philippines bothered to do. As the two men walked side by side toward the entrance of the library, they disappeared in the bright glare from floodlights that had been rushed to the location only a day earlier to enhance security. Both men squinted into the powerful white beams of light and realized that the uniformed guards at the library would certainly be able to see them. So they decided to act. The larger of the two men, Ahmed J. Ahmed, carried a large canvas bag containing a powerful bomb. When he attempted to set the device's timer in the dark, using a ten-cent butane lighter for illumination, he set the timer backward instead of forward, initiating a blinding flash of light and an overwhelming wind of heat that explosively cracked through the Pacific night with the might of thunder. Ahmed was torn to shreds by the powerful bomb, made of PETN, a rubbery high-explosive agent.* The heat of the blast vaporized his clothes and skin, and the force of the explosion tore apart his head, his limbs, and his extremities and flung them fifty yards away. But because Ahmed was so big, he was able to absorb enough destructive power from the explosion to spare the life of his partner, Sa'ad Kadhim. Kadhim was not spared completely, however. When Ahmed disintegrated into pink mist and bone fragments, much of the Iraqi became embedded in his partner's muscular frame. He was burned over a fair portion of his body, and the destructive concussion wave that removed oxygen from his lungs and battered his head like two giant metal hands clapping made him twist and writhe in absolute agony. A taxi driver saw Kadhim walking around in a daze of pain and sped him to Makati Medical Center, one of the finest hospitals in all Manila.

SPECIAL AGENT BRENDON PAT O'HANLON, THE DIPLOMATIC SECURITY Service regional security officer, or RSO, at the U.S. embassy in Manila, knew that a building like the Thomas Jefferson Cultural Center

---

*Investigators believe that the PETN device was smuggled into Manila through the diplomatic pouch of the Iraqi embassy in Manila, located down the street from the targeted U.S. library.

would be hit. A veteran of America's most vulnerable hotspots overseas, from Saigon to Cairo and a dozen desolate stops in between,
O'Hanlon was a robust, barrel-shaped man who just knew that once
the bombs began to fall over Baghdad, bombs would be used against
American diplomatic posts and facilities overseas. Saddam Hussein
had no choice but to resort to terrorism, O'Hanlon warned at embassy crisis management meetings with the ambassador and other
Foreign Service personnel. And the only place that Saddam could
strike, O'Hanlon ventured to guess, was Europe, where there was a
strong Middle East terrorist network already in place, or in Asia, in a
country like the Philippines, where many Middle Easterners worked
and studied. DSS special agents are taught from their first day out of
training to be resourceful and to seize the initiative. Good agents, instructors in the training branch insist, must trust their gut instincts
and follow their hunches. A sixth sense told O'Hanlon that the Philippines, *his post*, was one of the Asian posts that were going to be hit.[1]
Special Agent Mike Evanoff, one of O'Hanlon's deputies, realized the
severity of the attack when he reached the bomb scene along with assistant RSO Mike Young. The mangled pieces of Ahmed's corpse were
spread throughout the area, with the torso left smoldering inside a
three-foot crater. The street was awash with the unforgettable stench
of blood and smoldering iron. The bomb had been a big one and, if
strategically placed, could have killed dozens of innocent people.
Searching through the bloody mess, Evanoff was able to uncover what
looked like a bank passbook. It was, in fact, an Iraqi passport caked by
blood and tissue specks, issued in the name of Ahmed J. Ahmed, passport number 072203.

AHMED AND KADHIM WERE NO STRANGERS TO THE THOMAS JEFFERSON
Cultural Center. The two had already paid a visit to the library a few
days earlier to, in the RSO's words, "case the joint for attack." The
library was usually crowded with university students and Manila residents simply interested in going through the *New York Times* on mi-
crofilm. To prevent a possible bombing attack, the RSO's office went
to great pains to ensure that no one was allowed into the building with

a bag or a briefcase, and that no Middle Eastern visitors would be allowed entry into the building, even those with valid college ID cards. "We told the guards to do thorough checks on anyone trying to come into the building," O'Hanlon remembered, "even if it meant checking them for hemorrhoids!" O'Hanlon had good reason for concern. A few days earlier, Iraqi terrorists had tossed an explosive device into the garden of the U.S. embassy in Jakarta, Indonesia. The bomb, a fairly sophisticated device by local Indonesian anarchist standards, had failed to detonate. But still, the failed bombing had sent a wave of heightened awareness throughout U.S. diplomatic facilities in the Far East.

The two Middle Eastern men were physically searched when they entered the building, and their bags received meticulous scrutiny. Although the contracted security guard did not want to let the two Arab men inside the building, Pat O'Hanlon ran with his gut instinct and gave the OK—*If these were the bad guys,* O'Hanlon thought, *let me give them an inch of rope so that they can hang themselves.* Their student IDs were photocopied and both men, venturing inside the library ostensibly to do research, stood nervously by the Xerox machine scanning the security arrangements and looking at emergency exits. Both young men possessed Jordanian passports and Palestinian identity cards, though in the Middle East, those were as easy to come by as a falafel and a bottle of 7-Up. Their paperwork looked genuine, but somehow suspicious. A Hercules Team, or countersurveillance guards from the indigenous Filipino force that protected the outside of the embassy, monitored their every move and even followed them outside the door. The two men stood watch over the facility for nearly fifteen minutes before disappearing into the congested streets of Manila, walking nervously toward a bustling intersection and a row of shops.

Pat O'Hanlon and his crew of assistant RSOs knew that it was only a matter of time before the library or the embassy would be attacked, so when the DSS special agents learned of the explosion outside the library that Saturday night, it did not spark surprise. The photocopied IDs taken at the library were run against U.S. law enforcement criminal databases, as well as against the records of the Philippines Bureau of Investigations. The photocopies were also run to friendly embassies, whose countries might have an interest in—and records of—Middle

Eastern terrorists active in Asia. O'Hanlon and his staff also went to
their contacts in the local police departments—Manila had several
agencies vying for control of the city—as well as to their local foreign
service national investigators, or FSNIs, for help. With the cooperation
of the local power company, all streetlights surrounding the library
were shut and powerful searchlights, the kind used at POW camps,
directed out toward the street. "Anyone looking at the building was
immediately blinded by the bright light," O'Hanlon recalled, "but we
could see out." The Diplomatic Security Service Command Center in
Washington, D.C., had been alerted through an urgent telegram that
U.S. facilities were likely to be hit. It was just a matter of time until
the trigger was pulled, or the fuse lit. A few minutes after 6:00 P.M. on
the night of January 19, the phone rang inside the RSO's office at the
embassy.

Cops live by their hunches, and O'Hanlon trusted his sixth sense.
Upon hearing reports that one man, possibly a Caucasian, had been
rushed to a hospital, the RSO ordered Evanoff to Makati Medical Center to start his search for a wounded man. The emergency room was
its typical chaos that Saturday evening—Manila drivers were quite
good at hitting pedestrians and one another and keeping the emergency room doctors and nurses busy twenty-four hours a day. In a
ward reserved for trauma care, Evanoff came across a small army of
policemen, cordoning off the area where the badly burned Middle
Eastern male was being cared for. O'Hanlon had always told Evanoff
that he should carry his credentials and DSS gold shield *wherever* he
went in Manila. "The cops run the streets of the city," O'Hanlon told
his deputy. "Your badge might just get you through a jam or a situation
when being a cop might be helpful." Evanoff flashed his tin at the
Manila cops, but they were adamant about denying him access to the
Iraqi. DSS agents are taught to improvise and adapt, so Evanoff offered
one of the policemen "special assistance" with a tourist visa application
at the embassy. The Filipino cop happily accepted the bargain. Evanoff
sifted through the Iraqi's effects, including his passport, and looked
over the badly injured man. Kadhim must have thought that the DSS
special agent was a doctor, because he grabbed his white polo shirt and
handed him a crumpled-up piece of paper with a Manila telephone

number scribbled on it. Evanoff called the number in to O'Hanlon, who ran it against files for possible hits on the embassy's system. The telephone number came back gold. It was the telephone exchange for the security office at the Iraqi embassy.

News of an Iraqi connection to the failed bombing suddenly became a matter of life and death to the RSO's office. What targets could be next? How many teams of bombers were out and about in Manila? Filipino police rushed to the U.S. embassy immediately, as well as to the homes of the diplomatic community, to cordon off all access to traffic. *We have to speak to this guy*, O'Hanlon thought. *We need to find out what his people are up to.*

U.S. intelligence assets in the embassy were also mobilized immediately following the bombing, though much to O'Hanlon's surprise, nobody at the embassy spoke Arabic. Using his New York charm and calling in a few favors, O'Hanlon located an Arabic speaker who could help interrogate the wounded Iraqi as he assembled an investigative team to uncover what was left of the network in Manila.

Passport and visa fraud is the service's criminal bread and butter, and O'Hanlon took an immediate interest in the wounded man's travel papers. Both Ahmed and Kadhim's passports—travel papers on thin cheap paper that looked like they were made in a Baghdad printing press—were sequential. The passports were completely in Arabic—no French or English, as with Syrian or Jordanian passports—and they appeared to be brand new. The documents were special editions from the Iraqi intelligence services; it was as if the teams sent overseas to carry out terrorist operations had received a special batch fresh off the presses.

Both Ahmed and Kadhim also had airline tickets in their immediate possession—both for flights from Manila to Bangkok later that evening.

Even before O'Hanlon could get back to the embassy and send out an urgent cable to the command center, Evanoff, in a resourceful style that would have made his DSS instructors proud, managed to find a contact who was able to produce, in record time, a copy of the Philippines immigration entry roster. The roster highlighted every Arab male who entered the Philippines since August 4, 1990, two days after Iraq's invasion of Kuwait. The deputy security officer looked at the two Iraqi passports and then checked them against the computer print-out. There were a total of six similar Iraqi passport holders who had entered the Philippines recently; four of them had already left the country on flights to Thailand earlier that week. Only the Mutt and Jeff bombers were still in the country.

Realizing that a major Iraqi terrorist cell was operating in Asia, possibly one belonging to Iraq's *al-Istikhbarat al-Askariyyalon,* or Military Intelligence, O'Hanlon rushed back to the embassy to send a "flash" cable to Washington and to his fellow RSOs stationed in embassies around Asia. In the coded world of top-secret communications, a flash was a message indicating war was imminent, and O'Hanlon, as the RSO, was not authorized to send it. But with Irish brash and the urgency of a cop determined to get the word out, the RSO's office in Manila informed Washington, D.C., and every embassy from Islamabad to Seoul that there were teams of agents maneuvering through Asia tasked with targeting American embassies and installations.

The next morning, on a warm January morning in Bangkok, a man walked into the American Embassy on 120 Wireless Road, with information on some suspicious Arabs living in a flophouse at the edge of town. He demanded to speak to the CIA station chief, though protocol demanded that the walk-in be channeled through the embassy's regional security officer. Within hours, Thai SWAT teams were raiding possible safe houses throughout the city as Iraqi operatives with passport numbers in sequences like the two men in Manila were rounded up. Within days, DSS special agents based in embassies throughout Asia, the Middle East, and Europe were examining immigration records along with their counterparts in local law enforcement. Dozens of senior Iraqi agents assigned to blow up embassies, aircraft, and other American-related targets were arrested and, as in the case of Sa'ad Kadhim, secretly whisked back to Baghdad in a covert human bazaar of captured operatives in exchange for Filipino and Thai guest workers that Saddam Hussein was holding hostage.

DSS special agents like to say that the world is their precinct. Indeed, by keeping watch in such far-flung posts as Jakarta, Bangkok, and Manila, the agents had managed to save a great many American lives that winter. The CIA took a bow for the DSS operations in Asia, but that was par for the course. Most federal agencies, from the intelligence services to the FBI, often took credit for the work that DSS did overseas.

The need remained for the United States to be resolute and on guard against an Iraqi-led underground army of terrorists dispatched to the four corners of the world. The overall American intelligence and law enforcement assessment that winter was that the United States faced a clear and present danger from state-sponsored terrorist groups eager to expand the scope and battlefield of Operation Desert Storm to a global arena. The obvious enemies of America were Iraq, Libya, and Iran's puppets in Lebanon. Their war against America was overseas, and many in the halls of power in Washington believed that once Saddam Hussein was defeated, the threat would dissipate into pillars of smoke rising into the skies over Iraq. The thinking was that once Baghdad was punished, countries like Iran, Libya, and Syria would be deterred forever.

The assessment was wrong. State sponsors, in the early 1990s, were giving way to transnational movements fueled by religious rage that could not be bullied or bartered with. In November 1990, three months before the Iraqi attacks in Asia, the first shots of a long and bloody terrorist war were fired not in Baghdad or Beirut, not in Manila or even Bangkok. The shots were fired in midtown Manhattan, the heart of New York City, and the afterblast from that opening salvo is still heard to this day.

To anyone who lived in Jersey City, New Jersey, just across the Hudson River from downtown Manhattan, the majesty of the Twin Towers of the World Trade Center was a sight of immeasurable power and confidence. Residents of the gritty middle-class town often wondered how yuppies in the 212 area code of Manhattan could be suckered into paying $2,000-a-month rents for studio apartments in the shadows of the 110-story towers when the view from across the river, where rents were so much cheaper, was simply awe-inspiring. Some Jersey City residents, even patrol officers from the Jersey City Police

Department, would drive to Liberty State Park in the shadow of the Statue of Liberty just to sit and stare at the twin towers at dusk, when the towers were bathed in a purpled and orange shower of light, and at dawn, when a unique halolike brightness covered the tandem of steel and glass. "You looked at those buildings and it was America," claimed a Jersey City Police Officer. "They were living and breathing symbols of greatness."

The towers could be seen everywhere in Jersey City. Commuters heading to the Journal Square station of the Port Authority Trans-Hudson, or PATH, train for the quick seven-minute ride under the river to the bowels of the World Trade Center could almost see their offices in the building as they clutched a cup of coffee and a copy of the *Newark Star-Ledger*. To them, as well, the towers were as much a symbol of power and pride as a place where thousands of them worked. The towers could also be seen from the rear window of the al-Salaam mosque, a beat-up second-story walk-up religious center on the 2800 block of Kennedy Boulevard that attracted a large group of worshipers. To several of the faithful in the mosque, the twin towers were symbols of American arrogance and transgression. The sermons inside the shabby mosque were provocative and incendiary. A blind Egyptian cleric was the mosque's star attraction. He spoke of religious purity and the evil of American liberty and its support of the Zionists. The cleric often spoke of the need for a holy war to wash the Western world clean with the blood of the nonbelievers.

On the night of November 5, 1990, El Sayyid Nosair, a thirty-five-year-old Egyptian-born electrician and one of the mosque's most faithful sons, traveled to New York City from his home in New Jersey for a special night out. He was dressed for the occasion. Wearing a red leisure suit and white patent leather shoes, Nosair certainly stood out. But for a man known by some to be a hothead, a bitter introvert who allowed the troubles of the world to stew inside of him, he seemed at peace that November evening. Nosair had a cherubic face that offered a beguiling smile. It was cool in New York City that night, and traffic around the Marriott East Side on Lexington Avenue between 48th and 49th streets was heavy. Gridlock was part of the New York City landscape. So, too, was the endless line of yellow taxicabs jockeying for position in and around the hotels of midtown, praying for a fare to JFK.

Without trepidation, Nosair entered a second-floor ballroom at the Marriott to listen to a speech by a very special visitor from the Middle East who, like Nosair, had allowed religion to shape his political vision and destiny.

Nosair's mission that night was to assassinate militant Israeli rabbi Meir Kahane.

Kahane, too, was a man driven by a fanatic belief in God and interpretations of the Bible. The Brooklyn-born rabbi was the founder of the radical Jewish Defense League, or JDL, an organization that used terrorist tactics to defend Jewish interests in New York and other cities, as well as to protest the Soviet Union's treatment of its Jewish citizens. Rabbi Kahane emigrated to Israel in 1971, formed the Kach political party shortly thereafter, and ran for the Israeli parliament, or Knesset, in 1976 and 1980. In 1984, Kahane won a single seat for himself in the Knesset on a political platform demanding Jewish sovereignty over all of Israel—including the Gaza Strip and West Bank—and the expulsion of *all* Arabs, both Palestinian and Israeli citizens, from the Jewish state.

In 1988 the Knesset voted to bar Kahane from running for political office, banning all political parties that espoused racial views and edicts. With his parliamentary career in ruins, and the Israeli secret service, the Shin Bet, monitoring his supporters, Kahane assumed the life of a political activist, often raising funds for his causes on speaking tours throughout Jewish communities in North America and Western Europe.

Kahane's speech at the Marriott East Side the night of November 5, 1990, came at a time of heightened anti-Arab sentiment in the United States—and of great fear in the Jewish community. Iraq had threatened to launch missiles and, possibly, weapons of mass destruction against Israel, should the anti-Saddam coalition launch an attack to get Iraqi forces out of Kuwait.

Inside New York City, there was a heightened sense of fear about terrorists doing the unthinkable and striking inside the United States.

At the city's John F. Kennedy International Airport, police officers patrolled terminals with shotguns and machine guns. Tactical patrols protected Penn and Grand Central rail terminals from possible terrorist
attacks. There were fears that Iraqi agents, perhaps coming across the
border from Canada, would poison the city's drinking water or even
unleash anthrax spores through its twisting maze of subway tunnels.
The New York City Police Department and the FBI, in their combined
Joint Terrorism Task Force, or JTTF, feared possible Iraqi terrorist
attacks against the United Nations, or even against NYPD headquarters at One Police Plaza near City Hall. They did not think about
sending additional officers to a hotel in midtown Manhattan.

El Sayyid Nosair had planned much of his operation meticulously.
He assumed that people in the crowd—even possible Jewish Defense
League thugs on hand to protect Kahane—would not be able to identify him as an Egyptian. Nosair believed that, with his olive complexion
and a yarmulke acquired for the operation, he would be able to pass
himself off as a Sephardic Jew—perhaps even an Israeli. He also assumed—correctly—that security would be lax.

New York City was, of course, home turf for the silver-haired rabbi
from Kings County whose oratory skills and verbal eloquence peaked
in his incendiary diatribes against Arabs and Palestinians. New York
City was still the Jewish capital of the world. More Jews lived in the
New York metropolitan area than lived in both Tel Aviv and Jerusalem
combined. If ever there were a place where Rabbi Meir Kahane could
feel safe, it was inside a hotel ballroom in the borough of Manhattan.

Nosair had trained for the mission in midtown for months before
that fateful night. He studied the art of guerrilla warfare from his
friends in the mosque who were veterans of the war in Afghanistan.
Nosair also went shooting, along with other Middle Eastern friends,
in open-air firing ranges in rural northern Pennsylvania and in Nau-
gatuck, Connecticut.

At the end of Rabbi Kahane's speech, following wild applause and
the chanting of "*Am Yisroel Chai,*" or "The Israeli People Live!" the
devout rushed to embrace the man who had militarized right-wing
Jewish thinking in the Diaspora. Few paid attention to the oddly
dressed Sephardic Jew walking to the stage. Nosair removed the yar-

mulke he wore and drew a Brazilian-made Taurus 9mm pistol from a holster nestled in the small of his back. Without a word or a message, he aimed his weapon at Kahane and fired once. The round was well placed. It blew through Kahane's neck and sliced through his carotid artery. The rabbi was dead a few moments later.

Nosair did not seem interested in killing more people that night, nor did he want to be arrested in order to address a larger political agenda. He wanted to escape. Nosair raced out of the Marriott East Side onto Lexington Avenue, pursued by a dozen of Kahane's supporters yelling "Stop the Arab scum! He assassinated Kahane!" Midtown traffic suddenly froze. People stopped and looked to see what the commotion was about. It was hard not to notice the bearded Middle Easterner, dressed as if he was heading to an Egyptian revival of *Saturday Night Fever,* running for his life. What El Sayyid Nosair could not envision was the comic chain of events that characterized his thwarted escape. Overtaken by confusion and fear, Nosair hopped into what he thought was his getaway car—a taxi driven by a redheaded friend from the mosque who just happened to be a cab driver. Instead, with his heart racing and adrenaline blocking his judgment, Nosair had entered the wrong cab. The driver, separated from his passenger by a bullet-proof partition, leapt out of his vehicle. Running down 48th Street, confused, immersed in the closing world of lights and sounds crashing in around him, Nosair struggled to escape. Instead, he came across a Postal Police officer named Carlos Acosta.[2] The sight of a badge and a uniform must have terrified Nosair. He raised his automatic at the police officer and fired, hitting Acosta in the chest. Acosta, however, managed to return fire. He unholstered his .357 revolver and fired one round that hit Nosair in the chin. The assassin was placed in cuffs and rushed to Bellevue Hospital.

When he was arrested and subsequently tried, the popular consensus in New York City was absolute—a fanatic Arab had killed a fanatic Jew. Case closed. Many in the NYPD figured the assassination of Kahane to be a clear-cut example of hate and rage mixed together with the lethal effects of a 9mm bullet. But Nosair was far more than a lone gunman, and the FBI field office in New York City was worried about him. On November 8, 1990, FBI and Jersey State Police troopers raided Nosair's New Jersey home. Investigators could not believe what they had found. Reams and reams of classified material, sensitive military documents from the U.S. Army's Special Operation Command in Fort Bragg, North Carolina, were uncovered. The apartment looked like a billboard for an Islamic revolution, littered with countless cassettes of Arabic prayer sermons. More ominously, though, investigators found the actual plans for the destruction of skyscrapers in New York City. The FBI and prosecutors at the time could not fathom that the blueprints found in Nosair's apartment were plans for future operations. Many in law enforcement viewed the Egyptian as a lone-wolf zealot.

EL SAYYID NOSAIR WAS THE FIRST WARRIOR OF A JIHAD, OR HOLY WAR, TO be launched against the United States from within. The origins of El Sayyid Nosair's rage can be traced to a mysterious Palestinian cleric named Abdullah Azzam. Abdullah Yusuf Azzam was born near the West Bank town of Jenin in 1941. A prodigious academic who studied throughout the area, from Jordan to Syrian, Azzam became a teacher, specializing in the intrinsic justice of the *sharia*, or Islamic law. Azzam became preoccupied with religious warfare. "Jihad and the rifle alone: no negotiations, no conferences, and no dialogues" was his motto.

As a man in his late twenties, Azzam had already earned a reputation as a spellbinding orator in the mosques and gathering halls of the West Bank and the lower Damascus salient. His sermons, laced with hate-filled diatribes against the Jews, were a combination of modern Arabic poetry combined with the blood libel of Eastern European anti-Semitism. Even in his early years, Azzam's interpretation of modern history harked back the Christian crusades, insisting on the necessity for Arab states to avenge the humiliation and indignity they had suffered at the hands of crusaders and later Western powers. Speaking in the mosques of the West Bank, often under the watchful eyes of Jordanian security men who feared his fiery antimonarchy sermons, Azzam had hoped to spark a fundamentalist Islamic guerrilla campaign to eradicate Israel and create an Islamic Palestine. The June 1967 War destroyed Azzam's dreams forever. Like tens of thousands of other Pal-

estinians fleeing the West Bank across the bombed-out bridges span-
ning the Jordan River, Azzam entered Jordan a refugee. He quickly
joined the ranks of the clandestine and outlawed Jordanian Muslim
Brotherhood and soon made contacts with compatriots in Egypt. Inside the mosques of Amman and Cairo, in secretive meetings held at
great risk, men seeking a greater Islamic nation, an Arab superstate
with the *sharia* as its code, gathered to discuss strategy. Azzam often
spoke of an unforgiving military strategy that would be required to
bring the name of Allah back to the nonbelievers.

But in 1970, a different type of war was fought in Jordan. Palestinian
guerrillas, who had used the Hashemite Kingdom as a base of operations from which to launch terrorist attacks against Israel and targets
in Western Europe, were defeated in a brutal civil war by Jordanian
forces. The bloodletting, known in Arabic as *ailul al-Aswad*, or "Black
September," forced Palestinian radicals to flee. Most escaped to Lebanon. Azzam ventured to al-Azhar University in Cairo, eventually obtaining his Ph.D. in principles of Islamic jurisprudence in 1973.

In the mid-1970s, Sheikh Abdullah Azzam traveled to Saudi Arabia
to take a teaching position at King Abdul-Aziz University in Jeddah.
But the academic position would be short-lived. In 1979, Azzam abandoned the Arabian peninsula for a one-way ticket to Islamabad and
then moved on to Peshawar. In Pakistan, Azzam founded the Beit-ul-
Ansar, better known to the CIA and other Western intelligence agencies as the Mujahadeen Services Bureau. The bureau's original objective was to offer assistance to the Afghani jihad and the mujahadeen
and to support the many Muslim volunteers flocking to the Afghani
frontier. Soon, the "bureau" began to train volunteers itching for blood
in what was turning into a modern-day countercrusade against the
Soviet invader. Then the bureau, with Azzam at the helm, began to
recruit volunteers around the Arab world and to campaign for cash to
fund the jihad. Azzam viewed the war as an opportunity to establish
Khilafah, or "Allah's rule on earth," which he believed to be the responsibility of each and every Muslim.

For all his anti-Western diatribes and venom, Azzam was pragmatic.
The lanky figure with the fire of hell in his belly was aided in his cause
by Western men who spoke with northern Virginia accents, men who

represented "the Company." The CIA agents, called "Virginia Farm Boys" in some Mujahadeen circles, were supporters of Azzam's bureau, allies bringing weaponry and cash. Azzam did not refuse American help. "The enemy of my enemy is my friend" has been the currency of day-to-day life in the Near East for centuries. Abdullah Azzam and the Afghan Arabs knew how to make the most out of this ancient wisdom.

Another visitor to Azzam's bureau offering the promise of cash, guns, ammunition, and infrastructure was a lanky Saudi millionaire named Osama bin Laden, who ventured to Pakistan and Afghanistan shortly after the Soviet invasion.

OSAMA BIN MUHAMMAD BIN AWAD BIN LADEN WAS BORN IN 1955, THE youngest of some twenty sons of one of Saudi Arabia's wealthiest and most prominent families. His father, a Yemeni immigrant, was a businessman builder who earned the trust of the Saudi royal family and virtual exclusivity on all construction contracts in the kingdom. The family quickly became one of the richest in the kingdom, surpassed, perhaps, only by the royal family. Osama bin Laden's mother was reported to have been a Syrian-born beauty and his father's favorite—he had three other wives. Little has been recorded on Osama bin Laden's early life, but it is known to have been one immersed in luxury and opulence. In 1968, when the young bin Laden was only thirteen, his father was killed in a helicopter crash, and the family fortune was distributed among the fifty children, wives, and other dependents. It is said that bin Laden inherited over $50 million upon his father's death, as well as shares in the Bin Laden Group, the family's multinational construction conglomerate. Several reports have listed the young bin Laden as a deeply pious teenager completely immersed in Islamic studies. Other reports indicate that he was a typical spoiled Arab millionaire, traveling to Beirut, the sexual and alcohol paradise of Dubai, and other places in the area for some good naughty fun.

What is known about Osama bin Laden is that the year 1979 was a turning point in his life. The Ayatollah Khomeini had seized power in Iran, forging the Islamic revolution, Egypt had signed a peace treaty with Israel, and the Soviets had invaded Afghanistan. Initially, the young bin Laden was reluctant to join the fight in Afghanistan—palatial homes and Filipino servant women, chosen for their beauty rather than their domestic skills, were hard to give up. Bin Laden traveled, studied, and, were it not for the Soviet invasion of Afghanistan, seemed destined for a life of splendor inside the kingdom.

Osama bin Laden is known to have spent the first few years of the war in Afghanistan raising cold hard cash for the war effort against the Soviets. His fund-raising effort was centered on Saudi Arabia. He hit up members of the royal family and business associates of his father. The who's who of the Saudi political and business spectrum shoved dollars and dinars into bin Laden's war chest. The money was transferred through hundreds of money transferring enterprises, facilitated by a system known as *Hawala*, located throughout the Middle East, the Persian Gulf, and the Asian subcontinent to locations inside Peshawar and Afghanistan. *Hawala*, literally the "transfer of debt," dates back to the prophet Mohammed, who encouraged the free movement of goods and the development of markets. Moslems were the first to use promissory notes and assignment, or transfer of debts via bills of exchange, and *Hawala* is an extension of that practice. *Hawala* consists of transferring money, usually across borders and even continents, without the physical or electronic transfer of the actual funds. For an organization that would, in years to come, live—and die—by secrecy, the age-old *Hawala* apparatus allowed money transfers to remain paperless, wireless, and without any fingerprints that could one day be used in a court of law. Money changers received cash in one country— no questions asked—and then a dealer in another country, contacted by a phone call, a letter, an e-mail, or even a messenger knowing a predetermined codeword, would dispense the transferred amount, minus a minimal fee and commission, to a recipient.

FOR BIN LADEN, THE WAR IN AFGHANISTAN CREATED A RIFT OF RAGE AND anger inside his soul that would, for the next twenty-two years, be expressed through violence and savagery. As time went on, and the war in Afghanistan intensified, bin Laden sought a more active role for himself. In 1984, bin Laden moved to Peshawar to fight against the Soviets. He began to don military jackets over his traditional robes and was always seen, day and night, clutching a captured Soviet-made assault rifle. Some say that bin Laden killed a Russian soldier, in hand-to-hand combat, to seize the weapon.[3] The truth behind bin Laden's combat record remains a mystery, one often wrapped in folklore. But in a fight to the death against a superpower, folklore is important.

Through the Bin Laden Group, Osama bin Laden had earth-moving equipment, trucks, and other construction tools brought to the Pakistani frontier so that they could be smuggled into Afghanistan. The bin Laden equipment would be used to build roads and to burrow caves. Some of the most sophisticated and elaborate defensive tunnels and bunkers were built in Soviet-occupied Afghanistan with Osama bin Laden's money. Often, bin Laden would supervise the effort personally.

Azzam and bin Laden established a recruiting office that they called the Maktab al-Khidamat, or MAK. The MAK advertised all over the Arab world for young Muslims to come fight in Afghanistan; it set up branch recruiting offices all over the world, including in the United States and Europe. Bin Laden paid for the transportation of the new recruits to Afghanistan and set up very sophisticated facilities to train them. The Pakistani government donated land and resources, while bin Laden brought in experts on guerrilla warfare, sabotage, and covert operations from all over the world.

With bin Laden's cash and Azzam's zeal, the march toward jihad was a furious one. Azzam became such a hero among the Islamic militant movement around the Middle East that Hamas, the fundamentalist Islamic Palestinian movement, named their West Bank terrorist squads the Abdullah Azzam Brigades. Azzam also traveled the world seeking more cash and more men for the war. According to noted journalist Steve Emerson, "Between 1985 and 1989, Azzam and his top aide, Palestinian Sheikh Tamim al-Adnani, visited dozens of American cities, exhorting their followers to pick up the sword against the enemies of Islam."[4]

The international army assembled in Pakistan and Afghanistan was over 20,000 strong. Men came from Libya, Tunisia, Algeria, Morocco, Saudi Arabia, Palestine, Jordan, Somalia, Sudan, Ethiopia, Madagascar, Lebanon, Syria, Iraq, the Persian Gulf states, Yemen, Kashmir, Chechnya, Kosovo, Bosnia, Turkey, Indonesia, and even the Philippines. Azzam wanted to coordinate the multiethnic force of holy warriors for the next stage of the struggle, but bin Laden wanted to create a covert network of operatives for future operations. Slowly, bin Laden began to steal much of Azzam's thunder, and the relationship became fractious. While Azzam labored to improve the conditions in mujahadeen front-line clinics, bin Laden began networking with the international who's who of Islamic militancy that would flock to Pakistan's border with Afghanistan for a look of their own.

Inevitably, bin Laden and Azzam began to compete for prominence and control of the movement. Osama bin Laden wanted to continue the work of the jihad and take the fight to Saudi Arabia and beyond. Azzam continued to focus on support to Muslims in Afghanistan to create a base of operations for the next step. In the end it was bin Laden's vision that prevailed. On November 24, 1989, three bombs planted along a mountainous route in Afghanistan that Abdullah Azzam regularly traveled to on the way to his mosque detonated as he passed. Sheikh Azzam was killed, along with two of his sons. Rumors have consistently linked Osama bin Laden to Azzam's assassination, though there has never been any definitive proof. Nevertheless, with Azzam dead, it was bin Laden who would lead the global effort.

Interestingly enough, bin Laden would carry on Azzam's vision and create an organization called al-Qaeda, or "the Base," a loosely organized network that would continue the struggle of a global holy war. Al-Qaeda would not be a terrorist organization in the conventional sense of the word. Unlike other terrorist groups, such as the Provisional IRA, the Basque ETA, and the various Palestinian groups, al-Qaeda's quest was not regional. Al-Qaeda was not after national liberation or political autonomy. Unlike other terrorist groups, such as Hezbollah or the Popular Front for the Liberation of Palestine General Command, al-Qaeda did not require a state sponsor to furnish its foot soldiers with guns, explosives, safe houses, and documents. Instead, al-Qaeda was designed as a multinational corporation with offices, or branches, in virtually every country on earth. Osama bin Laden was the corporation's founder and CEO, his lieutenants served as chief executive council, and the many veterans of the war in Afghanistan, returning to their homes in the four corners of the world, would serve as the company's loosely knit but highly dedicated staff. Like any successful multinational corporation, bin Laden's al-Qaeda had global ambitions and, in nations like Afghanistan and Sudan, he had "business-friendly" headquarters from which to operate.

Osama bin Laden had envisioned al-Qaeda as a springboard for a global Islamic underground movement to topple corrupt regimes not adhering to Islamic principles. To get his struggle off the ground, Osama bin Laden looked no further than Egypt, and the fearless and visionary Egyptian lieutenants who had served with him in Afghanistan.

THE SOVIET INVASION OF AFGHANISTAN PROVIDED MANY OF THE DISILlusioned zealot-wannabes throughout the Arab world with a cause. A monolithic atheist empire, a superpower that since the revolution of 1917 had systematically persecuted its own Muslim minority, was now attacking a defenseless and primitive people who believed that Allah was the One True God and Mohammed His Messenger. The Soviet invasion of Afghanistan and the attempts, by the Soviet military and their Afghani puppets, to install a Communist regime in Kabul outraged Muslims all over the world. In response, Muslim volunteers flocked to the Khyber Pass to take arms in the holy struggle. But the volunteers who flocked to the camps to pledge their faith on the banana-clip magazine of an AK-47 assault rifle were focused on Afghanistan. The vision of a global jihad came to the volunteers courtesy of the Egyptians.

Cairo had, for centuries, been considered the capital of the Arab world, and Egypt, with its forty million souls, long considered the dominant Arab power. But modern Egypt had never been truly able to profess its power and greatness in this century. Dominated by the Ottoman Turks and then the British, Egypt was a country beset by poverty and strife, desperately clinging to the tatters of papyrus and the Pyramids as symbols of a long-departed greatness. Poverty, and a sense of diminished greatness, helped spark the reemergence of fundamentalist Islam. The emergence of Islamic political zeal in Egypt did not appear with the conquering Arab army that, with Lawrence of Arabia at the helm, liberated the Arabian Peninsula and what is today Jordan and Syria from Turkish rule. The rush of fundamentalist Islam began in the universities and mosques of the greater Cairo metropolis as an answer to foreign occupation and a quest for empowerment.

The Muslim Brotherhood Society was founded in March 1928 in Isma'aliya, Egypt, by Hassan al-Banna, a firebrand and cleric who would soon build one of the largest political parties in Egypt whose goal was to build a society based solely on the *sharia*. The Egyptian branch of the Brotherhood Society was, in essence, a movement of national liberation inasmuch as it worked for the liberation of Egypt from Western control and non-Islamic influences. It would not be long until British forces in Egypt found themselves the target of the Brotherhood in random and violent hit-and-run attacks. Brotherhood terrorist cells were known for their brutality and random indiscriminate attacks. British troops garrisoned in Egypt feared "the Brothers."

The war in Palestine, from 1936 to 1949, transformed the Muslim Brotherhood into an accepted tool of the greater Arab struggle against the fledgling state of Israel. By March 1948, Hassan al-Banna claimed to have 1,500 Brotherhood volunteers in Palestine. At the same time, the Egyptian military, originally wary of the threat the Brotherhood posed to the regime of King Farouk, authorized the training of volunteers for the fight in Palestine in order for them to wage a jihad. Camps were opened up along the border near Gaza and contacts made with local fundamentalists. Following the war, Egypt annexed the Gaza Strip and took under its control the 750,000 Palestinians living there, subjecting the local populace to an often repressive occupation. Gaza was the definition of misery: crowded, poor, unsanitary, and underdeveloped beyond mere neglect to the point of malice. There was no industry in Gaza, no hope for work, and often no hope at all. The power and promise of Islam became the sole hope to many, and the only way most of the refugee population had to vent their anger and rage.

The establishment of the state of Israel in May 1948 transformed the Muslim Brotherhood into a political force to be reckoned with not only in Egypt. On December 28, 1948, King Farouk's prime minister, Mahmud Fahmi Noqrashi, was assassinated by Brotherhood gunmen in Cairo. The Brotherhood, outraged that the Egyptian monarchy had led the Arab world to a humiliating defeat against the upstart Jewish state, began to call openly for a resurrection that would bring Islamic rule to Egypt. Although secret police operatives working for King Farouk assassinated Hassan al-Banna in Cairo a year later, the 1948 debacle would continue to breed revolution inside Egypt. In 1952, with tacit support of the Brotherhood, Colonel Gamel Abdul Nasser seized power in a military coup. But Nasser, a socialist cut from pragmatic cloth, angered the fundamentalists when he allied himself with the Soviet Union and Socialist regimes throughout the world for the struggle against Israel.

Nasser would ban the Muslim Brotherhood and dispatch his secret service agents to the slums of Cairo and the villages around the Nile Delta to round up the activists. The Muslim Brotherhood responded by launching several unsuccessful assassination attempts against him. Nasser vowed to crush the underground movement as part of his effort to make Egypt a great and modern state. In 1966, Nasser ordered the execution of Sayyid Qutb, one of the founders of transnational Islamic fundamentalism, and the Brotherhood military commander. Other Brotherhood leaders would soon find themselves swinging from the gallows in Egypt's most desolate maximum-security prisons.

June 1967 would be a watershed year for the underground Islamic fundamentalist movement in Egypt. In May, in daring moves designed to rally the Arab world behind him, Egyptian President Nasser sent his armies into the demilitarized Sinai Desert, closed the Straits of Tiran in the Red Sea to Israeli shipping, and vowed to push the Jewish state into the sea. On June 4, 1967, the upstart state of Israel struck first, launching a multipronged series of preemptive air strikes against targets in Egypt, Jordan, Syria, and Iraq. In six days of combat, an Arab army of some one million men was vanquished by Israel's citizen-soldiers. Egypt lost the Gaza Strip and the Sinai Desert. Jordan lost the West Bank of the Jordan River, and Syria lost the Golan Heights. Secular Arab nationalism had disintegrated over the smoldering desert battlefields of Sinai, and was disgraced by the Star of David flying over the al-Aqsa mosque in Jerusalem, from which Muslims believe the Prophet Mohammed ascended to heaven.

The 1967 calamity brought new life to fundamentalist Islamic movements in Egypt. Young men flocked to the mosques and to the Islamic universities to seek answers to yet another humiliating defeat at the hands of the Western powers. Crowds of angry young men, some openly expressing their desire to fight in a global holy war, flocked to hear the sermons of such noted orators of the cause as Sheikh Omar Abdel Rahman, a blind cleric who was becoming famous throughout North Africa for his calls for a pan-Arab Islamic revolution.

Sheikh Omar Abdel Rahman was born in May 1938 into a poverty-stricken family in the Nile Delta. Blinded by diabetes when he was ten months old, Rahman was offered few choices in life. Egypt did not help its crippled. They were often discarded in the trash piles of poverty and indifference. Islamic studies was one of the few options the young blind boy had. And the young Rahman was a brilliant religious student. By age eleven, it has been reported, he had already memorized a braille copy of the Koran.[5] Egypt's 1967 military debacle changed the twenty-nine-year-old Islamic student forever. He was outraged by the national humiliation from a war he, as a blind cripple, could not fight in; the military defeat left him zealous and bitter. Most of his rage was directed against the political leadership, or the "New Pharaohs," as they were known in the mosques of southern Cairo.

One such man who attended Rahman's sermons was Dr. Ayman al-Zawahiri, a young up-and-coming physician from a prominent Egyptian family. Born into wealth and prestige, al-Zawahiri forsook a promising medical career, money, and family to become one of the founding members of al-Jihad, a highly secretive underground movement dedicated to establishing Islamic rule in Egypt. There would eventually be two sects of the al-Jihad group—Zawahiri's faction, considered the fanatical movement, and something called Vanguards of Conquest (*Talaa' al-Fateh*) led by Ahmad Husayn Agiza. Both al-Jihad groups accepted Sheikh Omar Abdel Rahman as their spiritual mentor, though Zawahiri was a proponent of the *Takfir wa Hijra*, or "Anathema and Exile," the bleakest offshoot of fundamentalist Islamic thought, which condoned the killing of both Westerners and Muslims alike in purifying the earth of nonbelievers and traitors.

Another Egyptian group was the *al-Gama'a al-Islamiyah*, a terrorist faction that emerged as a phenomenon rather than an organized group, mainly in Egyptian jails, and later on in some of the Egyptian universities, during the early 1970s. Following the release of most of the Islamic prisoners from the Egyptian jails by President Sadat after 1971, several groups of militants began to organize themselves. These militant groups or cells took names such as the Islamic Liberation Party, Excommunication and Emigration, and Saved from the Inferno. Each cell operated separately and was self-contained, a fact that allowed the organization to be structured but at the same time loosely organized.

Initially, the Muslim Brotherhood accepted the rule of Nasser's successor, Anwar es-Sadat, who assumed power after Nasser succumbed to a fatal heart attack in September 1970 while brokering a cease-fire between Palestinian guerrillas and Jordanian troops attempting to evict them from the Hashemite Kingdom during the Black September crisis. Sadat, realizing the potential of the Islamic underground to wreak havoc, instituted the *sharia* as the law throughout Egypt and pardoned all Brotherhood leaders imprisoned by the government in the mid-1960s. But the movement worked best underground. Faithful members of the cause were recruited from inside the Egyptian military and officer corps. The tide and rage of Islamic zeal inside the Egyptian military reached its zenith during the October 1973 Arab-Israeli war. Launched during Ramadan, the Muslim holy month of fasting and prayer, the initial Egyptian and Syrian offensive scored impressive battlefield successes before Israel managed to turn the tide of the war. After eighteen days of brutal fighting that risked superpower involvement, Israeli tanks were an hour's drive from Damascus and well on the road to Cairo.

It was the aftermath of the 1973 fighting and Egyptian President Sadat's acceptance of a unilateral Egyptian-led diplomatic solution to the Arab-Israeli conflict that marked a turning point for the underground Islamic movements in Egypt. President Sadat's acceptance of the Jewish state was viewed by the clerics, especially the fundamentalist clerics like Sheikh Rahman, as unforgivable religious treason. Although blind and physically hesitant in his movements and gestures, Sheikh

Rahman was a mesmerizing orator, and his sermons on Islamic betrayal at the hands of the modern Arab state sparked furious applause from the poor and disenfranchised, and the ire of the security police. Sheikh Rahman would soon become a regular at the headquarters of the *Jihaz amn al Daula*, or Egyptian State Security. When President Sadat prepared his historic flight to Israel to seek peace, Rahman would become a threat to Egyptian national security.

That Sadat would venture to a Jerusalem under Israeli control was viewed by members of al-Jihad as incomprehensible betrayal. In signing a peace treaty with the state of Israel in March 1979, Sadat was signing his own death warrant. Many in the lower ranks of the service were sympathetic to the fundamentalists, and the peace accords with the Israelis pushed many into becoming active operatives in the Brotherhood. In a complex assassination operation that required the coordination and complicity of the many arms of the Muslim Brotherhood movement, Egyptian President Anwar es-Sadat was murdered on October 6, 1981, as he sat in a reviewing stand in central Cairo commemorating the eighth anniversary of the crossing of the Suez Canal. The terrorists, leaping from transport trucks participating in the military parade, fired their AK-47 rifles with great precision as they riddled the velvet-draped presidential section of the stand. Dozens of grenades were tossed and dozens were killed in the chaotic gun battle that ensued—all televised live to forty million viewers inside Egypt.

Over 2,500 men—from imams as old as eighty and suspects as young as twelve—were arrested by Egyptian authorities and tried in chaotic courts where the verdict was usually "guilty." Those directly responsible for the assassination were executed. Those even circumstantially connected were imprisoned. Hell awaited the hundreds of men who escaped execution only to find themselves inside the docket of an Egyptian courtroom. Life in an Egyptian prison was harsh and brutal for common criminals. According to reports by Amnesty International, there were "widespread and indiscriminate" incidents of torture and ill-treatment in Egyptian police stations and detention centers. Prison life was nightmarish for enemies of the state implicated in the assassination of Sadat. Torture was a daily activity. Prisoners were tortured with electric shocks, beatings, whippings, suspension by the wrists or ankles, suspension in contorted positions from a horizontal pole. They were also subjected to various forms of psychological torture. Prisoners were often threatened with death, including mock firing squads. Many were threatened with rape and sexual torture. Some male prisoners were even raped by guards and interrogators. Often, security service interrogators threatened to rape the wives, sisters, and daughters of those being questioned. "Do you want to know the difference between life in prison four hundred years ago and life in prison today?" an Egyptian secret service officer said in a Cairo meeting with U.S. intelligence officers. "Today you get a plastic bucket to shit in!"

Dr. Ayman al-Zawahiri was sentenced to three years of prison time for his role in the Sadat assassination. He was convicted only on weapons charges, though his role in the killing was far more involved.

The brutalization endured in Egyptian prisons hardened the fundamentalist operatives beyond Western comprehension. Men whose faiths saw them through the most barbaric of treatments had survived and, ominously, had lived to fight another day. Many of those let out of Mubarak's jails went underground, heading to the untouchable universe of Cairo's slums and religious schools. Other militants set up bases of operation in southern Egypt, or in Sudan, where the Islamic call to arms was finding a sympathetic ear. Others, including Dr. al-Zawahiri, petitioned the Egyptian government to provide them with exit visas to Pakistan, where they could join a fight—any fight, in fact—in the name of Islam. By 1985, the stream of Egyptian volunteers to bin Laden's Arab army had swelled. Some Western intelligence organizations believe that over 2,000 Egyptian holy warriors ventured to Afghanistan to fight the Soviets.

According to reports, Osama bin Laden met Dr. Ayman al-Zawahiri in Afghanistan. Osama bin Laden provided money, arms, and facilities to the Arabic-speaking warriors; Dr. al-Zawahiri provided medical care to wounded mujahadeen. The two men were ideally suited to one another's visions. Osama bin Laden was the banker, the facilitator, the Robin Hood of the Islamic revival who could turn a rabble into an army that could vanquish a superpower. Dr. Ayman al-Zawahiri was an ingenious plotter. If ever there was a terrorist field marshal who knew how to coordinate and manipulate small cells of operatives for a larger cause, it was al-Zawahiri. And al-Zawahiri knew, if there was one religious leader who could lead the call for an underground Islamic movement, it would be Sheikh Rahman. Soon, the blind Egyptian cleric, looking out of place in his white robes in a land where the AK-47 ruled, began his journey to Peshawar.

THE ONE ELEMENT OF TRUE GENIUS LINKING BIN LADEN AND AL-ZAWAHIRI was their understanding of just how small a place the world had become. Jihad emissaries, recruiting fighters and raising cash in Western Europe and the United States, had set up headquarters, mosques as covers, and a myriad of travel agencies, financial institutions, and other businesses that could all service the cause in Afghanistan. Middle Eastern migration to Western Europe, to cities like Hamburg, London, Manchester, and Brussels, provided an endless address book of safe houses and facilitators throughout the continent. In the United States the network was even larger. Not only was there a vibrant Arab presence in New York City and New Jersey, but in Tampa, Chicago, and even the American heartland, Oklahoma City. Culturally, Afghanistan might be 2,000 years away from the reality of America's modern technologically advanced society, but it was only a fifteen-hour flight with a good connection through London or Frankfurt. Money could be transferred between accounts in hours, if not minutes, and phone service, even to remote stretches of Peshawar and Jalalabad, made communications effortless.

By 1989, after Azzam's death, the organization that bin Laden and the fire-spewing "martyr" from Jenin had begun and that bin Laden had transformed into a truly global underground army was ready to spring into action. By 1990, with much of the fighting over in Afghanistan, bin Laden returned to Saudi Arabia. The monarchy, bin Laden would argue in sermons, was corrupt and not true to the Islamic principles incumbent upon the kingdom as caretakers of the holy sites of Mecca and Medina. Osama bin Laden, the Yemeni, a perennial outsider in a kingdom that tolerated only its own inner circle, would use his charisma and wealth to change the face of a kingdom that just happened to fuel much of the modern world.

The other Arab veterans of the Afghanistan fighting, riding a high of ballistic victory, returned home to Algeria, to Egypt, to Sudan, to Yemen, and to Palestine. They also returned to the United States.

MANY OF THE ARAB AFGHANS CRISSCROSSED THE NEAR EAST AND NORTH America during those critical years in the mid-1980s. Some of the travelers were Arab émigrés who were permanent residents in the United States and green-card holders; others were naturalized U.S. citizens. The Afghan Arabs sent emissaries to the Arab Diaspora communities of Brooklyn, Jersey City, Detroit, and Chicago to raise money for the struggle. Impassioned speakers, including key officers in bin Laden's network, lectured the faithful at conferences in Marriott hotels, Holiday Inns, and even inside the homes of wealthy Muslims. The talk was of the struggle against the Soviets and, invariably, the Zionists. Money was always raised. Sometimes, volunteers would follow, as well. One such volunteer was Mahmoud Abouhalima.

Born in 1959, in a ragtag slum suburb of Alexandria that was fertile ground for future operatives in al-Jihad and the *al-Gama'a al-Islamiyah*, Mahmoud Abouhalima was a man who stood out in a crowd. Well over six feet tall and the owner of orange-red locks and a bright red beard— a parting gift to his ancestors from the Crusaders, as an Egyptian security official liked to joke—he was a man who was easy to notice in a cause where notoriety generally bought a one-way ticket to the torture chambers of the Egyptian *Muchabarat*. And, in the Egypt of October 1981, notoriety often got you killed. Abouhalima was granted a tourist visa to Germany and settled in Munich, where he married a German girl, got divorced, and then found another German bride— though this one was a willing convert to Islam. In 1986, they moved to New York.

Like millions of other permanent tourists who come to the United States each and every year to live and work in the cash-only world of undocumented-immigrant status, Mahmoud Abouhalima and his German bride allowed their tourist visas to expire. Fortunately for them, their papers ran out at a time when the U.S. federal government was offering an amnesty for "visitors" to the United States with expired papers. The Abouhalimas applied for amnesty from the Immigration and Naturalization Service and, in 1988, were awarded temporary legal residence. Abouhalima, like so many Arab immigrants before him, obtained a hack license from the Taxi and Limousine Commission and picked up fares for a living.

According to an article in *Time* magazine by Richard Behar, Abouhalima's cab was a mini-mosque and jihad recruitment center. Abouhalima's cab was filled with copies of the Koran and other Islamic decorations. Anyone hapless enough to enter his taxi—he is reported to have been cited over a dozen times for traffic violations and suspended licenses—was assaulted by cassettes of fiery sermons from Egypt calling for the death of President Hosni Mubarak, Israel, the United States, and just about anything else that was non-Islamic. Many of the sermons were by a man he had come to idolize—Sheikh Omar Abdel Rahman. Abouhalima also volunteered to work at the al-Kifah refugee center in Brooklyn, funneling men and money to the Arabs fighting in Afghanistan. Watching his Palestinian, Algerian, Jordanian, and Egyptian brothers travel to Pakistan on discounted tickets on Pakistan International Airlines arranged through the refugee center, Abouhalima wanted to be much more than a circumstantial Islamic holy warrior who just happened to escape Egypt by the skin of his teeth. Abouhalima became friendly with Mustafa Shalabi, a member of the al-Gama'a al-Islamiyah on the run from the Egyptian authorities who just happened to be the New York City agent who ran the al-Kifah refugee center in Brooklyn. Abouhalima and Shalabi became close friends. Within months, Abouhalima ventured to Afghanistan to join forces with the mujahadeen.

In Afghanistan, during his numerous trips to the embattled land in the late 1980s, Abouhalima soon found himself in a training camp with other fellow Arab volunteers learning how to strip apart and then assemble an AK-47 in less than ten seconds, and learning how to lay an ambush for Soviet armored personnel carriers. The Arab soldiers were equipped lavishly. The United States and the Central Intelligence Agency invested close to $3.3 billion in the foreign volunteers; Saudi Arabia was reported to have matched the CIA dollar for dollar.[6] The Arabs were disliked by their Afghan comrades. The Arabs kept to themselves. They felt and acted superior to the illiterate rabble who had been fighting the Soviets since 1979. But the Arabs were fierce—truly fanatical—on the battlefield. According to one Middle Eastern intelligence veteran, "They would attack without quarter and without warning. Russians who were lucky were killed when the first RPG was launched and the first 7.62mm bullets impacted the convoy. Those wounded by the combat and left to die became miserable experiments of what knives and petrol could do to the dwindling remains of a human life."[7]

Some of the Arabs came to Afghanistan for the duration. Others, like middle-aged American businessmen traveling to Florida for baseball fantasy camp, came on one-month vacations of close-quarter bloodletting before heading back to the bodegas and yellow cabs of New York City, where they could earn enough money for yet another plane ticket and another month of combat.

It is reported that Mahmoud Abouhalima made several trips to Pakistan in 1989 and 1990. The entry turnstile into the United States provided the global jihad network with enormous opportunities.

In early May 1990, Sheikh Omar Abdel Rahman's representatives walked into the U.S. embassy in Sudan on the tree-lined Sharia Ali Abdul Latif in Khartoum and sought an entry visa for him to the United States. Sheikh Rahman, at the behest of the Egyptian authorities, had been on a terrorist watch list for his role in the assassination of Anwar es-Sadat and his involvement with the al-Jihad movement since 1987. On May 10, 1990, Rahman was granted a one-year visa to enter the United States. He arrived at John F. Kennedy International Airport in July. It remains a mystery to this day how, despite his record in Egypt, Rahman ended up in the United States, shuttling between the al-Salaam mosque in Jersey City and the al-Kifah refugee center in Brooklyn's Arab Atlantic Avenue enclave, though his apparent enlistment by the CIA as an "asset" in rallying the troops in Afghanistan appears to have played a crucial role in his earning the right to visit the United States.

"Nobody ever gave a second thought to the mosque in the bustling shopping district of Jersey City," claimed an officer in the Jersey City Police Department's Emergency Service Unit. "There were so many

Arab residents of that part of town, who knew what they were up to?"[8] In New York City the traveling holy warriors sparked little interest or concern from local cops; NYPD Intelligence Division detectives were far more concerned with Jewish vigilante operations against Arab-owned businesses on Brooklyn's Atlantic Avenue than they were with mysterious guerrilla veterans milling about the al-Kifah refugee center.

In November 1990, shortly after the assassination of Rabbi Meir Kahane, the sheikh's visa was supposed to have been revoked by the State Department, though miscommunication with the Immigration and Naturalization Service resulted in Rahman being approved for permanent residency status.

Sheikh Rahman, in his religious robes, dark glasses, and white turban, became a source of inspiration to Arabs in the New York City metropolitan area who felt disenfranchised in their new homes and alienated in a strange culture. Rahman struck a raw nerve among those who were homesick and those who were pious but felt strange about expressing their religious beliefs in a city that was moving forward, rather than backward in time. Many of the young and middle-aged men who ventured to Sheikh Rahman's sermons felt powerless in the United States. Tales of the fighting in Afghanistan and the mysterious Saudi millionaire who abandoned wealth and luxury for a cave and an AK-47 assault rifle sparked fantasy and religious pride.

Mahmoud Abouhalima became Sheikh Omar Abdel Rahman's part-time bodyguard and chauffeur. Others who flocked to worship with the sheikh and become one of his followers included El Sayyid Nosair; Nosair's first cousin, Ibrahim Elgabrowny; and Nidal Ayyad, a Kuwaiti-born chemical engineer who worked for Allied Signal, the giant Morristown, New Jersey, chemical company. Another member of the inner circle was Wadih el Hage, a Lebanese native and naturalized U.S. citizen. Initially el Hage was a devout follower of Abdullah Azzam but came to know—and work for—Osama bin Laden. While many in the Brooklyn al-Kifah crew were always wary of not overstepping the bounds of criminal behavior in order to avoid possible deportation, el Hage was known to boast that his American passport allowed him to travel around the world without hindrance.

Another key member of the inner circle was Emad Salem, a former

Egyptian Army intelligence officer who had converted to the side of the "righteous." Salem was, in fact, an informant supplying the FBI with information on this growing underground group traveling back and forth between Jersey City and Brooklyn.

August 2, 1990, was a turning point. On August 2, 1990, America became the target.

The Iraqi invasion of Kuwait on August 2, 1990, had some of the earmarkings of another Third World act of bloodshed that would quickly be forgotten by the international media. War was no stranger to the region, and Iraqi strongman Saddam Hussein had always squabbled with his weaker neighbors over border disputes, oil exports, and the other Byzantine elements of bravado that marked Middle Eastern politics. But the Iraqi invasion wasn't just a ten-hour incursion designed to intimidate and extort. This was a full-fledged bayonet-driven takeover, and the Emir of Kuwait, and the billions his country possessed and produced, appeared to be just a staging area for a grander scheme to dominate the world's oil supply.

In the Middle East, especially inside the fundamentalist corner of the Arab world, the Iraqi invasion was seen as a mixed blessing. The emirs, shahs, kings, and sultans of the Persian Gulf were rich theocratic rulers who had lost their way in pursuit of American military protection and the almighty dollar. Saddam Hussein wasn't a righteous Muslim by any stretch of the imagination, but he did, some argued, expose the leaders of the oil-rich Gulf States and of the Saudi royal family as nothing more than *munafaqeen*—the Arabic term for hated hypocrites. Arab might and Islamic justice were, in a moment of crisis, abandoned to allow 300,000 American soldiers—infidels the lot of them—to tread on holy Saudi soil. To many fundamentalist Muslims, the Saudi royal family had perpetrated treason and blasphemy by permitting American soldiers, Christians and Jews, to enter the kingdom in defense of oil and cash. The United States of America, in the eyes of many fundamentalist Islamic leaders, was not defending an Arab state, but rather occupying the holy cities of Mecca and Medina.

The continuous presence of U.S. soldiers in Saudi Arabia in the autumn of 1990 was an escalating source of hatred and anger inside the mind of Osama bin Laden. It was a call to arms inside the al-

Salaam and the Abu Bakr mosques in Jersey City and Brooklyn. The assassination of Rabbi Meir Kahane was a convenient crime of opportunity sparked by hatred and blind faith. Behind it were the teachings and fatwas, or religious-sanctioned homicide contracts, called for by Sheikh Rahman.

Sheikh Rahman availed himself to members of his flock, who often contacted him about religious questions—they even phoned the blind cleric, a man with two wives, about marital advice. Nosair was one of the Sheikh's most persistent callers. According to federal authorities, Nosair recorded some of his telephone conversations with Rahman, including a discussion in which the two discussed their impotent anger over the growing influx of Jews emigrating to Israel from the Soviet Union and the difficulties that portended for destroying the Jewish state.

El Sayyid Nosair's involvement in the Kahane assassination was an opening salvo in the fundamentalist religious attack that was slowly building inside the United States of America. The Kahane killing should have been seen as a harbinger of much worse to come. Instead, it sparked nothing more than a series of ignored reports by an FBI informant and the belief, strongly held by many in law enforcement, that whatever happened in Jerusalem and Beirut and Bogotá could never happen inside the United States.

The case of El Sayyid Nosair became a rallying point for the followers of Sheikh Rahman. The sheikh's followers and Nosair's fellow guerrillas were seen protesting Nosair's trial each day of the proceedings outside the Manhattan criminal courts building. Often arguing— and sometimes fighting—with Kahane supporters, the Arabs constantly demanded that Nosair be found innocent and returned to his community. News cameras captured the faces of Mohammed Salameh, Mahmoud Abouhalima, and Ibrahim Elgabrowny outside the court. Often they were dressed in combat fatigues that they had worn in Afghanistan. They brandished the Koran in anger and defiance.

Remarkably, El Sayyid Nosair was not convicted of murdering Rabbi Kahane—defended by legendary left-wing attorney William Kunstler, Nosair was instead convicted of weapons charges and sentenced to the maximum sentence of seven to twenty-two years behind bars. Inside the al-Salaam mosque, and at the al-Kifah refugee center in Brooklyn, the followers of Sheikh Rahman organized inexpensive bus trips— lunch not included—for followers to visit "Brother" El Sayyid Nosair in Attica State Penitentiary. Even from behind the cold brick walls of prison, Nosair continued to plot future "operations." Nosair openly talked about killing judges and politicians, as well as other bombings throughout the New York metropolitan area.

FROM THE SECOND-STORY WINDOW OF THE AL-SALAAM MOSQUE, WHERE Sheikh Omar Abdel Rahman preached a great carnage that he envisioned in the United States on most evenings during the week, downtown Jersey City was basked by the bright lights from a picture-postcard view of the World Trade Center. The two buildings were also inescapable from the Abu Bakr mosque and the al-Kifah refugee center. They were symbols of American power and might, and had become, just like Anwar es-Sadat, a symbol of betrayal.

Whether there was any direct involvement between Sheikh Omar Abdel Rahman's New York–area network and Osama bin Laden's Afghan Arab network in Afghanistan remains a mystery to this day. The assassination of a militant rabbi might have been a small victory, but it would hardly satisfy the call to arms from the mosques of Jersey City, Cairo, and Peshawar. But the material confiscated in Nosair's apartment, including sketches and drawings of skyscrapers, could have provided a tantalizing clue that Rahman's followers had destructive plans for New York City. Notes kept by Nosair, and seized by the FBI, called for attacks on the enemies of Islam by destroying their high buildings, their statues, their entire tourist infrastructure. However, a sketch of a skyscraper erupting in a ball of fire and some rambling notations in Arabic of killings in New York were far from hard evidence of a genuine plot. If Sheikh Rahman's calls for a holy war against the United States were to be realized, the men in Brooklyn and Jersey City needed expert help. The faithful at the al-Salaam mosque were zealous but they were not professional. For the war to truly begin, they would need outside assistance.

In the world of the global jihad, help was always a phone call away.

Chapter 2

"THE TRAVELER"

WELCOME TO NEW YORK'S JOHN F. KENNEDY INTERNATIONAL AIR-PORT—GATEWAY TO THE UNITED STATES OF AMERICA!

The sign in the concourse area of the airport's sprawling IAB, or International Arrivals Building, said it all. No matter what country you came from, no matter what language you spoke, if you were flying into the United States, your first glimpse of America would more likely than not be the inside of a terminal building located in a southern stretch of Queens County. The IAB was where most international flights from smaller European countries and the Third World were processed. It was a chaotic building of awaiting relatives, émigré cab drivers seeking a Japanese mark for a $250 cab ride into Manhattan, and people in all shapes, colors, and sizes. And that was *outside* the Customs Hall.

Inside the secure area of the IAB, where flights from the four corners of the world were funneled, the multicultural mosaic that was New York City was concentrated in a chaotic sea of human faces passing through immigration and customs and entering the United States of America through the frenetic and ungovernable mess of the airport's arrival and parking area. It was not uncommon to find flights from Tel Aviv and Cairo landing simultaneously at the IAB, with Israelis and Egyptians huddled together in seemingly endless lines of complaints echoed jointly in angry Hebrew and Arabic. Europeans, Africans,

Asians, Arabs, Israelis, Turks, Indians, and Russians passed through the twisting, roped-off barriers twenty-four hours a day past a formidable wall of inspectors from the U.S. Immigration and Naturalization Service. From São Paolo to Sri Lanka, entry into the United States was a coveted blessing bestowed upon only the most fortunate of souls. Here at JFK, being on line to present one's passport to the uniformed inspectors at the passport control booths represented the final barrier that separated dreams of the Promised Land from Third World misery. The immigration line at JFK was the last tension-filled step that made promise, fortune, and the American dream seem so tangible.

To an experienced mind trained to detect and manipulate chinks in an enemy's armor, however, the immigration line at JFK was an insignificant barrier to cross.

According to one veteran INS inspector, "Anyone with half a brain and a set of balls had, with the flimsiest of documents, a fifty-fifty chance of walking through the terminal, fetching a cab, and disappearing forever into New York City. Anyone with any degree of talent could walk through the terminal and out into oblivion without anyone being the wiser." For years, the Immigration and Naturalization Service had been known as the paper tiger of federal law enforcement. In an interview with *Newsweek* magazine years later, even agency spokesman Russ Bergeron claimed that the Immigration and Naturalization Service had "languished for decades."[1] Inspectors were promoted through an old-boy network of nepotism and favors. An inspector who brought too many discrepancies in entry documentation to his supervisors and sent too many individuals for interviews with senior agents was considered an "NFL," or "Nine for Life," a reference to the government rank that individual would be saddled with for the duration of his career with the agency. Corruption and apathy were system-wide.

The malaise at JFK, the literal first line of America's defense, was not lost to Afghan Arab veterans who traveled frequently in and out of the airport on trips to and from Egypt, Sudan, Yemen, Saudi Arabia, and Pakistan. "In Pakistan, at Abdullah Azzam's bureau and inside bin Laden's training camps, operatives were often required to donate their original passports to the organization," reflected a former supervisor with the DSS Counterterrorism Division. "If they needed someone to travel to the United States on a genuine passport, the person could walk past immigration without a problem as long as the ages were similar and a beard or glasses masked any physical differences." Veterans of the Afghanistan fighting often traveled to and from New York City armed with a friend's passport, or the travel documents of someone they never knew, picked up at one of the dispatch centers in Peshawar set up by Abdullah Azzam and financed by Osama bin Laden.

The two young men sitting inside the belly of Pakistan International Airlines Flight PK702 that warm September morning were fairly confident that immigration would not be a problem at JFK. American law enforcement was not looked upon as a menacing obstacle. The Pakistani Boeing 747-200 flying from Karachi to New York City was, as always, packed to capacity with over 400 men, women, and children. Some of the passengers wore Western dress. Most did not. Luggage often consisted of plastic bags crammed with their most important essentials, stuffed without mercy into overhead compartments or underneath narrow seats. The suitcases that were checked into the cargo hold were large and always heavy. Often, passengers simply checked in cardboard boxes sealed with tape. The fourteen-hour haul from Karachi was a rough flight. Bathrooms often clogged and, by the time the aircraft was over Eastern Europe, failed to function altogether. When the aircraft finally touched down at JFK, passengers pushed and ran toward the immigration line in a 200-meter sprint down red carpeted lanes that passed I LOVE NY posters toward a barrier separating those with U.S. passports and green cards from those without. By the time the INS inspectors had processed the first 200 passengers of the plane, scheduled to land together with three European carriers and an E1 A1 jet, those checking passports would be weary-eyed and dizzy.

Pakistan International Airlines Flight PK702 landed at John F. Kennedy International Airport at just after 5:00 P.M. on September 1, 1992. It had been a typical summer's day in New York City—warm, very humid, with the threat of a thundershower an ever-present fear. It had been a long journey for the two men. They had flown together from Peshawar on Pakistan International Airlines Flight PK339 to Karachi and then, after a brief layover, boarded the flight to New York City.

The two men, who sat together on the flight and talked quietly for the duration of the haul to New York City, wore the silk tribal gowns and vests that were typical of Afghan refugees. Both were unkempt. They wore sandals and seemed in no hurry to push and jockey for position on the lengthy line. In fact, at the entrance to the long line of individuals hoping to cross through immigration and fetch their bags, the two men split up without even a good-bye handshake.

Both men must have had a great deal of contempt for the INS inspectors they would soon come up against. Although both possessed valid travel documents, they had used photograph-substituted passports from the United Kingdom and Sweden to purchase their tickets and board the flight in Karachi for New York City. But at one point during the flight, the two men stowed away their valid identification and substituted flimsy forgeries.

The first of the two to present his documents at the passport check was, according to law enforcement officials, the diversion. His name was Ahmad Ajaj, a twenty-five-year-old Palestinian living in Texas and working as a Domino's Pizza deliveryman. Ajaj had attempted to live the American dream only to find himself alienated and disenfranchised. Lanky, with emaciated jowls, Ajaj had traveled to and from Pakistan from his home in Houston before that September afternoon. He had volunteered for the fight in Afghanistan and had trained in the camps in Pakistan to be a mujahadeen. According to reports, he had also traveled to the United Arab Emirates, a freewheeling Disneyland of Arab commerce and terrorist traffic called, in Jordanian intelligence circles, "The Hub of the AK-47 and Semtex Crowd." Ajaj had also ventured to Saudi Arabia, where he studied at Islamic schools and training facilities.

Ahmad Ajaj was the operation's travel facilitator—it was his job to personally escort the operation's commander and chief bomb builder into the United States. Ajaj had a five-year student visa for the United States, though he was traveling to and from the Asian subcontinent on a Jordanian passport he had received in Houston. The passport's owner, who had just been naturalized as a U.S. citizen and was eligible to get a U.S. passport, no longer needed his Jordanian documentation and its U.S. entry visa. The Jordanian immigrant handed his old passport to the eager Palestinian who, in Houston, was known to talk of his brave battles against Israeli forces in Jerusalem. In reality, Ajaj's claims of defending the al-Aqsa mosque were nothing more than fantasy.

The Jordanian passport with its U.S. visa would have allowed him to pass through unhindered and without undue scrutiny by INS agents. But either Ajaj was trying to hide any evidence of his own arrival into the United States, or his role that September afternoon was to cause a scene at the airport. Walking up to the booth of INS Inspector Cathy Bethom, Ajaj removed a battered Swedish passport bearing the name Khurram Khan from his teeth. INS inspectors hated when Third World travelers handed them passports with teeth marks and dripping saliva. As Bethom looked at Ajaj, inspecting his demeanor and facial patterns, he scowled and seemed perturbed.

The passport belonged to an actual Swedish citizen, a European of Middle Eastern descent who had surrendered his original passport at the front gate of a training camp in Pakistan. The Swedish passport was a useful tool to hand in at the PIA check-in counter at Karachi International Airport—Swedish citizens did not require a visa to enter into the United States. But the passport's original bearer looked *nothing* like Ajaj, so Ajaj had used children's glue to paste a photo of himself over the image of the passport's original owner. The immigration officer in Karachi must have seen that it was a fake, but corruption was rife in Pakistan—especially at airports and border crossings. The photo substitution was so bad, so amateurish, in fact, that Inspector Bethom was able to remove the photo with her fingernails.

Ajaj raised a holy ruckus at Bethom's primary interview, the initial process of having one's passport checked. He began to curse, he screamed, and he even threatened violence. With the help of several inspectors, Ajaj was dragged to an interview room, where an INS Special Operations inspector was summoned to conduct a secondary interview, determining what was to be done with the Middle Easterner without true documentation.

Inside a holding room at the IAB, Ajaj was strip-searched and his bags were searched as well. Ahmed Ajaj was the stereotypical terrorist who should have raised a giant red flag in the hallways of the Department of Justice. But the INS investigation of the wiry Palestinian was almost as amateurish as the glued-on photo on his bad Swedish passport. Bomb-building materials in Arabic and English were found in his suitcases, as were two passports—the genuine Jordanian passport with the U.S. visa and a stolen British passport, the one the other traveler had used to get out of Pakistan, also modified with a poorly pasted-on photo. Both passports had Pakistan International Airlines boarding cards, for seats 26A and 26B, inserted inside, and both sported Karachi International Airport immigration stamps, indicating that the bearers of those passports left Pakistan on September 1.

Ajaj had been a good soldier. He had completed his mission almost as planned, in a fashion almost too good to believe. His job was to act as a loud and boisterous diversion affording his "human package" the opportunity to slip through JFK. The human package must have been important for the cause to sacrifice an operative. That operative, in the moments before PK702 flew over Long Island, New York, on its final approach to Runway 22L at JFK International Airport, handed his British passport to Ajaj for safekeeping. It would no longer be needed. Even as he was being led away to a federal immigration detention center in downtown Manhattan, Ajaj remained defiant. He knew that the Americans had apprehended the wrong man. He knew he would be the one to laugh last.

The INS handling of Ahmed Ajaj, after Inspector Betham successfully pinpointed the doctored passport and detained him, was, in the words of one former federal law enforcement official who served in New York City, "like having the Keystone Kops manning the floodgates, and it was embarrassing." The INS often failed to investigate and prosecute cases of individuals with terrorist connections. In fact, they prosecuted and deported only the most severe violators for fraudulent entry into the United States. The Diplomatic Security Service was never called to play a role in the Ajaj matter, because the service was, remarkably, rarely called in such matters. Simple cases of illegal entry into the United States were usually handled solely by INS. And, long before enhanced penalties involving cases of document fraud connected to terrorist acts that would have guaranteed a twenty-year prison term were in place, the INS was not on guard for terrorists attempting to enter the United States. The INS tended to summon DSS only in cases when a fraudulent American passport or forged American entry visa might be found. Airport inspectors working for the Immigration and Naturalization Service do not have the authority to arrest American citizens.

To this day, DSS agents, including veterans from the agency's counterterrorism division, are convinced that had they had the chance to review the paperwork of the two highly suspect Arab men that September afternoon, one of the most audacious terrorist operations ever launched inside the United States would have been thwarted.[2]

UP UNTIL HE HAD ENTERED THE LONG LINE OF FLIGHT PK702 PASSENGERS waiting to pass through immigration, Ajaj's travel partner was a Kuwaiti-born Pakistani national who spoke Arabic with a unique West Bank Palestinian accent. Unlike Ajaj, who threw what veteran INS inspectors called a "subcontinent shit fit," the Pakistani walked calmly, almost respectfully, toward the window of Inspector Martha Morales. The young bearded man in his Afghani robes smiled in polite reverence at the INS inspector, and handed her a Grade-A counterfeit Iraqi passport in the name of Ramzi Ahmed Yousef. "I would like to request political asylum," Yousef stated in a low and apologetic voice. "I will be killed if I go back to Iraq."

Two incidents from one flight was odd, even by the wacky standards of flights from Pakistan, though INS investigators saw no connection between the two young Arab men who had sat next to one another on the flight from Karachi. Unlike Ajaj, Yousef was quiet, pleasant, and in awe of the treatment he received. He spoke in a Middle Eastern accent that sparkled with the slightest British nuance. He did not appear to be threatening, though the inspector who conducted his interview seemed somewhat unsure of the veracity of the Iraqi's claim. Ajaj, conveniently enough, had been the last detainee assigned to the holding facility, and the makeshift immigration jail was now filled to capacity. The INS supervisor at the airport that afternoon ignored the report filed by the secondary investigator. Airline passengers, the Immigration and Naturalization Service hierarchy demanded, were to be referred to as "customers." And the customer was always right. Cases that could not be definitively resolved at the airport, or at a detention facility, were, in the words of one INS inspector, "to be removed expeditiously."

Yousef received a thorough interview by a secondary inspector, and then by an asylum officer. It was the asylum officer who would have to make the determination if Yousef was adjudged to have credible fear of persecution, death, or imprisonment. The criteria were incredibly subjective, and anyone deemed close to fitting the bill—or putting on one hell of an acting performance—would be entitled to a formal hearing before an immigration judge. Yousef aced audition after audition. He was, reportedly, held at the airport for seventy-two hours while INS officials pondered his case. The primary case agent, Martha Morales, had serious doubts about the Iraqi with the charming and humble personality. His story, no matter how many times he went through his routine, was suspect, and he had a "bad" passport. But, as the main detention facility in downtown Manhattan on Varick Street was full, and he did not confess to being an aggravated felon, or a criminal convicted of a crime of moral turpitude, the asylum officer handed the grateful Iraqi a "Walk in 240" form, releasing the individual on his own recognizance and trusting him to show up for the hearing some six months to a year and a half down the road at 26 Federal Plaza in Manhattan to plead his case for political asylum. Ninety percent of those issued with the release never showed up for their hearings. Yousef did not ruin the INS percentage rate. Without as much as having to show how he would support himself before his hearing and without having to prove where he would stay until then, Ramzi Ahmed Yousef was released, handed his bags, and delivered to the United States of America through the meeting hall of JFK's International Arrivals Building.

The name of Ramzi Ahmed Yousef would stick—as would the photograph taken from his confiscated fake Iraqi passport. When he grabbed his suitcase and walked through the International Arrivals Building to look for ground transportation, Abdul Basit Mahmoud Abdul Karim had become Ramzi Yousef.

Yousef took a cab from the airport to Atlantic Avenue in Brooklyn, the heart of the Arab émigré community in New York City, and went to the al-Kifah refugee center.

RAMZI AHMED YOUSEF WAS THE KIND OF YOUNG MAN WHO, WITH THE proper goals and a nice wife, could have been a rising star on the corporate ladder of success. Potential is a dangerous character trait in the tumultuous world of the global Islamic jihad, and Yousef was seen as a man with an unlimited future in the bin Laden underground in Afghanistan.

Little is known about Ramzi Yousef. His real name is Abdul Basit Mahmoud Abdul Karim.[3] The son of Pakistani laborers, Yousef was born in Kuwait and grew up in Pakistan—claims of him being an Iraqi, a Baluchi, an Iranian, and an Arab are incorrect, though it is believed that his mother is Palestinian (he has a grandmother still living in the Israeli port city of Haifa). Unlike in the United States, Kuwaiti citizenship is not a birthright. The majority of the people in Kuwait, in fact, are foreign laborers who keep the oil-rich emirate running, so citizenship and all it entails—free housing, free education, government allowances, and health care—is not offered to the sons and daughters of Pakistani builders, Lebanese nurses, Egyptian street sweepers, and Filipino domestic servants. Besides his birth on April 27, 1968, little is known about Ramzi Yousef's childhood other than that he was a gifted student who went to Fahaheel High School in Kuwait City.[4] Like many in Kuwait, even children of foreign workers, Ramzi Yousef traveled overseas for his university studies.

In the autumn of 1986 Ramzi Yousef enrolled at the Swansea Institute in Wales. At Swansea, Yousef majored in electrical engineering; he also spent months at the Oxford College of Further Education to bolster his English-language skills. Yousef's fellow students remember the Kuwaiti-born Pakistani as "temperamental and volatile."[5] Others remember him as a playboy-wanabee who tried to take maximum advantage of his exotic good looks with the local females.

Like all foreign students, Yousef was fingerprinted by the local police upon his entry into enrollment at Swansea. It was the first piece of a multisectional puzzle of evidence that the wily Yousef would leave around the world.

Four years later, now fluent in English and far more savvy than he was before his first overseas trip, Yousef returned to Kuwait City equipped with an engineering degree. He returned to a Kuwait that was living on borrowed time.

Oddly enough, in a footnote to his life story that still puzzles investigators, Yousef was able to leave Kuwait City after the Iraqi invasion. On August 26, 1990, three weeks after the Iraqi military seized the emirate, many of Kuwait's able-bodied male population had been arrested or executed or, if they were rich native-born sons, had driven their Cadillac, Mercedes, and BMW sedans across the desert into Saudi Arabia. In a Kuwait under the most brutal of Iraqi occupations, Ramzi Yousef managed to bypass the Iraqi intelligence services and Republican Guard roadblocks to get himself into Iran.

Perhaps it was his Palestinian heritage that allowed him to move freely in occupied Kuwait. The Palestinians, led by PLO Chairman Yasir Arafat, openly embraced the Iraqi occupation and Iraqi strongman Saddam Hussein. The Palestinian residents of Kuwait, resentful for years that they were the engineers and oil-drillers who made Kuwait so wealthy but were always second-class laborers never offered Kuwaiti citizenship, were willing collaborators with the Iraqi forces.

The Islamic Republic of Iran was not Yousef's final destination, however. Yousef found his way to Pakistan, *his*—by nationality anyway— Pakistan. He made his way to Peshawar and then into Afghanistan, where he became a willing recruit for the Egyptian, Palestinian, and Saudi men running Osama bin Laden's al-Qaeda network. Yousef was quite different from many of his comrades in al-Qaeda. He was cool and calculating. The Afghan Arabs were impulsive. They had earned their stripes of valor on the battlefields of Kabul, Jalalabad, and Khost. Yousef had potential for tasks far more important than ambushing a Soviet convoy of Zil trucks and BMP armored personnel carriers.

Yousef's electrical engineering studies were put to their maximum potential use. According to several reports, and the beliefs of Pakistani investigators, Ramzi Yousef attended bomb-making and terrorism instructional courses while in Afghanistan and Pakistan with al-Qaeda.[6]

Yousef was a bomb-building prodigy. He was also a natural deep-cover operative. Terrorist headhunters possess an uncanny knack of being able to tell which man will fit into foreign surroundings and survive, and which one will be looked at warily by local law enforcement. Being a good terrorist required confidence, and Yousef was as cocky as they came. He was the kind of man al-Qaeda had sought. Witty, urbane, and very cognizant of his appearance, Yousef was a yuppie for Allah. He was also incredibly resourceful and a terrific liar, skills that would be crucial in excelling in the intricate terrorist tradecraft that built operational cells, procured safe houses, obtained phony driver's licenses and stolen ATM cards, and developed an underground persona that kept law enforcement away until it was too late. Yousef was such a promising pupil that his commanders dispatched him throughout Asia to act as a recruiter for new fighters for the cause. Yousef's commanders in al-Qaeda wanted him to set up operational bases for the organization in the Far East. Al-Qaeda was going global in 1992, and Asia was fertile ground for a terrorist front line.

In April 1992, according to intelligence reports, Yousef returned to Pakistan from the Far East via Iraq. Iraq was a clever ruse. If he was ever captured or implicated in a crime, the Iraqi connection would deflect attention away from Pakistan. Iraq was also one of those countries that were full of covert opportunities, and like any yuppie eager to invest in the market or buy a time share, Yousef was aggressively opportunistic in all his "business" ventures.

Yousef remained in Pakistan until September 1, 1992, when he was brought to New York City to carry out a most sensitive mission for the cause.

ARRIVING AT THE AL-KIFAH REFUGEE CENTER, YOUSEF MET MAHMOUD Abouhalima. It is unclear if the two had met in Pakistan or whether, in the many surreptitious phone calls placed by the Sheikh's followers, through numbers in Germany, to telephone numbers in Pakistan and Saudi Arabia, Abouhalima had been forewarned about Yousef's arrival. Abouhalima introduced Yousef to everyone as "Rashid the Iraqi," a special visitor from "overseas." Many in the al-Kifah refugee center were wary of newcomers. Old-timers could be trusted. New faces could be FBI, CIA, Mossad, Egyptian intelligence, even agents for Saddam. Atlantic Avenue was always a "sensitive" stretch of Brooklyn's northern precincts. Patrol officers were routinely called to break up disputes, sometimes violent ones, between Yemenis and Egyptians, Syrians and Lebanese. And when responding, precinct officers always had to be wary of compromising FBI or other governmental intelligence-gathering agencies, staked out in front of Yemeni social clubs and Palestinian coffeehouses. As one veteran Brooklyn cop stated, "In World War Two there were places of espionage and intrigue like Stockholm, Lisbon, Casablanca, and Istanbul. Well, we have Atlantic Avenue!"[7]

The immigrants tended to trust only their own kind unless a newcomer came with a recommendation. Sheikh Rahman, apparently, had thrown out a large welcome mat for the traveler from Karachi. According to Simon Reeve, in his meticulously documented book *The New Jackals*, Yousef slept on the floor of Abouhalima's Brooklyn apartment his first free night in New York. Eventually he moved in with Mohammed Salameh into his Jersey City apartment on Kensington Avenue in the heart of the city's Arab section. Salameh, a Palestinian, was a wide-eyed follower of Sheikh Rahman who, after being forced to flee the West Bank as a child in the 1967 war, and living as a refugee in Jordan, was itching to be a player in an operation—any operation—that would strike out against Israel. And if Israel couldn't be attacked, then Israel's primary ally and supplier of weapons would do just fine.

The exact manner in which the threads of the bombing plot were woven together into a military operation designed to topple both towers of the World Trade Center remains a mystery to this day. Many of the men who listened to Sheikh Rahman's every word, swallowing up the hatred and the contempt with an endless appetite, were foot soldiers. They had pulled triggers, pulled pins on grenades, and maybe even shot down a Soviet helicopter or two. Mahmoud Abouhalima, the hulking redheaded giant, was rumored to have cleared Soviet landmines using nothing more than a wooden stick and unyielding faith and courage. Foot soldiers obey orders, storm an enemy fortification, and fight to the death. They don't create operational plans nor, like master artisans, do they conjure up recipes and mixtures to create an explosive agent so powerful, it could result in the death of over 250,000 people in the blinding flash of detonation.

From the apartment building in Jersey City, where the smell of the Arab kitchen permeated the air like a walk through the bazaar in Kuwait, Yousef's true objective was clear. One didn't have to travel far or look hard to see what enemy position was most vulnerable and most visible. The lights from the Twin Towers cast a bright blanket of warmth over Jersey City at night. After dinner—Yousef would cook—when Mahmoud Abouhalima would come to visit his two friends and talk about the "operation," the bright light from across the Hudson River was inescapable. Destroying the towers, Yousef envisioned, would change the view from across the Hudson forever.

The FBI, through its informant inside the Sheikh Rahman inner circle, had grown concerned over the band of zealots shuttling back and forth between Jersey City, Brooklyn, and visits to El Sayyid Nosair in Attica. But Emad Salem was pulled off the case. Salem was a difficult source to control. He apparently made inappropriate advances to Special Agent Nancy Floyd, and he was also reported to have taped conversations with Floyd's partner, Special Agent John Anticev.[8] But in September 1992, just after Yousef's arrival in the United States, federal law enforcement was once again interested in El Sayyid Nosair and his supporters, whom Salem had been monitoring for the bureau.

Sheikh Rahman's enmity toward the United States was nothing compared to his absolute hatred for the regime of Egyptian President Hosni Mubarak. Mubarak, Sadat's successor and, in the eyes of the fundamentalists, stooge, was the true enemy of Islam. Mubarak's security forces in 1992 were waging a brutal campaign against the fundamentalist underground. The war had intensified following the return of hundreds of Afghan Arab veterans eager to put their combat skills to good use. The Egyptian fundamentalist terrorist groups wanted Mubarak dead. Egyptian military intelligence, with information possibly obtained from Emad Salem, had learned of Sheikh Rahman's influence and power in New York City. In the fall of 1992, with Mubarak scheduled to address the United Nations at the opening of the General Assembly, Egyptian authorities were concerned that Rahman's supporters would attempt to assassinate Mubarak in Manhattan.

So the FBI, at the behest of the U.S. Secret Service, summoned over twenty of Sheikh Rahman's followers to their field office at 26 Federal Plaza for fingerprinting and intimidation. FBI surveillance photos of the group were even posted on the wall in the waiting area where the motley crew of cab drivers and handymen were questioned and warned.[9]

Men like Mahmoud Abouhalima and Ibrahim Elgabrowny were not intimidated by the bureau. After all, they came from a country where the security services attached electrodes to one's genitalia if information was needed. Ramzi Yousef's operation would continue unhindered. It was time for "Field Marshal Yousef" to take command and rally the troops.

RAMZI AHMED YOUSEF'S MOST BRILLIANT TALENT LAY IN HIS ABILITY TO rally men behind him and delegate authority for a scheme that few of his cohorts could truly appreciate. Nidal Ayyad was a required tool for the operation. A chemical engineer, he had access to the raw materials needed to build a homemade explosive device and could act as a convenient cover in case Yousef's bomb-building procurement list required corporate legitimacy. Together with his helper Salameh, Yousef, using a phone book's worth of aliases, procured enormous quantities of chemicals from a company called City Chemical, including 1,000 pounds of urea, 105 gallons of nitric acid, and 60 gallons of sulfuric acid.[10] The materials were stored in an industrial storage facility, Space Station Storage, near the Bayonne border.

On January 1, 1993, Ramzi Yousef and Mohammed Salameh moved into an apartment at 40 Pamrapo Avenue, on the fringe of the Arab quarter's frontier, which served as the bomb factory. For the next month, Yousef and his helpers from the al-Kifah refugee center and the al-Salaam mosque built one of the most ingenious—and powerful—improvised explosive devices ever constructed in the United States.

It was ironic that the ragtag army of impoverished holy warriors that worked with Yousef in building and delivering his bomb were, for the most part, individuals who were buying into the promise of the

American dream. They were immigrants engaged in a holy struggle but protected, as their cries of injustice indicated during the El Sayid Nosair trial, by the constitutional rights of democracy.

In January 1993, Sheikh Rahman's sermon of the week focused on the evils of America and the great carnage that would soon befall the evil land of Satan and the Jews. As Rahman fired up the crowded mosque with warnings of death and destruction, Ramzi Ahmed Yousef took the PATH train from Jersey City to Manhattan for a visit to the consulate general of the Islamic Republic of Pakistan at 12 East 65th Street on New York's upscale Upper East Side. Dressed in a suit and tie, Yousef walked into the townhouse holding his genuine birth certificate in the name of Abdul Basit and relating a story that he had lost his passport in New York City. Eager to help out the stranded citizen, the consulate general's office quickly arranged for a new passport to be issued. With a passport in hand, Yousef ventured to the Pakistan International Airlines ticket office at 505 Eighth Avenue on the West Side. Paying in cash, he purchased a business-class ticket for the flight to Karachi leaving New York City on the night of February 26, 1993.

Ramzi Yousef's mission to New York City was coming to an end.

On the morning of February 26, 1993, Ramzi Ahmed Yousef was sitting inside a bright yellow one-ton Ford F350 Econoline van, rented a week earlier by Mohammed Salameh and Nidal Ayyad in Jersey City, New Jersey, heading for the Holland Tunnel and the quick commute into lower Manhattan. Eyad Ismoil, a Jordanian who had entered the United States two years earlier on a student visa for Wichita State University in Kansas, was driving the vehicle; Salameh, whose incompetence had already sparked furious spasms of rage from Yousef, had crashed a car with Yousef inside a month earlier. Mahmoud Abouhalima and Mohammed Salameh are believed to have followed in close pursuit in a red Oldsmobile sedan that Nidal Ayyad had rented a few days earlier. The Ryder van, Alabama license plate XA70668, entered Tower One of the World Trade Center at just after 11:00 A.M. The van had been meticulously loaded all of the night before with large cardboard boxes containing an ingenious witch's brew of urea and sulfuric acid, fused together with four large containers of nitroglycerine propelled by compressed hydrogen cylinders. Federal investigators believe that the bomb consisted of 1,500 pounds of homemade fertilizer-based explosive urea nitrate. The fusing system consisted of two twenty-minute lengths of nonelectric burning-type fuse, which, when reaching a lead azide blaster, would initiate the explosion. The device was ingenious, and it could have been far more diabolical. Ramzi Yousef, ostensibly, had hoped to place chemical agents inside his device to increase its lethal capacity. According to federal investigators, Yousef had wanted to use hydrogen cyanide in the bomb, but in the end it was too expensive to implement.[11]

The Ryder truck was parked underneath West Street, below the PATH tracks, approximately ten feet from the south wall of Tower One, near support column K31/8, directly underneath the northeast corner of the Vista Hotel. Yousef scanned the public parking garage carefully, and lit the fuse carefully. Fearing some sort of mishap, he had designed his initiator with a multitiered backup once the fuse was lit. Yousef and Ismoil walked quickly out of Level B-2 of the parking garage and into the backseat of the rented Oldsmobile. The gang wanted to be through the Holland Tunnel and back in New Jersey when the Ryder truck evaporated into a fireball of destruction causing the support beams of Tower One to buckle and collapse and crush Tower Two.

The weather was nasty that Friday afternoon. It was bitter cold, with the mercury hovering at just above freezing. Snow flurries were in the air. It was windy.

It was just about noon on February 26, 1993, when Sergeant Juan Garcia of the NYPD's Emergency Service Unit Truck Two found himself tied into a support beam atop a bridge overlooking the Mosholu Parkway in the Bronx. Truck Two, whose area of responsibility covered Manhattan North from 59th Street uptown to the Bronx border, river to river, was responding to a distraught male, a "jumper," threatening to commit suicide by hurling himself onto the pavement below. Sergeant Garcia loved rescues. Even though the Emergency Service Unit was also the department's tactical SWAT team, one of its primary missions was emergency rescues of motorists trapped in their vehicles, or burning jetliners, and people who simply needed their lives saved. Jumpers were one of their responsibilities.

At 12:18 P.M., as Garcia was attempting to create a dialogue of trust with the hapless soul looking to end it all in the Bronx, the Special Operations Division radio frequency flashed an emergency call. "Adam-One, Truck One, Adam-Two, Truck Two, we are receiving confirmed reports of a 10-33 [NYPD code for explosion] from underneath the World Trade Center." Within seconds, the jumper was abandoned by the emergency cops flying south, down the Henry Hudson Parkway, toward the shimmering silver towers of the World Trade Center. They would soon be joined by hundreds of rescue workers.

Every one of the NYPD's Emergency Service Units responded to the explosion at the World Trade Center. Smoke billowed through broken sheets of glass. Dark puffs of smoke were even seen emanating out of the observation deck. ESU officers, flown to the top of the deck by NYPD choppers, rappelled down to the rooftop to assist in the rescue. The Fire Department of New York (FDNY) responded to the incident with eighty-four engine companies, sixty truck companies, twenty-eight battalion chiefs, nine deputy chiefs, five rescue companies, and twenty-six other specialized units comprising nearly 50 percent of the department's resources.

The explosion underneath the World Trade Center was massive. Six people inside the garage were killed by the thunderous blast. More than 1,000 people in the towers were wounded by acrid smoke and flying glass or suffered injuries in the chaotic rush to flee the buildings. More than 50,000 people were evacuated. It was, perhaps, naïve for Yousef to think that he could topple one building onto the next. FBI postblast experts were able to determine that a crater some 150 feet in diameter, and five stories deep, had been burrowed out by Yousef's bomb. Bomb assessment experts were able to assess, from damage to vehicles in the parking garage, that the explosive agent had a velocity of detonation of between 14,000 and 15,000 feet per second. The damage that the powerful explosion initiated was mind-boggling. The blast had created over 2,500 cubic yards of debris weighing in excess of

6,800 tons. Some 2 million gallons of water and sewage were pumped out of the crime scene. The explosion had caused over $600 million in property damage.

Two Bureau of Alcohol, Tobacco, and Firearms (ATF) National Response Teams assisted the New York City Police Department and the FBI in the investigation. Also participating in the investigation were the U.S. Secret Service, the U.S. Customs Service (whose New York field offices were based in the World Trade Center), the U.S. Department of Defense, the Port Authority of New York and New Jersey, and the New York and New Jersey State Police. Detectives from the NYPD Bomb Squad and the NYPD Emergency Service Unit were at "ground zero" throughout the investigation. At the time, it was the largest criminal investigation in the history of American law enforcement.

At just after 6:00 p.m. on the evening of February 26, 1993, Ramzi Yousef sat in the backseat of a yellow cab, grinding through the wet winter's traffic, southbound on the Van Wyck Expressway toward John F. Kennedy International Airport's International Departures Terminal. The airport was its usual bustling epicenter of crisscrossing taxis and arriving and departing passengers juggling luggage. Security at the airport was tighter than usual. An explosion underneath the World Trade Center sparked added interest from the police and federal authorities. But what would the responding patrol officers be looking for? Would FBI agents assigned to the airport be looking for anyone in particular? Which terminal should they have focused on? Some six hours after the explosion had buckled six stories of rubble and steel underneath the Vista Hotel in a crater of death and an elevating smoke cloud, the true cause of the blast had yet to be determined. FDNY officials were still checking out the possibility of the explosion coming from a faulty electrical transformer. NYPD, ATF, and FBI officials, at a command post in downtown Manhattan, were fielding phone calls from every psycho and his mother claiming responsibility for the blast. Callers claiming to represent a dozen Arab and Palestinian groups contacted police and news organizations to stake responsibility for the bombing. Many in law enforcement believed that the Serbs, or possibly Russian organized crime, were involved.

Ramzi Ahmed Yousef, wearing a custom-fitted green twill suit, checked in at the Pakistan International Airlines counter just as news reports filtered in to the local networks that the 5th Battalion of the Arab Liberation Army had taken credit for the World Trade Center bombing. He handed his legitimate Pakistani passport in the name of Abdul Basit and business-class ticket to the young woman at the counter and checked his bag for PK 716, with a connection through Manchester for Islamabad and Karachi.

The Pakistani aircraft taxied on runway 4R that crisp evening. Air traffic control was congested but manageable. As nearly 500 NYPD Emergency Service Unit officers, firemen, and FBI and ATF agents attempted to descend into the fiery pit of destruction underneath the Twin Towers, Ramzi Ahmed Yousef reclined in a window seat and relished having pulled off the crime of the century and a great escape. Yousef was far from the dictionary definition of the courageous leader. As he crossed the Atlantic en route to life on the run and with ambitions that dwarfed even the attempted destruction of the World Trade Center, his cell of operatives and wannabe holy warriors were left without escape and without a fight. Perhaps Yousef wanted it that way. How fitting a cover for a man so brilliant and devious—to have the authorities arrest and humiliate a bumbling force of amateurs.

Some sixteen hours later, Ramzi Ahmed Yousef walked through the immigration hall in the Jinnah terminal at Karachi's Quaid-e-Azam International Airport. There was no need to claim political asylum, no need to be walked through and facilitated, as had been done for him at New York's John F. Kennedy International Airport. Unlike his departure from Karachi some six months earlier, his arrival did not require bribing an immigration official. Ramzi Ahmed Yousef was, once again, Abdul Basit, and he was just another traveler returning home.

Yousef vanished from Karachi International Airport that night. He either took a flight to Quetta, where he had family, or ventured, by rail or by bus, to the North-West Frontier to Peshawar, where he could report to his masters about the operation in New York City.

When DSS special agents based in the United States and throughout the world first heard the news that a bomb had torn through the basement of the World Trade Center, the first thought was Hezbollah. Hezbollah, the Lebanese Shiite "Party of God," had turned truck bombing into an art form. The Israeli Air Force, using an American-built AH-64 Apache chopper and an American-built Hellfire missile, had, almost a year to the day before the World Trade Center blast, assassinated Hezbollah military leader Abbas Assawi in an aerial ambush on a twisting mountain road in southern Lebanon. "This had to be revenge for that," one DSS agent based in Cairo immediately told himself. "Who else blew up American buildings?"

Special Agent Scott Stewart was one of the first DSS agents dispatched to New York City to investigate the terrorist angle of the blast underneath the Twin Towers. News of the World Trade Center bombing came as a complete surprise to the veteran agent assigned to the DSS Counterterrorism Division.

The Counterterrorism Division had since 1985 been the sole U.S. law enforcement entity to actively travel the planet hunting down terrorists and investigating bombings, kidnappings, assassinations, and hijackings. "The FBI does have a presence overseas in their legal attaché, or LEGAT, program," Stewart said, "but they were always based in the real world capitals of Europe and Asia, like London, Paris, Rome, and Bangkok. We were the ones who were in places like Beirut, Sierra Leone, Sana'a, and Karachi. Our RSOs were there and we had, in our travels, developed and nurtured the local contacts who could help us out. These were contacts, incredibly important assets, that the FBI simply did not have. We were in the Karachis of the world. The FBI wasn't."[12]

Stewart had just returned from Aden, Yemen, when Yousef's bomb tore through the basement underneath the Vista Hotel. He had led a small team of investigators sifting through forensic evidence of the December 29, 1992, bombing of the Gold Mihor Hotel, as well as a sophisticated rocket attack against the U.S. embassy in Sana'a. The hotel, a rest stop for U.S. servicemen assigned to Operation Restore

Hope in Somalia, was hit by a sophisticated bomb that killed an Austrian tourist and seriously injured his wife. "Yemenis had traditionally settled family scores with bombs," Stewart recalled, "but the timing device on this one was very sophisticated and it caught our attention." Initial focus in Aden centered on a Libyan or Iraqi connection. Yemen was a hotbed of activity for Arab intelligence services and Middle Eastern terrorist groups. Whoever built the bomb that tore through the hotel in Aden possessed skill, sophisticated tools, and equipment often used by Middle Eastern security services. Even the rocket attack against the embassy in Sana'a left the telltale signs of a sophisticated terrorist group at work. The rocket, a U.S.-built M-20 bazooka round, was fired from the launching tube with a book of matches taped around the end of a piece of time fuse and stuffed into the rocket. The projectile was fired from an empty field across the street from the embassy. Special agents in the DSS Counterterrorism Division had taken a course in IEDs, or improvised explosive devices, from the CIA some months earlier—the same sort of class that agency training officers had offered their Arab legions fighting in Afghanistan. In Yemen, less than two months before Yousef's bomb would rip through the parking area underneath the Vista Hotel, the bin Laden terrorist network hit its first target. But Aden and Sana'a were far from the mass media outlets of New York City. Few paid attention to the attacks or to who might have perpetrated them.

Special agents assigned to the Counterterrorism Division were the Diplomatic Security Service's specialists in dealing with any acts of terrorism committed overseas, as well as with acts of terrorism committed domestically that involved fraudulent passports and visas. The DSS Counterterrorism Division relished its top-secret reputation. Few in the service knew that they existed, and even fewer knew what they did. The division's small nook on the fifth floor of a nondescript building near the main headquarters of the State Department on C Street, in the section of Washington, D.C., known as Foggy Bottom, was affectionately known as the "Cone of Silence," a reference to *Get Smart*, the 1960s TV show about spies in the nation's capital. But there was nothing amusing about the work they did. Special agents assigned to the division knew just about everything there was to know about various terrorist groups' tradecraft, modus operandi, and personalities.

Some agents in the unit knew everything to be known about Hezbollah in Lebanon. They had been dispatched to the smoldering ruins of the two U.S. embassies that were blown up by suicide bombers, as well as to the deadly catacombs of the marine barracks destroyed in Beirut in 1983. There were agents who knew everything about the Popular Front for the Liberation of Palestine General Command and its leader, Ahmed Jibril, the mastermind of the destruction of Pan Am Flight 103 over Lockerbie, Scotland. Two DSS agents, Daniel Emmet O'Connor, the site security manager at the embassy in Cyprus, and Ronald Lariviere, an assistant RSO based in Beirut, were among those killed high above the green plains of Scotland in December 1988. Special agents in the division knew more about Basque ETA bomb-builders than the Spanish authorities, and there were old South American hands in the division who were walking encyclopedias on guerrilla groups lurking in the jungles of the continent.

In March 1992, for example, following the Hezbollah bombing of the Israeli embassy in Buenos Aires, Argentina, DSS Special Agent Mike Parks, one of the founders of the agency's rewards program, led an investigative team from Washington, D.C., to the Argentine capital to help local authorities hunt for clues leading to the perpetrators responsible for the attack, which left nearly 30 people dead and over 100 wounded.

The Counterterrorism Division also fielded International Response Teams to help nations beset by terrorist attacks, primarily bombings, to investigate and prosecute those responsible. The International Response Teams consisted of DSS special agents, along with specialists from the FBI and, primarily, the Bureau of Alcohol, Tobacco, and Firearms, to conduct postblast investigations and to attempt to re-create the explosive devices used in an attack.

To serve inside the Counterterrorism Division, a DSS agent had to be resourceful, intuitive, and cognizant of the reality that the work of sifting through bombed-out buildings and treading on the remains of colleagues and compatriots was not easy. Stewart's trip to Yemen was living proof of that. Yemen was a nation that, after years of being divided into two separate states, had unified to create one lawless mess.

Even by Middle Eastern standards, according to one Jordanian intelligence officer, "The Yemeni authorities were corrupt and inefficient."[13] "Law and order" was a relative term depending on who was paid off, and by how much. Terrorists from all over the world found safe haven in both halves of the Yemeni puzzle. According to one veteran British intelligence officer with years of service in the Middle East, "Aden was the type of city where a Palestinian assassin could be found having lunch with a Provisional IRA bomb-builder in a café owned by the East German Stasi and served by a waiter on the Mossad's payroll." Sana'a, the capital, was even more cutthroat. For DSS special agents like Scott Stewart, getting any work done in Yemen—from building a criminal case to assembling material for a multiagency intelligence briefing—was most difficult, especially during Ramadan, when the entire government shut down its day-to-day operations.

Stewart was sent to New York City along with Darren Hushower, a DSS security engineering officer (SEO), to join high-ranking supervisors from the FBI and NYPD's Joint Terrorism Task Force team, who were busy assembling the first shreds of a criminal case as the crater that was once the building's basement smoldered. SEOs were often likened to "Q" in the James Bond films. They take care of most of the field agents' technical needs, from setting up covert video cameras for buy-and-busts in passport fraud investigations, to installing EGIS explosive-detection machines in high-threat embassies. Stewart and Hushower were, in fact, able to take one of the EGIS machines with them to New York in order to assist the JTTF investigators in determining which type of explosive had been used in the blast.

When both special agents arrived at the smoldering crater, nothing could have prepared them for the devastation and destruction underneath the World Trade Center. "When I walked down the cavern of smoke and debris only to find the hole of twisted metal and rubble, I was overcome by the destruction," Stewart remembered. "It was far worse than things I had seen overseas. The devastation was indescribable."[14]

"Everyone and his mother claimed responsibility for the bombing," recalled an NYPD detective assigned to the Emergency Service Unit. "Every nut from Billings to Bensonhurst was looking for his fifteen minutes of fame." Initially, in fact, much of the federal focus centered on Serb nationalists. The war in Bosnia was raging at full force, and U.S. policy was against the Bosnian Serbs. Terrorist bombers from the former Yugoslavia had, after all, been active New York City. On December 29, 1975, Croatian nationalists planted a bomb in the main terminal of New York's La Guardia Airport that killed eleven people and injured over seventy-five. Nearly a year later, on September 11, 1976, Croatian terrorists struck again in New York City. A powerful bomb that had been planted in Grand Central Station exploded in a fireball of destruction that killed a detective from the NYPD's Bomb Squad and wounded over thirty cops and civilians. Police wondered, *Did the Serbs have the wherewithal and the stupidity to strike out at the heart of New York City?*

At the request of the NYPD-FBI Joint Terrorist Task Force, DSS was asked to contact its RSO in Belgrade and Zagreb and to follow up on leads and other theories.

The DSS Counterterrorism Division had worked closely with the NYPD-FBI Joint Terrorism Task Force before. Each year, for the opening of the United Nations General Assembly in New York City, the Counterterrorism Division was responsible for organizing the intelligence that agents in the field would need to coordinate the protection of the foreign ministers or members of international royalty who would come to midtown Manhattan for the annual event. Many of the dignitaries that DSS was tasked with protecting were high-threat, such as the Israeli and Cuban foreign ministers, and the Counterterrorism Division would investigate terrorists believed to be operating in the United States in order to prevent possible assassination or kidnapping attempts. UNGAs, as the United Nations General Assemblies were known, were chaotic exercises in motorcade madness. Often DSS, with manpower backup from the U.S. Marshals Service and the Bureau of Alcohol, Tobacco, and Firearms, would maneuver, manipulate, and safeguard over forty motorcades crisscrossing the gridlocked avenues and crosstown streets of New York City.

Immediately following the bombing of the World Trade Center, the NYPD-FBI Joint Terrorism Task Force requisitioned two DSS agents from the New York field office to join its ranks.

DSS special agents in the Counterterrorism Division knew many of the FBI agents from the advance work performed annually in New York City. Relations were good between the two agencies. They would have to be. The investigation would take the JTTF from theories on a Balkan connection to the realization that an international Islamic plot, with Pakistan and Afghanistan at its vortex, had just struck at a prominent symbol of American business and economic might.

THE TRUE BREAK IN THE INVESTIGATION OF THE WORLD TRADE CENTER bombing came on February 28, two days after the blast when, amid the rubble and destruction in the six-story-deep crater, agents from the Bureau of Alcohol, Tobacco, and Firearms, along with detectives from the NYPD's Bomb Squad, came across a differential from the van that transported the bomb. From its position and appearance, the agents strongly suspected that the fragment had come from the vehicle that carried the bomb. Upon closer examination, the twisted piece of metal, once scrutinized by ATF, NYPD, and FBI chemists, revealed a Vehicle Identification Number, or VIN, that had been etched onto the metal. A routine vehicle check revealed that the VIN, number LHA75633, belonged to a Ford F350 Econoline van purchased by the Ryder rental corporation. ATF bomb techs had assessed, from their initial view of ground zero, that the bomb that caused the damage must have weighed about 1,500 pounds. The Econoline van was just the vehicle to carry such a payload. An Econoline van with an identification number corresponding to the number of the missing vehicle had just been listed in a nationwide computer directory of stolen vehicles.

Special Agent Scott Stewart was in the smoking bowels of the World Trade Center when the differential was found. He would be joining other federal agents shortly thereafter knocking down doors and bringing in suspects.

Mohammed Salameh had, in the effort to retrieve his $400 deposit on the Ryder rental truck, reported the vehicle stolen the day before and had obtained an official report. When the assigned FBI agents first contacted the Ryder office in Jersey City, the clerk said that the man who rented the vehicle, a Middle Easterner named Mohammed Salameh, claimed it stolen and would be back the next day to retrieve his money. The Middle Eastern connection warranted an immediate records check. The name Mohammed Salameh came back as hot. His name lit up the FBI computer like a Roman candle. Salameh's name was prominent among the part-time *mujahadeen* who had become known to the authorities following the Kahane killing.

FBI and New Jersey State Police tactical units laid ambush to the Ryder office. When Salameh showed up, desperate for his money, he was arrested. Arrest warrants were issued for other members of the Rahman inner circle whose names first came up following the Kahane killing and who had been summoned to 26 Federal Plaza prior to Mubarak's arrival in New York City several months earlier.

MOHAMMED SALAMEH WILL FOREVER BE REMEMBERED AS THE *STUPID* TERrorist for not fleeing the country and risking arrest and eventual life in prison for a measly $400. But Salameh, like all his coconspirators, was dirt poor, and he desperately needed the $400 he had put down on the Ryder van. Salameh possessed an infant's ticket for a Royal Jordanian Airlines flight from New York to Queen Alia International Airport in Amman, through Amsterdam. The ticket had cost him only $65 and was originally acquired to obtain an entry visa into the Netherlands, but now Salameh needed to escape soon—before federal authorities could uncover the Jersey City connection to the bombing attack. Rahman's jihad foot soldiers, led by the masterful Yousef, were visionaries. But they were frugal and operating on a shoestring budget.

The Middle Eastern connection was of special significance to Special Agent Stewart. He remembered walking through the markets of northern Yemen, past stalls in the souk where $100 could buy you a .50 caliber heavy machine gun. Some of the most popular sale items had been audiocassette sermons of Sheikh Omar Abdel Rahman. Now, blocks away from the al-Salaam mosque, Stewart felt as if he were back in Yemen.

Later that day, with Salameh in custody, the other members of the viper's nest of part-time operatives were rounded up. In the afternoon of March 4, 1993, Scott Stewart donned a DSS raid jacket—a blue windbreaker with the words POLICE, DSS, and FEDERAL AGENT emblazoned in yellow reflective tape on the back and front—as he joined ATF, NYPD, INS, and FBI agents to storm the Brooklyn apartment of El Sayyid Nosair's first cousin Ibrahim Elgabrowny. Angry and abusive, Elgabrowny seemed more concerned with getting "Eat shit" and "Go fuck yourselves" out in proper English than with the prospect of being implicated in what was then the most all-encompassing criminal investigation in the history of American law enforcement. Elgabrowny refused to cooperate. In fact, he pushed and struck an ATF agent, Tom Kelly.

As the federal agents manhandled the Egyptian and frisked him, they came across a bulge inside a hidden pocket on his leather jacket. The agents removed the item, fearing a gun, but were shocked to see that it was a folded manila envelope holding several Nicaraguan passports, Nicaraguan *cédulas* (national ID cards), Nicaraguan birth certificates, and drivers' licenses. As Scott Stewart began to examine the passports and papers, a bizarre conspiracy suddenly became a lot stranger.

The Nicaraguan documents were genuine—they were not fakes and they were not stolen. Upon a closer look, though, Stewart was shocked to find that the passports with Hispanic names contained corresponding photographs of Elgabrowny, as well as El Sayyid Nosair, his wife, and their two children. Having traveled extensively throughout Central America, Stewart realized that the viper's nest of operatives slowly being rounded up were not merely radicals connected, by plot or by circumstance, to El Sayyid Nosair and Sheikh Abdel Rahman. The Sandinista government in Nicaragua was in its waning hours, and the country's intelligence service had been issuing genuine passports to many Basque ETA, Italian Red Brigade, and Palestinian terrorists who had trained and even fought in Nicaragua. But these documents, Stewart assessed, were not espionage-grade papers. Instead, he assumed, they were issued by a corrupt government official eager to make a few hundred dollars.

The passports were to be used to usher Nosair to freedom. In Elgabrowny's apartment, investigators uncovered documents and operation blueprints for a mujahadeen-style commando assault against Attica State Penitentiary in Wyoming County, New York, to rescue his imprisoned cousin. Attica, one of the darkest and most feared holes in New York State, was 350 miles and an eight-hour road trip away from downtown Brooklyn. The plan called for a truck crammed with explosives to ram the main gate of the prison while an assault force killed most of the correction officers and rescued "Brother Nosair." The plan was grandiose and a fantasy of militant fervor taking precedence over tactics and reality. But federal law enforcement officials were convinced that the Jersey City cell would definitely have attempted the operation.

Another grandiose plan that Elgabrowny had sketched out, found on papers discovered in his home and corroborated by information gleaned from FBI informant Salem, involved kidnapping former U.S. Secretary of State Henry Kissinger and holding him hostage unless El Sayyid Nosair was released and flown out of the United States.[15]

When the FBI commenced its prosecution of the World Trade Center conspirators, agents assigned to the JTTF did not even realize that they could prosecute individuals for fraudulent foreign passports and visas and indict them on charges that were virtually 100 percent convictable. Federal assistant U.S. attorneys, or AUSAs, are known to *adore* the Diplomatic Security Service, because most of the cases it brings to the attorney's office are guaranteed convictions. In order to make a passport valid—even a fake one—the bearer of that document must sign underneath his or her photograph. It is impossible to deny that the individual did not know what he was signing, so most passport cases are adjudicated with plea bargains. The pleas and convictions look impressive on an up-and-coming AUSA's list of accomplishments. And passport cases come with heavy jail time. A person in possession of a fake or fraudulent passport could receive a twenty-year sentence of hard federal time.

Out of the thirty-nine federal counts arising from the World Trade Center bombing, nine were for violation of the passport laws.[16]

Special agents from the Counterterrorism Division almost invited themselves into the initial phase of the investigation against the World Trade Center bombers. Special Agent Scott Stewart, along with Special Agent Jim Dolan from the New York field office, went to the office of the assistant U.S. attorney in lower Manhattan leading the investigation and said, "If you guys don't know that much about document fraud, we'll be happy to help you out." With the blessing of the FBI and the U.S. attorney's office, Stewart and the Counterterrorism Division began to look at both the Ajaj and Elgabrowny cases. Ahmed Ajaj was on the tail end of a six-month plea bargain with the INS over his poorly doctored-up Swedish passport. Looking at the evidence, Stewart was able to make a definitive link between Ajaj, Mohammed Salameh and his cohorts, and the man the world had come to know as Ramzi Yousef. The visa fraud investigation into Ajaj uncovered enough evidence to tie him to the conspiracy.

Once Salameh had been arrested, phone records of incoming and outgoing phone calls were examined and traced. One number came up repeatedly—a federal detention center in New York City. The time of the phone calls in question linked Salameh to Ajaj. All phone calls made inside federal holding facilities were recorded, and the transcripts revealed the extent of the bomb-building conspiracy. Salameh was heard frequently on the tape, as was another individual speaking Arabic with a unique accent. An international connection had finally been established.

Searching the evidence seized from Ahmed Ajaj at John F. Kennedy International Airport on September 1, 1992, Stewart was naturally taken aback by the bomb-building manuals and the other terrorist paraphernalia. He was also taken aback by a lead that had never truly been followed up. In Ajaj's bags Stewart found two boarding passes—in the false names used by both Ajaj and Yousef to board the aircraft in Karachi. Up until the DSS personal involvement, there had been rumors of a missing link—a mysterious man simply known as "Rashid the Iraqi." Doing a bit of detective work through the often maddening world of federal law enforcement bureaucracy, Stewart and his team of DSS investigators searched immigration for any "hits" indicating Iraqis entering the United States. One hit resonated loudly—Ramzi Ahmed Yousef. Yousef, Stewart would soon discover, had come in on the same flight as Ajaj. The coincidence was too remarkable to be circumstantial.

Stewart, with the help of DSS agents in Pakistan, contacted the travel agent in Islamabad where the airline tickets that Ajaj and Yousef used to fly to New York City were purchased. A check of the Pakistan

International Airlines computer indicated that a man by the name of Abdul Basit had *also* flown to Karachi on February 26, 1993. His passport, the records revealed, had been issued in New York City only weeks before. An international database search of fingerprints revealed that Abdul Basit was on record in Great Britain. The data were readily available inside the Files of M15, Britain's domestic counterespionage and counterterrorist intelligence agency. The prints matched those taken from the Jersey City storage facility and the apartment shared with Mohammed Salameh.

An international manhunt was underway.

THROUGHOUT 1993, FEDERAL PROSECUTORS BUILT AN IRONCLAD CASE against the World Trade Center conspirators. There were still many questions that needed to be answered, and many inside the U.S. intelligence community and federal law enforcement believed that a state—either Iraq or Iran—must have sponsored the bombing. The motley crew of bombers remained stoic in their silence. Even Mohammed Salameh, a man who became the butt of many jokes as the Bozo the Clown of international terrorism and was called, by NYPD detectives, "Carlos the Jackass," refused to cut a deal and betray his cell, his sheikh, and his religion.

As the conspirators sat inside their heavily guarded cells inside the Manhattan Correction Center, attempted to coordinate their defenses, and wondered where they had failed, their commander and bomb-builder was halfway across the world embarking on a series of operations that, in retrospect, could have made the bombing of the Twin Towers appear to be nothing more than an office fire.

FOUR MEN INVOLVED IN THE WORLD TRADE CENTER BOMBING PLOT MAN-aged to flee the United States. Ramzi Yousef was the first, followed by Abdul Rahman Yasin. Born in the American heartland, though he had spent most of his life in Iraq, the epileptic Yasin was a minor player in the conspiracy—relegated to the menial task of mixing the chemicals used to build the bomb. The FBI initially held the Bloomington, In-diana, native, then released him on the grounds he cooperated. Yasin took his American passport and fled to Baghdad, where he remains a fugitive to this day. Eyad Ismoil, the twenty-one-year-old Kuwaiti-born Jordanian national who drove Yousef and the bomb-laden truck into Tower Number One and parked it next to support column K31/8 underneath the Vista Hotel, also fled.

Next to Yousef, the most important of the fleeing plotters to escape was Mahmoud Abouhalima. He would also be the first to be picked up by law enforcement.

The giant redheaded Arab departed the United States shortly after the blast, when federal authorities were still working the Serbian or Croatian angle to the bombing, traveling to the Saudi Arabian city of Jeddah and then, by ferry, to Egypt. Mohammed Salameh's arrest brought Arab attention to the bombing in New York. "We were embarrassed by the fact that some of our citizens were involved in these attacks, and we wanted to round them up before they could do more harm," claimed a Jordanian officer in military intelligence looking back at the investigation conducted in Amman following the February 26, 1993 bombing.[17] The embarrassment was far more evident in Egypt, where President Mubarak was outraged that his old nemesis, Sheikh Omar Abdel Rahman, was still painting Egypt's image to the world with the red brush of blood and terror. Mahmoud Abouhalima would be an easy man to find in his Alexandria slum. At over six feet tall, a towering and imposing figure whose red beard was a permanent giveaway, Abouhalima was compromised by an Egyptian secret service determined to show the world that it would not be a safe harbor for terrorists. There was too much at stake. Egypt lived or died on tourist dollars, drachmas, and Deutsche marks. It also lived on the four billion dollars a year that Washington pumped into the country.

Early one morning, inside a complex of single-family dwellings near Isma'aliya, plainclothes agents from the Muchabarat identified a house where informants had, for a fee, indicated that Abouhalima was holed up. Operators from Force 777, the Egyptian military's elite counterterrorist team, were flown up from Cairo to assault the location. Wearing black balaclava masks and clutching their AK-47 assault rifles and German-made Heckler and Koch MP5 submachine guns, the counterterrorist team slinked silently through the dirt roads and garbage-strewn alleys surrounding the house. Using an explosive charge on the house's front door, they quickly entered the location to find Mahmoud Abouhalima in bed, unarmed, and completely shocked that he had been captured.

Gagged, bound, and blindfolded, Abouhalima was helicoptered to Cairo and to a special section of the main headquarters belonging to the General Directorate of State Security Investigations. The interrogation sessions inside the basement of the directorate's headquarters were legendary in Egypt, and even the most hardcore Islamic militants feared the dark and damp rooms where agents armed with bamboo poles, hammers, and other tools of the trade exacted confessions from suspects by beating their testicles, knee joints, and any other point of the body that would create the most pain. According to reports, Egyptian security agents grudgingly and secretly admitted that Abouhalima was singled out for "special treatment."

Several days later, Abouhalima was escorted from the darkness of the windowless room he had been beaten in and was blindfolded and driven, in the sort of multivehicle motorcade usually reserved for President Mubarak or one of his ministers, to Heliopolis and a secure shack on the tarmac of Cairo International Airport. There, he was handed over to Special Agent Bob O'Brien, the RSO at the sprawling U.S. embassy in Cairo, who was waiting at the airport along with several of his assistant security officers. Mahmoud Abouhalima, the gigantic red-headed Afghan warrior known for his brash and unrelenting personality, was subdued and withdrawn. Some thirteen hours later, Abouhalima was back in New York City, being processed at the Manhattan Corrections Center in the shadows of the World Trade Center.

From inside the Cone of Silence, special agents assigned to the Diplomatic Security Service's Counterterrorism Division dispatched classified memos to RSOs in embassies throughout the Middle East, the Indian subcontinent, and Southeast Asia. DSS is an organization of contacts, and it hoped that somewhere, in Kuwait, in Qatar, in Pakistan, or in Lebanon, a police officer or a secret police official who had friends at the U.S. embassy would pick up on Yousef's whereabouts and, in the vernacular, drop a dime. But DSS had a far more lucrative secret weapon in its arsenal.

In 1984, the State Department, with the support of the U.S. Congress, created the "America's Counterterrorism Rewards Program," offering cold cash—and lots of it—for information leading to the arrest of a wanted terrorist fugitive. The program truly took off in 1990, when DSS assumed logistical command of the information coming in to Washington, D.C., and the rewards initiative was placed in the hands of the Counterterrorism Division. Who better to analyze and verify the anonymous tips that might lead law enforcement to those who were responsible for such crimes as the bombing of the marine barracks in Beirut in 1983 and the downing of Pan Am Flight 103? DSS possessed impressive intelligence dossiers on many of the world's top terrorists, and it had the tools—the RSOs based in some 150 posts overseas—to do much of the legwork.

DSS ran with the program like a defensive end intercepting a forward pass. Public service announcements with such stars as Charlton Heston and Charles Bronson were released in a myriad of voice-over translations in a dozen major languages. Ads and posters in indigenous languages were distributed to local law enforcement around the world. Money spoke louder than a slick Madison Avenue campaign, and in 1990 DSS joined forces with the Air Transport Association of America and the Air Line Pilots Association, International, to increase the war chest of each reward to $1 million in addition to what the State Department was already offering. A sizable chunk of the Rewards Program was handled, remarkably, by Special Agent Brad Smith, an intrepid force seeking justice who had been stricken by Lou Gehrig's disease, from a converted command post in his home in suburban Virginia.[18]

Inside the United States, the program received relatively light publicity. Much of what the program accomplished was preemptive, and work done behind the scenes, often covertly on an anonymous tip, did not make the front page of the *New York Times*. In one case, the details of which are still classified, a tip to the rewards program helped uncover an Iraqi terrorist cell operating in the Far East that was plotting to perpetrate airport massacres in Thailand and a few other Asian cities during the opening of the Gulf War. The terrorists, armed with grenades and automatic rifles, were, at a prearranged time, going to shoot up the check-in lines of several American airlines, hoping to kill as many American citizens as possible. An anonymous call to the rewards desk prompted action from the RSO's office in the embassy and local law enforcement. A single call had averted a massacre.

But the program needed a poster child. DSS needed to jump-start the program with a face that embodied evil and indifference to human suffering. Yousef's photograph, the one taken from his Iraqi passport, was a reward program director's dream. Yousef looked like the Hollywood stereotype of a Middle Eastern villain—he possessed the kind of face that people generally saw in a bad Chuck Norris B-movie sequel being blown away at the end of the film by the hero. Yousef also had an indescribable coldness to his profile, an arrogant and twisted nature that was personified by his broken nose and dark eyes. The photo of the man, staring confidently into the camera lens, almost in a dare, was chilling. The case of Ramzi Yousef was the first DSS Rewards Program multimillion-dollar campaign.

Ramzi Yousef's face was printed on posters, pamphlets, and matchboxes teasing anyone who came across the government-printed paraphernalia with a two-million-dollar bounty. The Counterterrorism Division even wanted to put Yousef's face on packs of cigarettes, though bureaucrats at the State Department feared that critics would charge the diplomatic corps with promoting smoking in Third World countries.

Information on the reward, and on the information required, was printed in a Babel of languages. Wanted posters and matchboxes were printed in Arabic and Urdu, Farsi and Pashtun. A farmer tending to his crops in Quetta might just come across a color copy of a twenty-dollar bill that, when opened, revealed a photo of Yousef and the tempting two-million-dollar cash prize. Ferry seamen in Abu Dhabi might just light up a Kent 100 with a match from a Ramzi Yousef matchbook. "Two million dollars was a mind-boggling amount of money to offer someone in Pakistan or in a poor Arab country," a DSS agent once claimed. "Hell, you could buy most of Pakistan for less than we were offering."

Anyone with information on Yousef, or even Abdul Rahman Yasin, was urged to call, write, or e-mail. The rewards program, nurtured with great care over the infant Internet, was one of the first truly technologically sophisticated initiatives ever launched by federal law enforcement.

ONLY A FEW MONTHS AFTER THE BOMBING OF THE WORLD TRADE CENTER, Ramzi Yousef became the most wanted man on the face of the earth. The DSS was determined to bring him to justice.

Chapter 3

AMBASSADOR OF THE APOCALYPSE

Along the rock-strewn cliffs of Afghanistan, overlooking roadways carved out by mules and horses, the fighters from the East were known as the masters of the heights. They were vicious and unforgiving in battle, even more so than the Arab volunteers who came from places like Egypt and Palestine and had hundreds of years of rage to dispense. They were especially renowned for kidnapping Soviet soldiers, especially those on sentry duty, and dragging their struggling bodies back to caves where they were stripped of their weapons and rations, barbarically tortured, and then mercifully executed with a rock to the head—why waste a 7.62mm round on a man who was already dead? Unlike most of the volunteers to the cause in Afghanistan, these warriors had grown up on a steady stream of American culture, Coca-Cola, and rock music. They wore blue jeans and U.S. Army camouflage fatigues. Unlike most of the foreign volunteers to the Afghan fighting, these warriors did not speak Arabic. They spoke a combination of Tagalog and tribal dialects from a distant group of 7,017 tropical and jungle islands in the Pacific, far from the desert hell of Afghanistan.

Hundreds of Muslim volunteers from the Philippines rushed to Pakistan and Afghanistan in the mid-1980s to battle the Soviet army. The fighting in Afghanistan prompted many Muslim youngsters, some who could not see a future for themselves in the Philippines, to earn their combat stripes in the holy war beside their Arab brethren. And earn

their stripes they did. Few representatives of the jihad had excelled on
the battlefield more impressively than the young and energetic fighters
from the Philippines. But with the war in Afghanistan over and the
Soviets vanquished, the Filipinos returned home on crowded flights
from Islamabad and Karachi to Manila and Cebu. Yet the al-Qaeda
terrorist network had far more ambitious plans for these legendary
guerrilla fighters. The Philippines had always promoted itself as the
nation where "Asia wore a smile." Osama bin Laden wanted the islands
to become an outpost where Islam waved a scimitar.

The Philippines, the only Christian nation in Asia, were ripe for a
surge in Islamic fundamentalism. The Philippines' seventy-nine million people were predominantly Roman Catholic—a legacy from the
centuries of Spanish colonial rule—with just about 10 percent of the
population being Protestant. Some 5 percent of the population, nearly
four million people, was Muslim, however. Islam had spread from the
Middle East through the mountain and desert wildernesses of Central
Asia to India and China. Arab merchants, emissaries from the flour-
ishing empire based in North Africa, the Levant, and the Arabian Peninsula, had spread the word of Islam to the Malay Peninsula and the
Indonesian archipelago in the late thirteenth, fourteenth, and fifteenth
centuries. Unlike the way Islam began in the Balkans and some areas
of Africa, where it was imposed through conquest and occupation, Islam was introduced to Southeast Asia through charm and promise.
Islam flourished in what is today Malaysia and Indonesia, with the vast
majority of the inhabitants converting to the faith. In the thousands of
islands that make up the Philippines, Islam entrenched a foothold for
itself in the south. The indigenous Muslims, also called Moros, were
Sunnis and created several thriving independent sultanates in Mindanao and Zamboanga. The Moros were largely successful in resisting
the Spanish conquest and even U.S. hegemony following the Spanish-
American War, when American control of the islands began. Even after
independence, in 1946, the Moros refused to consider themselves Filipinos. The Muslim minority in the south yearned for an independent
Muslim state, one governed by the *sharia*, where American influence
and Catholic land ownership would be banished. The more the central
government in Manila neglected the southern territory, the more pow-

erful a force Islam became. Many Moro students were also sent overseas to study Islam in Malaysia, Indonesia, and the Middle East,
especially in Saudi Arabia and in Egypt. The international influence,
coinciding with the onset of the Palestinian terrorist movement, lit a
long and lethal fuse. By the 1970s, with Muslim anger building everywhere, the Moros did what Filipinos have been doing for centuries
when they have been disenfranchised from power and legitimacy—they
staged a guerrilla insurrection.

The Moro National Liberation Front, or MNLF, was the first Filipino guerrilla force to openly challenge the central government in
Manila. The central government, led by President Ferdinand Marcos,
responded with martial law. The conflict was a long and bloody one.
It has been reported that thousands of soldiers and civilians were killed
in the brutal jungle fighting. Arab states such as Libya and Iraq openly
supported the MNLF, and they provided the guerrillas with money
and weaponry. But in 1976, with both sides involved in a bloody and
pointless stalemate, Libya and the Organization of Islamic Conferences
pushed the Marcos government to end the conflict. In December 1976,
the Philippine government and the MNLF negotiated a settlement.
Called the Tripoli Agreement, the settlement called a cease-fire and
granted autonomy to thirteen provinces where the majority of Muslims
lived. The Iranian revolution in 1979 once again sparked fundamentalist fervor among a population not satisfied with the fruits of self-
rule. In fact, in speeches in Teheran, the Ayatollah Khomeini prayed
openly for the success of the Muslim revolutionary struggle in the
Philippines.[1] The Soviet invasion of Afghanistan reversed all the progress those years of fighting and diplomatic effort had won for both
sides. The young and the angry were enchanted by tales of the fight
in Afghanistan, and many soon volunteered to join the struggle. Abdullah Azzam and Osama bin Laden arranged and subsidized airline
tickets to Pakistan, where the volunteers were ushered into the ranks
of the Afghan Arabs.

The most radical of those Afghan veterans returned to Mindanao
and Zamboanga empowered and itching for a new fight. In 1991, a
radical group that disapproved of the peace negotiations of the Muslims and the central government in Manila defected from the ranks of

the MNLF and formed the Abu Sayyaf Group, or "Bearer of the Sword." The group's primary objective was the establishment of an Islamic state in the southern Philippines where the strictest interpretations of the *sharia* would be adhered to. Abu Sayyaf's founder, Abduragak Abubakar Janjalani, was a veteran of the Afghan war who had come to admire the international spirit assembled in Pakistan by Sheikh Azzam. Muslim warriors from Algeria bunked in barracks together with those from Azerbaijan and the Maldives. Like the Communist volunteers who flocked to Spain during the Spanish Civil War, the Muslim volunteers who found their fight in Afghanistan viewed the experience romantically. Abdullah Azzam and Osama bin Laden had forged an international brotherhood dedicated to a common goal. The barren wasteland of Afghanistan was the first battlefield of that common goal. The Philippines, it was hoped, would be the cause's Southeast Asia outpost. The man selected to invite the Abu Sayyaf Group to join the global jihad was Ramzi Yousef.

YOUSEF HAD SUCCESSFULLY DISAPPEARED FROM NEW YORK CITY INTO THE human quicksand of Pakistan. From Karachi International Airport to Quetta, on to Rawalpindi and Islamabad, and then gingerly toward Peshawar and the lawless safety of Afghanistan, Ramzi Yousef vanished. He could have found safe haven inside an Afghani cave, or in a luxurious al-Qaeda safe house nestled in the Wasir Akbar Khan section of Kabul, the luxurious former diplomatic enclave where villas, restaurants, and high-end brothels flourished during even the most desperate hours of the war. Yousef could have traveled with Osama bin Laden's entourage to Sudan in 1993, living a relatively comfortable life in a villa with a pool protected by the fundamentalist regime of Hassan-al-Turabi, protected by 100 of bin Laden's most capable Palestinian, Saudi, and Egyptian bodyguards. The field general who nearly pulled off the destruction of the Twin Towers deserved no less.

But Yousef was too talented to be anywhere but in the field. His arrogance was a virtue in the global campaign, and English skills and the knack of lying were added bonuses. Ramzi Yousef, his commanders ventured to guess, was perhaps the one man in the organization with the talents to surpass the World Trade Center attack, and the balls to keep on trying. "Like all criminals, like all those who have cheated a pair of cuffs," a DSS agent would later say, Ramzi felt he was smarter than anyone else, better, and could never be caught!

OSAMA BIN LADEN'S DOCTRINE RELIED ON AL-QAEDA'S ABILITY TO SUPPORT Muslim uprisings throughout the world. It also relied on a flexible hit-and-run military strategy of striking at the United States in some remote corner of the world, and then evaporating into the smoke of a bombed-out target only to strike again 3,000 miles away.

Osama bin Laden and, more notably, Dr. Ayman Zawahiri understood that the glaring weakness of modern American society was its short-term memory. Shortly after the bombing of the World Trade Center, even after the June 1993 arrest of Sheikh Rahman and a new set of disciples for a planned simultaneous bombing campaign targeting the New York bridges and tunnels, as well as 26 Federal Plaza, the hole underneath the Vista Hotel was nothing more than a distant memory.

The United States was a mighty superpower, but often it was nothing more than a paper tiger that did not defend its interests. The United States did not strike out against those responsible for the suicide bombings of the two American embassies in Beirut and the marine barracks in 1983 and 1984, nor did the United States retaliate for the kidnapping of its citizens, and murder of its CIA station chief, in Lebanon. The United States, some four years later, did not retaliate for the bombing of Pan Am 103 over Lockerbie, Scotland. The deaths of even 200 Americans did not remain in the public consciousness for long. As long as attacks were spaced apart by time and location, al-Qaeda commanders believed, America could be slowly and meticulously bled to death, robbed of its will and resolve to fight.

Ramzi Yousef first ventured to the southern islands of the Philippines in 1992 as an emissary of al-Qaeda. Like the thousands of Christian missionaries before him, Yousef traveled to the tropics armed with books designed to show potential followers the light. Armed with terrorist training guides and bomb-building manuals, Yousef promoted the virtues of a terrorist brotherhood while training the troops in the trenches. According to G.,* a law enforcement commander working in the southern Philippines, "Yousef was a masterful teacher. His followers found him patient and charismatic. He taught them the basics of roadside ambushes and bomb-building. He also taught them safe-house acquisitions, identity theft, and assassination."[2] Perhaps most importantly, Yousef established a close link between al-Qaeda and the newly formed Abu Sayyaf Group. Yousef, according to reports, offered the Abu Sayyaf Group logistical support and the blessings of Sheikh Omar Abdel Rahman from New York City. In turn, Yousef wanted the Philippines to become a launching pad for a worldwide terrorist campaign.[3] The Filipino fundamentalists agreed.

AMERICAN LAW ENFORCEMENT IN 1993 HAD YET TO UNCOVER YOUSEF'S Southeast Asian history. They were too busy unraveling Sheikh Rahman's still vibrant terrorist underground in New York City. The FBI, now back to utilizing the services of Emad Salem, their on-again-off-again informant inside Rahman's inner circle, was able to find out details of a plot simply called "The Day of Terror." Operatives, including several close associates of the men indicted in the World Trade Center bombing, were plotting to, in a single day, murder thousands of innocent men, women, and children by simultaneously blowing up the United Nations complex, the Lincoln and Holland Tunnels connecting New Jersey with Manhattan, the George Washington Bridge, and 26 Federal Plaza (the federal office building in lower Manhattan that was headquarters to the FBI and DSS), as well as assassinate New York's senators and Egyptian President Hosni Mubarak. In June 1993, the cell, including Sheikh Rahman, had been apprehended by the NYPD-FBI Joint Terrorism Task Force. The U.S. Attorney's office was worried about the pending case against Rahman, so DSS prepared an undated complaint against the blind cleric for visa fraud, Title 18 U.S. Code, Section 1546, based upon the false statements made on his visa

*Identity withheld for security reasons.

application in Khartoum. If Rahman was acquitted on charges of seditious conspiracy, he would then be immediately charged with visa fraud. As a result of the Rahman case, the Diplomatic Security Service brought pressure upon Congress for enhanced penalties to be added to the statutes, so that terrorists charged with passport and visa fraud could receive a mandatory twenty years of federal time.

Ramzi Yousef remained the one prominent terrorist fugitive who had evaded justice.

THE GLOBAL SEARCH FOR RAMZI YOUSEF EMANATED FROM PAKISTAN AND spread out in a multidirectional dragnet. For the DSS and its RSOs, the search for Yousef was not restricted to climate or continent. News reports of Yousef filtered in to embassies across every time zone. RSOs in Doha, Qatar, met with counterparts in local intelligence and security to see if their confidential informants had heard *anything* about Ramzi Yousef. RSOs, often calling in favors, went with local cops in Cairo and Khartoum on arrests hoping that a walk-in to the embassy was right and that the World Trade Center bombing mastermind was, indeed, close enough to grab and cuff. There were reports of Yousef in Canada and Colombia, the West Bank and the United Kingdom. The man who had built the 2,000-pound bomb that tore through the concrete and steel skeleton underneath the Vista Hotel was everywhere and nowhere. He had managed to vanish into thin air.

Ramzi Yousef was, in fact, alive and well in the Pakistani city of Karachi, and he was busy advancing his résumé as the world's most famous terrorist.

FROM THE SPRING OF 1993 INTO THE WINTER OF 1994, THERE WERE CONflicting reports about Yousef's activities, whereabouts, and operations. Depending on which branch of Pakistani, Iranian, or Filipino intelligence can be believed, Ramzi Yousef was either a no-nonsense drill instructor inside Afghanistan and the Philippines, or he was a hardcore assassin plying his trade inside the tumultuous blood-soaked world of

Pakistani politics. Ramzi Yousef read about the "Day of Terror" arrests in New York City, it has been reported, while working inside a Karachi bomb factory.

According to several reports, Yousef found temporary safe haven in Karachi, working together with the *Sipah-e-Sahaba*, Pakistan (SSP), a fanatical terrorist group that was formed in 1982 as a reaction to the Iranian Revolution and increased Shiite militancy in Pakistan. Former Pakistani premier General Zia al-Haq has been credited with having nurtured the SSP as part of his efforts to appease the fundamentalist clerics, though the Saudi government also provided funding and infrastructure support. The SSP's primary mission was the killing of Shiites, and the robbery and looting of their property in Pakistan. Pakistani intelligence sources estimate that there are now today some 3,000 trained activists in Pakistan involved in the daily killing of Shiite Muslims on the streets of Islamabad, Lahore, and especially Karachi.

The SSP was allied to numerous fundamentalist factions fighting in Afghanistan, primarily to Saudi volunteers and units set up by Pakistani intelligence, though Yousef's link to the SSP remains circumstantial. He was, allegedly, building a bomb to be used in an assassination plot against Pakistani Prime Minister Benazir Bhutto when chemicals he was mixing blew up in his face. Yousef was disfigured by the blast and sustained scars on his fingers; he was treated in Karachi hospitals throughout the summer of 1993. Years later, Yousef would claim that he obtained the scars and the facial damage while training Muslim fighters about to head off to Sarajevo to battle the Serbs.[4] Few doubt that Yousef did, in fact, train Bosnian Serbs and other Arabs looking for a new jihad to wage in the blood-soaked landscape of the former Yugoslavia; Yousef, in fact, prided himself on the dribs and drabs of Serbo-Croatian he picked up while teaching in the camps. But his operations with the SSP remain credible. According to numerous reports, Yousef was also involved in bombing a Shiite religious shrine in Mashad, Iran, on June 20, 1994. Twenty-five people were killed in the bombing, and an additional 100 were wounded.

It is believed that Yousef was sent by al-Qaeda to the Philippines in order to escape the wrath of Iran's Ministry of Intelligence and Security, or *Vezarat-e Ettela'at va Amniate Keshvar*, the country's terrorist and special operations intelligence apparatus. The ministry, also known by its acronym of VEVAK, tortured and killed dissidents and enemies of the Islamic Republic of Iran with great efficiency.

WHATEVER YOUSEF WAS DOING FROM 1993 TO 1994, ONE FACT REMAINS clear—he was the al-Qaeda emissary to the Far East, laying the groundwork for a terrorist master strike that would have changed forever the face of international civilian aviation. The grandiose plan was to kill nearly 4,000 men, women, and children as they sat in airliners at a cruising altitude of 30,000 feet over the Pacific, and to assassinate both Pope John Paul II and President Bill Clinton. The master strike, one that would dwarf both the Skyjack Sunday in 1970 and the seizure of the Israeli Olympic team in Munich in 1972, was code-named "Bojinka," a Serbo-Croatian expression for "Big Bang."

Yousef arrived in the Philippines in August 1994, along with several close friends, some from his childhood in Kuwait, who would join him in his most audacious and cold-blooded terrorist attack yet. They included Khaled Shaikh Mohammed, a thirty-year-old friend of Yousef's from Kuwait; Wali Amin Shah, a veteran of the Afghan bloodletting; and, Abdul Hakim Murad, a twenty-seven-year-old childhood chum of Yousef's who was also a fully licensed commercial pilot.

Osama bin Laden and the al-Qaeda hierarchy were students of history. Few terrorist organizations in the last fifty years have been able to study the mistakes and successes of the world's top terrorist groups. Bin Laden and his lieutenants had seen the follies and missteps of Yasir Arafat and his Fatah movement in the Palestine Liberation Organization. Many former Arafat loyalists were now bin Laden sympathizers and they had learned—in surrender, and from inside Israeli jail cells—how poor planning, disloyalty, and marginal dedication could undermine an organization's chances for success against a military power like Israel.

Yet bin Laden had watched, with great interest, the rise of Hezbollah in Lebanon. The Shiite "Party of God" had mastered the tactic of slowly and unrelentingly bleeding an overwhelming foe to death. "Hezbollah wanted the United States out of Lebanon, so what did it do?" asked an Israeli intelligence officer who had worked against the Shiite terrorists for over a decade. "They slowly and meticulously bombed and kidnapped the Americans out."[5]

The Popular Front for the Liberation of Palestine General Command was another terrorist group that al-Qaeda hoped to emulate. Created by Ahmed Jibril, a former Syrian army captain, in 1968, the PFLP-GC was the world's first terrorist group to adopt technology into its arsenal. Jibril loved to tinker, and he understood that technology was an answer to increased security efforts by Israeli and Western security services. He had toyed with radio-controlled antitank missiles as a safe method for attacking Israeli schoolbuses traveling close to the Lebanese frontier and had also played with booby-trapped explosive devices camouflaged as everyday items. In 1970 Jibril tested, over the snow-capped Alps, a novel new approach to striking terror into the hearts of the flying public. Instead of hijacking aircraft to seek the release of jailed comrades or sending gunmen to shoot up a plane as it sat on the tarmac outside an international departures terminal, Jibril simply—and mysteriously—blew the aircraft out of the sky utilizing a small though potent supply of high explosives affixed to an altimeter device that would initiate a blast once the aircraft reached a certain altitude. A barometric bomb triggered by air pressure was a threat, at the time, that the fledging airport security industry had not imagined.

On February 21, 1970, one of Jibril's barometric bombs ripped through the cargo hold of a Swissair jet that had just taken off from Zurich en route to Tel Aviv and had reached an altitude of 14,000 feet. The aircraft crashed in a heavily wooded forest in Canton Aargau, killing all forty-one passengers and crew on board. A few hours later, an identical barometric bomb punched a hole through the rear cargo hold of an Austrian Airlines jet traveling from Frankfurt to Vienna on its way to Tel Aviv. Miraculously, the bomb failed to bring the jet down, and the pilot was able to bring the aircraft into a remote section of Frankfurt Airport to make an emergency landing. For the next three years, Ahmed Jibril tried unsuccessfully to bring down a series of El Al aircraft using similar explosive devices but was, for the most part, unsuccessful. Jibril's operatives had always secreted their bombs into the cargo holds of airliners utilizing young women, often strung-out teenagers, who had fallen in love with their Arab boyfriends. The boyfriends, charming revolutionaries promising the girls love, drugs, and the dangers of Middle Eastern intrigue, would hand the unsuspecting young women an El Al airline ticket to Tel Aviv, some cash, and a parcel that they wanted them to carry for them. The girls, known as mules, had no idea that their exotic Arab lovers were planning to turn them into flying bombs.

But the mules were often unreliable. Most were picked up by El Al security guards at the check-in line and their explosive devices uncovered. In the few instances where the bombs were actually slipped into the cargo hold, El Al's armor-reinforced fuselages were able to absorb the explosions, and the pilots were able to maneuver the aircraft, some seriously damaged, to Tel Aviv for a safe landing.

The jihad could not pin its hopes of success on impressionable junkies and whores or innocent dupes naïve enough to be tricked into carrying a radio crammed with explosives onboard an aircraft. Many airlines, especially those in the more secure airports of Asia, followed the El Al Israel Airlines policy of "profiling" passengers. Single females, especially young ones traveling alone, were likely to be targeted by security and immigration officials, for fear that they were smuggling narcotics or were unknowingly carrying a bomb onboard.

On December 21, 1988, one of Jibril's bombs ripped through Pan Am Flight 103, a Boeing 747, as it sailed to a cruising altitude of 30,000 feet over the Scottish town of Lockerbie. The flight, a connection from Frankfurt through London's Heathrow, to New York, was two hours late in leaving the British capital and, as a result, blew up over land, where investigators could piece together shards of fragments from the bomb to build a case against those responsible. Jibril's bomb was a very sophisticated piece of workmanship with *two* barometric switches—the first switch, the safety, was released on the first leg of the flight, when the bag containing the bomb flew from Malta to Frankfurt; the second switch, triggered when the aircraft hit a specific altitude, initiated a timer. Pan Am 103 carried 259 passengers and crew that fateful winter's solstice in 1988; eleven residents of Lockerbie were also killed in the crash.

Attempting to smuggle the bomb onboard an aircraft by interlining a suitcase, sending it through from one carrier to another, without a ticketed passenger flying onboard the same aircraft, had worked well for Pan Am 103, but airlines became aware of the ruse shortly thereafter, and aircraft were not permitted to take off unless each piece of checked-in luggage matched a ticketed passenger sitting inside the aircraft.

Yousef knew that the bombs would have to be brought onboard by an inner circle of cohorts he trusted. He also knew that the bombs would have to be small enough and innocuous enough to get by modern airport security systems.

Ramzi Yousef had always liked to tinker with explosives. One of the brightest pupils in the bomb-building clinics of Peshawar, Jalalabad, and Khost, Yousef was a grandmaster when it came to bomb design. The bomb he had built to topple one Twin Tower onto the next was a unique, ingenious design of industrial chemicals brewed carefully and meticulously to be economical and massive. Destroying an aircraft required a different sort of bomb-building expertise. It required a combination of size and payload, and it also required guile. Any device, no matter how big or small, had to be able to fool airport security guards and be undetectable by either human or machine.

Yousef had just the creation.

Guncotton provided Yousef with an obvious first step. This age-old, highly explosive compound, prepared by saturating cotton with nitric and sulfuric acids, is especially effective when used with electronically initiated detonators. But the mixture is volatile and quite sensitive to friction, shock, and fire. But soak the guncotton in nitroglycerin, the compound used to make dynamite, and the composite develops into a gelatinous agent that can be molded and fitted into the most innocent of everyday items. With the nitroglycerin serving as the explosive agent, and guncotton providing the stabilizer, a bomb can be an extremely lethal package of high-energy destruction. For a detonator, Yousef came up with the Casio Databank watch. Casio watches, known among policemen and soldiers as the sturdiest on the market, are tough and resilient. The Databank could be manipulated, with the use of small electrical wires, to initiate a charge that would result in an explosion. If it worked, the device would be undetectable by any security procedure or device in service anywhere in the world.

To test out his concoctions, and perfect them, Yousef and his cohorts randomly bombed targets throughout the Philippines. Test bombs were planted at the Miss Universe Pageant at the Philippine International Convention Center in 1994; a bomb was discarded along a stretch of Roxas Boulevard in Manila shortly thereafter, and a man who picked up the device was blown to bits. On November 13, 1994, Yousef and his cell bombed a Wendy's hamburger restaurant at the corner of Nagtahan and J. P. Laurel Street near Malacañang. On December 1, 1994, the cell bombed the Greenbelt Theater in Makati City.

Slipping his patented piece of genius past square-badge security guards was not a concern for Yousef—smuggling the two nine-volt batteries needed to power the device was. After attempting to come up with a variety of bizarre and exotic smuggling tricks, Yousef came up with a novel approach that he had learned in the terrorist training camps in Peshawar. The heels of a Western pair of shoes that were carefully carved out could hold a variety of contraband ranging from several 9mm or 7.62mm rounds of ammunition to nine-volt batteries. It was all so simple.

RAMZI YOUSEF HAD LEARNED ONE MORE BIT OF TRADECRAFT FROM HIS Palestinian mentors—the art of theater. Major multifaceted operations, especially those designed to be awe-inspiring spectacles of bloodshed and fear, should be carried out simultaneously in order to yield the most bang for the buck. On September 6, 1970, the Popular Front for the Liberation of Palestine hijacked four aircraft and flew them to Zarqa, in Jordan. The complex and highly coordinated operation, designed to paralyze international air travel in one coordinated attack, was designated as "Skyjack Sunday" in the media; images of the terrorists detonating the cockpits of the evacuated aircraft remain to this day a symbol forever etched into the international consciousness of the true power of international terrorism.

Ramzi Yousef attempted to combine the success of Skyjack Sunday with the destructive yield of the Pan Am Flight 103 bombing. Yousef had targeted eleven airliners for destruction along with the cold-blooded homicides of nearly 4,000 men, women, and children. All the airliners were to be American flag carriers, flying routes from Asia to Los Angeles, San Francisco, Honolulu, and New York City. It was to be the single bloodiest day in the history of terrorism.

OPERATION BOJINKA REQUIRED IMPECCABLE INTELLIGENCE, A LIBRARY OF passports, and, most important, bombs. Intelligence was easy enough to come by in the Philippines, especially for Yousef, who seemed to travel everywhere with a Toshiba laptop computer. Airline flight schedules were not classified state secrets. They could be obtained in airline guides, flight books, and even on-line, on the Internet. Khan Amin Shah, Yousef's trusted associate, would serve as Bojinka's chief forger and identity thief, acquiring and altering whatever travel documents could be obtained. The entire operation was financed through bank deposits made to the cell from a bank in Abu Dhabi.[6]

LIFE IN MANILA WAS GOOD FOR YOUSEF AND HIS CELL. ACCORDING TO sources inside the Filipino security services busy monitoring the Abu Sayyaf Group networks in the capital, Yousef and his operatives avoided the mosques and other Islamic centers in the city.[7] They ate out, enjoyed the numerous nightclubs and dance halls of Manila's notorious red light district, and easily blended in with the many Middle Easterners who studied, worked, and lived in the Philippines. They were known as big tippers in the sex bars located in Makati and the other red-light outposts in Manila. Yousef was always careful to avoid past mistakes. In New York City and New Jersey, for example, Sheikh Rahman's followers made it too easy for law enforcement to round up the entire cell of operatives. They congregated at places of worship that were compromised by informants and always under the watchful eyes of law enforcement and other government agencies. To evade public scrutiny and police attention, Yousef and his team would shed their Islamic practices and blend into the multiethnic Manila mosaic.

In order to avoid the watchful eye of the Filipino authorities, it was absolutely necessary for Yousef and his cell to be able to pass themselves off as everyday residents of Manila. Yet the success of Operation Bojinka was dependent on two technological factors. The bombs had to be secreted through airport security, past the check-in counter and pregate screeners, onto the aircraft. The bombs also had to work and be powerful enough to rip a gaping hole through the cabin and fuselage of a Boeing 747, causing the aircraft to be ripped apart by air pressure and to go into an out-of-control spin into the depths of the Pacific Ocean. The targeted flights would depart from Manila, from Bangkok, from Singapore, and from Jakarta. Operation Bojinka was designed to leave no clues, no telltale signs of a timer or bomb residue, and no short list of the usual suspects.

Part of the true horror of terrorism is its randomness and indiscriminate assault on life and property. To test his ability to secrete one bomb onboard an aircraft, let alone eleven, Ramzi Yousef randomly selected a flight that he felt confident would be a suitable experiment for the larger operation.

On December 10, 1994, Ramzi Yousef and another unidentified bomb-making expert[8] left the Josefa Apartments in Manila, hailed a jeepney taxicab from a nearby intersection, and traveled forty minutes through the wearisome hell of Manila traffic. Ninoy Aquino International Airport always required nerves of steel and the patience of a saint. Yousef and his accomplice patiently stood on a long, slow-moving line at the check-in counter for Philippine Airlines, paid the 500-peso airport tax, and filled out the departure card form; Yousef, according to reports, was traveling on a forged Italian passport.[9] Milling about the busy terminal, the two men made their way to the gate, boarding Philippine Airlines Flight 434 from Manila to Cebu City in the south, with a connection to Tokyo. Flight 434 was a commuter hop for domestic air travel over Philippine skies and then an international flight on to Tokyo, on one of the airline's busiest routes. At Cebu, some passengers would deplane at Mactan Cebu International

Airport, while others, primarily Japanese tourists and businessmen, would board the aircraft for the five-hour hop to Tokyo.

Ramzi Yousef sat in row 35F on the Philippine Airlines Boeing 747-200. It wasn't the one he had requested at the check-in counter in Manila. Seat 35F was in the middle of the second bank of seats of economy class, behind the wings, in the middle of a row of four seats. 35F was neither a window nor an aisle seat. Yousef was sandwiched in between a row of ordinary passengers and tourists. Comfort wasn't supposed to be an issue for the brief flight to Cebu—even in congested skies, the flight wasn't supposed to take longer than ninety minutes. But in the middle of the flight, Yousef politely asked a stewardess if he'd be permitted to move forward, toward seat 26I located at the base of the 747's wings. The stewardess agreed.[10]

Once the NO SMOKING and FASTEN SEATBELT signs had been extinguished and the flight reached a comfortable cruising altitude, Yousef quietly unfastened his seatbelt and walked toward the rear lavatories. In methodical fashion he removed two nine-volt batteries carved out of the heels of his shoes and rigged up his test bomb. He returned to his seat and, witnesses would later tell investigators, shoved an object inside the seat cushion next to the life jacket underneath his chair.[11]

When Flight 434 touched down at Mactan Cebu International Airport, most of those getting off the aircraft were in a hurry to rush for the shuttle that would take them to the Maribago Bluewater Beach Resort, one of Asia's finest, only fifteen minutes from the terminal. Yousef and his travel partner were in no hurry. They walked out of the airport and then walked back in. They boarded another flight an hour later back to Manila. By the time Flight 434 was cleaned, refueled, and loaded with new baggage, Ramzi Yousef was sitting inside a cramped and colorful Manila jeepney heading back to the Josefa Apartments.

Haruki Ikegami, a twenty-four-year-old engineer, had, fatefully, been issued seat 26I as he checked in his bags at Cebu. The Boeing 747-200 had reached a cruising altitude of about 35,000 feet some two hours into the flight when the first small clouds of white smoke began to float from underneath Ikegami's seat. A second or two later, the smoke turned into the blinding flash of a fireball. A muffled blast hid the telltale destructive power of Yousef's bomb, but not its effects. The bomb exploded vertically, splitting Haruki Ikegami in two from his crotch to his head and pouring his innards into his chair. According to one federal law-enforcement official who was privy to the U.S. Federal Aviation Administration investigation into the bombing of Flight 434, "The bomb was so powerful that it blew all of the victim's guts into the chair and into the ceiling, where his testicles were found. A man sitting behind Ikegami, who stretched his legs, had both limbs eviscerated by the force of the explosion. It was horrific."[12]

The blast also tore through a swath of cables leading from the cockpit to the wings and controlling the flaps. Miraculously, the pilot managed to regain control of the shaking aircraft and dumped its remaining fuel near the Okinawa shore. With 272 passengers and a crew of twenty onboard, Captain Ed Reyes managed to make an emergency landing in Okinawa.

Had the blast ripped across the cabin horizontally, it is almost certain that the aircraft would have come apart and plummeted into the Sea of Japan.

Yousef had, presumably, hoped to bring down Flight 434 over the Pacific to see just how well his homemade brew of nitroglycerin and guncotton, powered by a store-bought nine-volt battery and timed by a Casio Databank, would work. But Yousef had miscalculated. "The fuselage located directly around the wing structure is the strongest part of the plane," said Colonel Ed Gatumbato, a group commander of the Philippine National Police Aviation Security Special Operations Group, who was rushed to Okinawa to run the investigation into the blast for the Philippine national government. "By placing the bomb where he did, Yousef inadvertently saved the aircraft from being destroyed."[13]

Hours after the bomb exploded onboard Flight 434, a man with a heavy accent, believed to be Middle Eastern, called a news agency in the Philippines, and claimed responsibility for the attack in the name of the Abu Sayyaf Group. Colonel Gatumbato and his staff of investigators were able to piece together bits of Yousef's device. The shards of metal fragments and traces of nitroglycerine indicated that they were dealing with a sophisticated bomb-builder—not the fragmentation-grenade crowd that flocked to Mindanao and Zamboanga to serve with the Muslim guerrillas.

OPERATION BOJINKA WAS SLATED TO COINCIDE WITH THE ARRIVAL OF POPE John Paul II on January 12. In all, Yousef had hoped to target eleven airliners over a forty-eight-hour period departing from hubs in the Far East. Flights from Delta, United, and Northwest Airlines were marked for destruction. "Operation Bojinka" might have gone down in history as one of the most audacious and brilliantly planned terrorist strikes in history. It should have succeeded. But Murphy's Law had caught up to Yousef in embarrassing fashion.

Activity was furious inside Apartment 603 in the Josefa Apartments in Manila on the night of January 6, 1995. Time was running out for the Big Bang to be heard across the Pacific. Inside the bomb factory, Yousef, Shah, and Murad were busy assembling the components of the Bojinka bombs when routine turned into disaster.

Abdul Hakim Murad was a pilot by profession, not a bomb-builder. With the TV blaring, and the other members of the cell working on components of the bombs and devices as they drank soft drinks and smoked Marlboros, Murad decided to wash his hands in the sink where some of the chemical components of Yousef's bombs had been mixed hours earlier. When the water mixed with the chemical residue in the sink, it sparked an explosive reaction. A small fire broke out and the small apartment was engulfed by a choking acrid smoke. Yousef, Murad, and Shah were forced to flee into the street below as the fire brigade rushed to the scene.

Because the Josefa Apartments were only 350 meters from the Papal Nuncio and on the route of Pope John Paul II's motorcade through Manila, the fire alarm prompted the police duty commander that night, Captain Aida Mariscal, to take a drive to the location. Cops live and die on their hunches and, according to Mariscal, she had a sixth sense about the Josefa Apartments, especially with the Pope due to arrive shortly.[14] Yousef, Murad, and Shah were horrified to see the arriving police sector cars pull up in front of the apartment complex. All of the materials—from bombs to fake security badges—for Bojinka were in-side Apartment 603. Most importantly, Yousef's Toshiba laptop, with the precise details of the operation, was sitting on the living room's coffee table, next to a stack of Norwegian, Afghani, Saudi, and Pak-istani passports.

Yousef remained far behind the scenes as the fire brigade affixed hoses to outside pumps and battled the smoky blaze. He was just an-other curious onlooker brought to the curb by the lights and sirens and the acrid smoke. But he did order Murad back into the apartment to retrieve the computer and some of the other material related to Bojinka. Murad attempted to enter the apartment, but he was con-fronted by police. He tried to flee, but police had no difficulty in lo-cating the Arab male with a full beard running through the streets of Manila with smoldering clothes.

According to Captain Mariscal, Murad offered her the bribe of a lifetime to let him go.[15] There was, after all, two million U.S. dollars on the table for anyone leading authorities to Ramzi Yousef. And Mu-rad was wise in his efforts to seek one last gasp at freedom. Inside Apartment 603 police investigators uncovered a bomb factory stocked with beakers, gallons of sulfuric acid, nitric acid, glycerin, large cooking kettles, funnels, fuses, passports, flight schedules, airline tickets, and a series of Casio Databank watches and other circuity that, in a follow-up check, would match identically with the forensic evidence obtained from the charred remains of seat 26I on Flight 434.

And, of course, inside Apartment 603, police found a Toshiba laptop computer fully loaded with an as-yet-unexecuted manifesto titled "Bo-jinka." The contents of Yousef's laptop were encrypted, but once the code system of obtuse passwords was broken, the files revealed time-tables for both Delta and American airlines, as well as calculations to determine when to set the bomb timer for each flight.[16]

There was one more important piece of evidence found inside the flat. A partial fingerprint was found by detectives searching the terrorist nerve center for clues. The print would be run against local files, and against an Interpol and FBI database. The print was a familiar one, belonging to an old foe of U.S. law enforcement. It belonged to Ramzi Yousef.

RAMZI YOUSEF REALIZED THAT BOJINKA HAD BEEN COMPROMISED THE MO-
ment he dispatched Murad back into the smoldering apartment. Armed
with cash and an Iraqi passport, Yousef hailed a jeepney from Quirino
Avenue and rushed to the airport. He is reported to have purchased
some clothing along the way and washed his face and combed his hair
in order to deflect any suspicion from inquisitive ticket agents. He
bought a one-way ticket from Manila to Bangkok and disappeared into
the dark skies of a January night. Before Filipino investigators truly
realized the web they had uncovered, Yousef was in Thailand, in a safe
house, coordinating his safe passage back to Pakistan. Yousef was not
one to stick around and pick up the pieces of his destruction. With
Shah on the run and Murad in custody, Yousef abandoned his com-
panions, saving his skin once again.

According to Filipino press accounts, Abdul Hakim Murad, Ramzi
Yousef's childhood friend, received what Filipino investigators called a
"tactical interrogation." Agents from the National Bureau of Investigations brutally interrogated the stoic Murad. He taunted his inquis-
itors and even threatened them once he was released. But Murad wasn't
going anywhere, and his resilience was short-lived.

Abdul Hakim Murad's home for the following three months was a
small and cramped cell inside Philippine National Police Intelligence
Command headquarters in Camp Crame. According to noted Filipino
journalists Marites Vitug and Glenda Gloria, in their book *Under the
Crescent Moon*, Murad was tortured for weeks as counterintelligence
agents beat him with chairs and long pieces of wood. Water was forced
into his mouth and lit cigarettes were extinguished on his genitals.[17]
The interrogators even told Murad that they were agents for the Mossad, Israel's famed espionage service, and that once they were done
beating a confession out of him, they were going to ship him back to
Tel Aviv.

Two week after Murad's arrest, Wali Khan Amin Shah, the chubby
passport acquisition master and bomber's assistant, was arrested in
Kuala Lumpur, in an al-Qaeda safe house set up by Yousef in case
Bojinka disintegrated.

Within weeks, both Murad and Khan were shackled in chains and walked onto aircraft heading toward New York City escorted by heavily armed DSS agents. Only Yousef and Khaled Shaikh Mohammed managed to escape.

NEWS OF THE ARRESTS IN MANILA SPREAD THROUGHOUT SOUTHEAST Asia—especially to the airline hubs of Bangkok, Jakarta, and Singapore.

DSS Special Agent Dale "Chip" McElhattan was ideally suited to serve in the rigidly immaculate city-state of Singapore. Tall and gregarious, Chip McElhattan enjoyed the passive pleasure of Asian society and the opportunity to immerse himself in the local culture. Like most of the DSS agents dispatched overseas to serve in embassies and consulates, McElhattan knew that a warm disposition and accessibility to local law enforcement were the most effective ways to protect the embassy and its staff from harm. "If you want to be able to do your job well," McElhattan always told younger agents sent to his posts on TDY, or temporary duty assignments, "you have to visit your friends in the police when you *don't* need anything from them. Those visits, just to say hello or shoot the shit over a few beers, foster lasting friendships, and when you really need them, in times of crisis, they will respond."[18]

McElhattan developed a close-knit relationship with Singapore's intelligence service and law-enforcement hierarchy. An athlete, McElhattan so endeared himself to the Singapore Police Force's commanders that he was invited to play on their national water polo team. Singapore wasn't a high-threat post. Singapore was strictly law-and-order—no ifs, ands, or buts. Some old Asia hands, travelers with years of experience in the Far East, called Singapore "Disneyland with the Death Penalty." It was a country where crime and subversive activity were not tolerated and where international terrorism was considered a scourge worthy of death.

Singapore was an economic engine driven by commerce and trade. And Changi International Airport was central to the merchant state's international importance. It was often voted, by business and leisure travelers, the world's best airport.

McElhattan was ushered out of a sound sleep on the night of January 6, 1995, by a call from the FAA investigator working Flight 434 from Manila. It was, according McElhattan, one of those "oh shit" calls that cops always dread getting. Two of the airliners that Yousef was planning to blow up over the Pacific, McElhattan learned, were originating from Singapore. The bombers would plant their bombs on a first leg of a flight, possibly originating in Jakarta, Kuala Lumpur, or Bangkok, and the aircraft would blow up over the Pacific several hours after it lifted off the runway at Changi International Airport. The airlines targeted were Northwest and United.

The news galvanized McElhattan. RSOs like to view their posts as small towns where they are the sheriff. They might not be able to stop violence and terrorism outside of the city limits, but anything on their turf—especially acts perpetrated against Americans—is stopped at all costs. McElhattan also understood that two Boeing 747s had the capacity to hold nearly 900 people. Any attempt to bomb the planes out of the sky was mass murder. At 3:00 A.M., McElhattan grabbed his SIG-Sauer P228 9mm automatic, his badge, and his embassy ID and drove the twenty minutes to Changi International Airport.

McElhattan would need help, and he would require the skill to persuade security officials at the airport—a bustling hub with a highly capable police and counterterrorist force of its own—that a significant threat might be awaiting takeoff from Singapore. McElhattan had, in his years in Singapore, cultivated close ties with his counterparts in the Singapore Police Force. But middle-of-the-night calls to the airport were the exception, rather than the norm, and security officials at the airport needed to be sure that the threat was genuine before turning the two terminals upside down.

And these were threats to Singapore that, for McElhattan, made the phone call from Manila all the more ominous. Malaysia, a Muslim nation with economic and cultural ties to many Middle Eastern nations, is just one kilometer away across the causeway over the Straits of Johor. A second causeway links Tuas in Singapore with Geyland Patah. A vehicle and passenger ferry operates between north Changi and Tanjung Belungkor, east of Johor Bahru, and a daily high-speed catamaran links Singapore with Tioman Island. Singapore, in fact, is the southern terminus of Malaysia's rail system, and there are four trains a day to Kuala Lumpur. Most worrisome for McElhattan was the fact that there were three scheduled Iran Air flights a week from Teheran to Kuala Lumpur, Malaysia, making it effortless for a terrorist to cross the Malaysian straits along with the 60,000 other vehicles that make the quick ferry hop, park a car bomb in front of the U.S. embassy, return to Kuala Lumpur, and be in Teheran before the device detonated. McElhattan knew that Singapore's intelligence service, the Internal Security Department, or ISD, was a highly capable organization that had a firm grip on possible terrorist activity inside the country.

Inside the ultramodern high-tech masterpiece of Changi International Airport, McElhattan asked the police duty officer to summon a bomb-sniffing unit from the Singapore Defense Forces to thoroughly check every nook and crevice of the Northwest and United 747s scheduled to depart that morning. Dogs weren't perfect, but they were better than nothing. Because the men arrested in the Manila bomb factory were Middle Eastern, McElhattan manned a determined vigil next to the departure gates for both flights. Armed with nothing more than a detective's instincts and the trepidation that a good many innocent people might be in harm's way, McElhattan scanned the long line of travelers attempting to profile that one face, that one person connected to the Manila bomb-building cell. Profiling two packed-to-capacity flights was a daunting challenge for McElhattan, but the checks of all people boarding the two jumbo jets were handled in a thorough fashion.

Normal air travel over the Pacific was threatened in the days following Murad's arrest and the revelation of Yousef's cell. On January 14 a credible bomb threat that was relayed to Japanese counterterrorist police forced a United Airlines aircraft bound for Honolulu to return to Narita International Airport in Tokyo; the aircraft had originated in Manila and had stopped over in Tokyo to pick up passengers. Less than twelve hours later, a flight from Hong Kong was grounded by a bomb scare. And, a few weeks later, a United Airlines DC-10 flying from Bangkok to Tokyo was diverted to Taiwan following a bomb alert.

In Singapore, McElhattan ventured to Changi International Airport on numerous occasions each and every time a bomb threat to an American airliner was posted somewhere in Asia. The workload became so arduous that he summoned the assistance of Special Agent Jerry Tuller, the RSO in Kuala Lumpur, to assist him in profiling passengers boarding flights to the United States.

The simultaneous destruction of eleven airliners over the Pacific Ocean would have changed the face of international civil aviation forever. But Yousef had envisioned even more ambitious heights for his cells in Manila. He wanted to crash a commercial airliner full of passengers into CIA headquarters in Langley, Virginia. Al-Qaeda operations to date had all been remote-controlled attacks against American targets. Yousef's massive truck bomb parked underneath the World Trade Center was designed to detonate with timers that allowed the culprits to escape. Al-Qaeda had yet to adopt the suicidal attacks that were the trademark of Hezbollah and Hamas, but both Yousef and Murad had a novel idea. An airliner, flown to its target by a skilled pilot, could easily be turned into a flying guided missile.

Hijacking an airliner was considered entry-level basics for any terrorist worth his salt. And, Yousef and Murad ventured to guess, hostages on board a seized jetliner would be cooperative and unsuspecting of the fact that they were going to be part of a kamikaze suicide run into a predestined target. That target, Yousef and Murad conspired, was the headquarters of the Central Intelligence Agency in Langley, Virginia. Such a strike would be a public relations nightmare for the United States and an image-boosting bonanza for al-Qaeda. In attempting to destroy the Twin Towers of the World Trade Center, Yousef had hoped to eradicate an icon of America's economic dominance of the world. By destroying the headquarters of the CIA, the same organization that had so naïvely supported bin Laden and the Afghan Arabs during the war against the Soviets, the icon of America's global power would forever be bloodied and compromised.

Records show that Murad was a licensed commercial pilot who first studied at the Continental Flying School in Pasay City, the Philippines, from November 1990 to January 1991; in November 1991, he enrolled at the Emirates Flying School in Dubai, United Arab Emirates, where he later earned a private pilot license. He earned his commercial pilot license shortly thereafter at Coastal Aviation, located in New Bern, North Carolina, and also took flight classes in San Antonio, Texas, and Schenectady, New York.

Murad, Filipino investigators believe, had planned to hijack an aircraft *inside* the United States. During his confession, intelligence agents were able to surmise that Murad thought less of airport security inside the United States than he did even in Manila, which was considered lax by international standards. The hijacking was to follow the Bojinka bombings. Security agents at airports, investigators gathered from Murad, would be too busy looking for bombs on aircraft and would not be expecting a potential hijacker.[19]

The destruction of eleven airliners, or even half of those, would have been a tremendous victory for Ramzi Yousef, but it would have been a success even if three aircraft disintegrated over the Pacific. The suicide crash dive of a hijacked airliner into the heart of CIA headquarters would have been an encore act of insolence and in-your-face audacity the likes of which had never been seen before in the bloody history of international terrorism.

Yousef had also one final grandiose operation in mind for his operatives in the Philippines. He had hoped to assassinate the Pope.

After sifting through Apartment 603 and extracting information from Abdul Murad, Filipino investigators were able to learn the far-reaching plans of the cell compromised by the freak fire.

It is believed that the first intended assassination target for Yousef's cell was President Bill Clinton on November 12 or 13, 1994. Clinton, along with Secretary of State Warren Christopher, stopped in the Philippine capital for forty-eight hours prior to attending an APEC conference in Jakarta.

Filipino investigators believe that Yousef's cell had planned to attack President Clinton in Manila during his brief visit. Investigators remain unclear as to exactly how the assault was supposed to be executed, though internal reports speculate that the terrorists were planning on crashing a truck filled with explosives into the president's motorcade. Presidential security, often encompassing the efforts of several hundred agents from the U.S. Secret Service, as well as over 10,000 local police officers and military special forces operators, is a mind-boggling veil of armor and firepower. Any attack against Clinton certainly would have been a suicidal gesture, and it appears that Yousef was not ready to cut his terrorist career short. After all, there would still be another target of opportunity venturing to the Philippines in January worthy of al-Qaeda attention.

Some Filipino investigators have speculated that Yousef might have been concerned that the bomb intended to obliterate the president's armored Cadillac limousine would not have been powerful enough to achieve its objective. A lesson that Yousef learned from his failed attempt to topple the Twin Towers in 1993 was the need to test his devices before applying the genuine article to the target. The first of Yousef's experiments involved a small test of the device that his operatives were hoping to use against the papal motorcade in Manila. On December 1, 1994, a small, highly powerful improvised explosive device was set off inside the Kukui Greenbelt Theater in Manila. Several moviegoers were hurt by the blast, and physical damage to the theater was significant. Western Police Department bomb technicians were relieved that the highly sophisticated device, one made of TNT and equipped with a never-before-seen detonator and timer, had not killed anyone. At first, police thought that the bombing might have been a violent expression in an organized crime turf war over protection money, but the device was far too sophisticated for common thugs who were used to gasoline bombs.

Plots to kill both President Clinton and Pope John Paul II in Manila were fantastic. "It was," according to one Filipino intelligence officer, "like a bad scene from Frederick Forsyth's *Day of the Jackal* happening to *us*, and we didn't know how the chapter would play out. It was all very frightening."[20]

The bomb-building material was a surprising discovery for Filipino investigators. Yet they were most shocked by the Bibles, priest outfits, and photos of Pope John Paul II found inside one of the closets. The Pope was scheduled to land at Ninoy Aquino International Airport in less than seventy-two hours on a historic pilgrimage to the Philippines—a first leg on a multination tour of Asia. It was obvious to all that police had stumbled across a major bomb-building factory and terrorist safe house. But what exactly had been uncovered inside the apartment in Manila? Were the terrorists state-sponsored operatives, like the men uncovered in Manila during the opening hours of the Gulf War four years earlier? Was there a Palestinian connection? If the Pope was a target for a group of professional assassins, was the man in custody a driver, a support man, or the trigger man?

Perhaps most ominous was the fact that the Josefa Apartments were only 350 meters from the papal nuncio's office, where Pope John Paul II would be staying during his time in Manila.[21] Not only were possible assassins building bombs only a few minutes from where the Pope would be staying, but it was well within rifle range.

An Arab terrorist cell operating in downtown Manila, possibly plotting against the pontiff, had warranted the mobilization of 20,000 *additional* soldiers and policemen assigned to the papal security package. But was it enough? Earlier in the month, Filipino police had detained and then deported a group of eight Iranians who had arrived in Manila with spurious passports and incredible stories as to why they just happened to be visiting the Philippines. In all, some 100 foreigners were expelled from the country as possible security threats to the Pope.[22] What else was out there?

ANOTHER ELEMENT OF OPERATION BOJINKA THAT EMERGED FROM THE Murad interrogation was particularly troubling for DSS. The sprawling U.S. embassy in Manila, located behind a beachfront swath of land at 1201 Roxas Boulevard in Ermita, was targeted for attack. Murad refused to provide any additional details on the method by which the colonial-style complex would be assaulted. Perhaps he didn't know. Had Yousef laid the groundwork for a suicide operative from his cell to drive a dumptruck crammed with explosives through the front gate of the embassy, or had Yousef conspired with his allies in the Abu Sayyaf Group to launch a suicide assault, something akin to the Viet Cong attack against the U.S. embassy in Saigon that opened the 1968 Tet Offensive, against the American diplomatic post? Most DSS agents were intimate with the story of famed DSS veteran Leo Crampsey,

who fired an Italian Beretta submachine gun until the barrel was a
flaming red and beat back a band of VC sappers who had penetrated
the embassy grounds. Even if Yousef was on the run and many of his
operatives were under arrest, DSS agents were very wary of his Abu
Sayyaf Group legions. According to one senior official in the Philippine National Police, "ASG commanders looked to Yousef as a hero
of the jihad. Some guerrillas have admitted that Yousef trained them
in terrorism in Afghanistan and near Zamboanga in the Philippines."

MANILA HAD SUDDENLY BECOME THE CENTER OF AN INTERNATIONAL Islamic web of terror targeting U.S. interests, and DSS sent one of its
best special agents to spearhead the investigation and advance intelligence operations. In DSS, action meant Special Agent Fred Piry.

Piry, known in DSS circles simply as "Razor," was the kind of special
agent who often ruffled the feathers of old-school diplomats and paper-
pushing bureaucrats inside the slow-moving and thankless world of the
federal government, but he got things done. A former high-school
teacher, Piry had first wanted to join the Secret Service, but they
weren't hiring. He found an ad for a mysterious and unheard-of law-
enforcement arm of the State Department and joined DSS in 1988 as
a rookie assigned to the Washington field office. Piry was lucky, however. He was assigned to the service's elite tactical and instructional
vanguard, the Mobile Security Division, in the first year that the unit
was geared for special operations. "Up until my class in MSD, agents
were basically sent into the team on an individual basis," Piry recalled.
"They were uniquely trained but they weren't schooled as a cohesive
unit. When I went in, the guys with me went to Fort Bragg together,
we went to Hurlburt Field in Florida together with the air force, and
we went to all these courses as one. The emphasis of our emergency
and survival training wasn't for an Africa, for the social disorder–type
responses of protesters storming a wall. We were being trained to fight
terrorists. We had to learn the terrorist mindset, their tactics, and be
able to teach people so that we could counter them and defeat them
before they could strike. We developed skills for driving, surveillance,

shooting, and other counterterrorist types of missions."[23]

Piry traveled on numerous high-threat assignments to hotspots in the Middle East, South America, and Africa—from bringing the U.S. ambassador back to the embassy in Kuwait City following Operation Desert Storm to rooting out the sniper dens of Sarajevo. After the rough-and-tumble of MSD, Piry traveled to Beirut for a year as the assistant RSO. After Beirut, he joined the Counterterrorism Division.

One of the Cone of Silence alumni to have excelled on a global scale inside the Counter-Terrorism Division, Razor was a what-you-see-is-what-you-get DSS special agent. His often unkempt dirty-blond hair and bright blue eyes denoted a loner who was far more at ease in a Third World backwater clutching an automatic rifle while riding in a mud-soaked 4×4 than he was wearing a Brooks Brothers suit in the Foggy Bottom halls of power. He was most comfortable in places like the murky jungles and countryside of Haiti, hunting down a former presidential bodyguard wanted for the killing of three U.S. embassy employees and stealing the embassy payroll.

Less than seventy-two hours after returning from Port-Au-Prince, Piry was back at Dulles International Airport, his P228 holstered to his waist, and a case file in his hands. Piry was flying west, to Honolulu, where the FAA and the FBI were slowly assembling an investigatory team focusing on Philippines Air Flight 434. Shortly after arriving in Hawaii and beginning the painstaking task of sifting through reports and evidence, news of the fire in the Josefa Apartments reached the hastily set-up federal command post in Honolulu. Less than twenty-four hours later, Piry was inside Apartment 603, assisting investigators as they sifted through the bomb-making materials abandoned by Yousef and his crew. With years of experiences in places like Beirut, Piry knew that it was essential to catch Yousef and his deep-cover cells before they could strike once again.

LIFE IN THE FAR EAST RETURNED TO NORMAL IN FEBRUARY 1995. A MAJOR catastrophe had been miraculously averted. A plot to assassinate Pope John Paul II had also been foiled, as had the aspirations of men in

Khartoum, Cairo, and Kabul to draw first blood in a holy war between Islam and Christianity—a settling of old scores, from the times of the Crusaders, between East and West.

For Special Agent Fred Piry, the desire to head east and return home to his wife and children after a long separation was thwarted that blustery February. Piry was sent west to the beleaguered capital of Pakistan. Veterans of the Counter-Terrorism Division had always believed that the hunt for Ramzi Yousef would lead them toward Pakistan. Now, with Yousef on the run, DSS special agents could hope to apprehend the mastermind of the World Trade Center bombing and of Operation Bojinka before he could strike again.

Chapter 4

"THE STANS"

ach August, in twenty-two field offices in the United States and in embassies and consulates around the world, DSS special agents study a twelve-page document with both enthusiastic optimism and heart-sinking anguish. This much anticipated and often dreaded piece of bureaucratic paperwork is what's known in DSS vernacular as the "Bid List," and it details where many of the 1,200 men and women who work for DSS will be serving overseas and domestically starting the next summer.

Unlike most other jobs in federal law enforcement, DSS, like the Foreign Service, is required to send its agents globetrotting around the planet on an annual basis. The agency attempts to be fair and even-handed in assigning its special agents to domestic and overseas posts, but most have to serve in cities other than London, Paris, and Rome. The agency realizes that the strains of constant international travel, long hours of investigative and protective work, and TDY (temporary duty) assignments to God only knows where are hard enough on an unmarried special agent, let alone on one who is married and has children. The hierarchy is well aware that special agents forced into an assignment or a post they do not want will more often than not leave the job and return to a "normal" life in the civilian sector. So, to placate personal desires, likes and dislikes, passions and prejudices, DSS offers its personnel the option of bidding on a forward assignment in the hopes of making at least some of the agents happy. For a special agent serving overseas for six years straight and about to return to the U.S., a bid list can mean the difference between selecting the high cost of living associated with work in the New York field office, or the possibility of working in the more relaxed confines of New Orleans or Seattle. For the agent in New York who realizes that his days of dodging an overseas tour have come to an end, a particular bid list might just mean the difference between serving for three years in Brussels, versus ending up in the heart of downtown Sana'a, Yemen—or worse. And in DSS, there is always worse. Places like Ouagadougou, Burkina Faso; Bujumbura, Burundi; and N'djamena, Chad, often strike fear into the heart of a DSS agent anticipating the adventure of an overseas post while dreading its realities. Each year the bid list offers its share of treats and horrors. "Shall I be cold and miserable in Riga," asked an RSO in the Middle East, looking through the latest bid list, realizing he was going to remain overseas for another tour, "or should I be hot and miserable in Delhi? Do I want three years of ease or three years of excitement? What about my family?"

Each time the bid list is published, there are special agents who grumble and moan, "If they send me to Africa, I'm quitting." Or, "There is no way in hell that my wife will agree to go to Sofia!" But every summer, like birds migrating to a greater calling, DSS agents summon movers and real estate brokers for a federal pilgrimage to the four corners of the globe. Each and every year, DSS agents sell or rent their homes and pull their kids out of school.

DSS special agents are allowed to mark a bid list with fifteen overall picks as to where they want to go. They can mark off five posts with a high bid, meaning that they really want to go there, five posts of medium enthusiasm, and five of low choice. A low choice on a bid tends to translate as "please don't send me there." There is no apparent rule or reason in determining where DSS will eventually send an agent. An agent fluent in Spanish, who studied Latin American politics in college, can end up being sent to Tel Aviv. An agent who spoke Mandarin at home, and who was taught German in the army, can wind up looking through his Portuguese phrasebook en route to a simmering two years of joy in Luanda, Angola. A Far East hand can end up in El

Salvador, and a Francophile might just wind up in Jakarta. The bid list is Russian roulette, designed and perfected by the State Department for the Foreign Service.

If there is one absolute about the bid list, if there is one certainty that has become a tradition year after year, it is that few DSS special agents ever bid on the "Stans." The "Stans," that affectionate blanket term for all countries in Central Asia, include the former Soviet republics of Kazakhstan, Kyrgyzstan, Tajikistan, Turkmenistan, and Uzbekistan. The "Stans" are desolate, dark, and dreary outposts mixing the New World Order and Old World disorder. Cities are remote, amenities virtually nonexistent. Work requires the patience of a saint while dealing with the flickering embers of Soviet-style bureaucracy tempered by tribal hatreds permitted to express themselves for the first time in fifty years.

And then, of course, there is the beacon of the "Stans"—Pakistan. "I'd rather go spend a year in Algiers, Beirut, Kosovo, or Bogotá, on a hardship tour away from my family, away from everything," reflected one DSS veteran who has spent more time than he cares to remember on TDYs to the former Soviet republics, "than be in the Stans . . . *especially Pakistan!*"

One DSS special agent who most emphatically did not bid on Pakistan was Jeff Riner—a forty-year-old investigator with silver hair, glasses, and seven years on the job.[1] Like many who find their way into this field through the maze of federal job opportunities, Riner stumbled upon DSS by accident and word of mouth. As an investigator with the Defense Investigative Service, he conducted background checks for the Department of Defense while yearning to be a "real" cop—and a federal one to boot. He had considered jobs with the FBI, the DEA, and the Naval Investigative Service, but DSS called first. After a stint in the Federal Law Enforcement Training Center in Glynco, Georgia, Riner traveled to Washington, D.C., for advance agent training.

After receiving his gold shield and his gun, he was assigned to the Washington field office (WFO), a vast pool of manpower for dignitary protection and foreign TDY assignments. Before he could learn the ropes, however, and before he could break in the chair that barely fit into the cubicle that was his office, he found himself assigned to a jump team that was part of the secretary of state's detail. With less than three days on the job, and very little idea of what he was doing, the spanking new DSS special agent found himself on the tarmac in San Salvador, El Salvador, in a land beset by war and conflict, awaiting the arrival of U.S. Secretary of State George Shultz. "We wore our bulletproof vests on the plane down there, and when we arrived at the airport we could hear gunfire in the hills. We were escorted to the embassy, my first time in an embassy, and then briefed on the secretary of state's trip. Two days later, in a massive motorcade, guns at the ready, we ferried our chief diplomat through narrow roadways and choke points, only to learn that we were in a *dummy* motorcade, and because of the high threat level, Shultz was being ferried to his location by helicopter. And then it hit me. This is for real. I am in the shit!"[2]

DSS likes to get its young agents off and running with a bang—because it has to. "Unlike the Secret Service, for example," says a DSS veteran serving in Europe, "our guys don't have the luxury of spending their first five years on the job doing 'halls and walls' on protection details. In our world, agents are literally graduated, given a shield, a gun, a diplomatic passport, and an airline ticket to a Third World airport. Welcome to Diplomatic Security."

Riner spent a year at WFO, and was then assigned to SD, the secretary of state's protective detail. Working in SD was a grind. It was three grueling years of incessant travel and frayed nerves. "It was all very exciting in those early years," Riner recalls. "We traveled around the world, were put up in luxury hotels, and we got to see a lot of famous people. But in retrospect, it was blood money. Because of our limited personnel we often had to work twenty-hour days, three weeks at a time, and then come home only to go out twenty-four hours later and do it all over again."[3]

But there are limits to what even a strong character can bear. For Jeff Riner, this came following a three-week trip around the Middle East where the last stop was Cairo. After working a midnight shift, he boarded a flight to Dulles International for the twelve-hour-long haul. It was just after dawn when the cab pulled up in front of his family's suburban Washington, D.C., home. His wife and children were waiting for the husband and father whom they hadn't seen in nearly a month. But before he could even his embrace his kids, Jeff's wife hugged him and said, "I don't know how to tell you this, but you got a call from the Operations Center. They want you to go overseas again." Within twenty-four hours, Riner was back on a flight to Cairo. His protective mechanisms completely shot, his ability to withstand the long separations no longer resolute, he felt exhausted and burnt out for the first time in his lengthy career.

Travel, long stretches away from his wife and children, plus the exhaustive wear and tear of living constantly out of a suitcase, takes its toll on a young agent. Divorce rates in the DSS are among the highest in federal law enforcement. Riner had to tell the SAC, the special agent in charge of the secretary of state detail, that he needed to settle down for a bit. As a reward for his nonstop travel, he was offered a slot in the Dallas field office—a major hub of DSS criminal investigations. Working in Texas and investigating passport cases felt to Riner like a reward. It made up for the countless hours spent arguing with the Shin Bet about how security should be handled in a command post at Jerusalem's King David Hotel, racing through the avenues of Brussels in a motorcade to NATO headquarters, and standing guard in an arrival hall in some Third World airport.

When it inevitably came time to bid on his next overseas post, Riner hoped for a chance to serve in Greece. His wife's family had emigrated from the area, and he thought it would be the perfect fit, both for his professional and personal life. Greece was considered marginal high-threat, mainly because of the "November 17" terrorist groups that had targeted American diplomats and military officers for assassination. But Greece was also marginally Europe and a great way to score points for possible promotion by serving in a threat-filled environment, without having to endure the primitive amenities of a Lagos or Kuala Lumpur. Like many DSS agents about to go overseas for their first extended tour at a post, he felt eagerness and trepidation following the submitting of his bids. He bid high on some other European countries, and on a few in the Middle East. What he got was Pakistan.

The Riners did what many DSS families do before embarking to a "new" post—they located the country on a map and then raced to the library to begin a hurried learning process. Still, their preparations were important. The study was useful. But all the books, videotapes, and magazine articles in the world could not prepare Special Agent Jeff Riner for the twenty-four months of snarled, violent, corrupt, and simmering high-threat reality that is the Islamic Republic of Pakistan.

PAKISTAN, IT HAS BEEN WRITTEN, IS A LAND OF ISLAMIC RELIGIOUS FAITH. In reality, it is a stepchild of the best and worst intentions of postcolonialism, a country carved out of British India, designed to prevent murderous rioting from becoming genocide. Pakistan's birth was a bloody trauma accompanied by the displacement of millions of refugees. Its fifty-plus-year history has been equally as traumatic. It has endured disastrous wars with its overbearing neighbor, India, barbaric internal strife, and wholesale corruption. Pakistan has been unable to turn its mosaic of cultures into a productive society. While other countries in Southeast Asia blossomed with high-tech and manufacturing boom years, Pakistan grew poorer. As India developed into a regional superpower, both in military might and high-tech expertise, Pakistan sank into ethnic strife and governmental coups and countercoups. Five major ethnic groups, the Punjabis, Sindhis, Pashtun, Muhajirs, and Baluchis, make up the most of its 148 million souls. Hatred and violence between them is rampant. Pakistan is the seventh most populated nation in the world, with an annual growth rate of nearly 3 percent.

In the years since the 1979 Soviet invasion of Afghanistan, the near-hypnotic messages of fundamentalist Islam have flowed through the backwaters of Pakistan with the force of riptides passing through a narrow stream. Islam expounded reasons for these people's poverty and misery. The imams in the mosques and in countless *madrassas*, or Islamic schools, in the nation's teeming cities, impoverished towns, and remote villages began preaching the madly romantic lure of a holy war against all that is not Islamic. Pakistan's demographic reality, with the filthy cities of Karachi and Lahore among the most densely populated in the world, makes it a perfect breeding ground for fundamentalist fervor. Adult literacy teeters below 40 percent. Over half of Pakistan's population is under the age of fifteen.[4]

And Islam's victory in Afghanistan, against the world's most ruthless superpower, brought a new racial mix to this already flammable landscape. Islamic terrorist groups from all over the world began looking to Pakistan and its lawless Peshawar province as a mini terrorist state from which the global jihad would be staged, trained, and fought. The presence of some three million refugees just to the northwest of Pakistan and near the cities and towns to the south has had a weighty impact on Pakistan's demographics. Once the Soviet Union invaded Afghanistan in 1979, refugees began streaming over the borders into Pakistan. Their influx had profound social consequences. Afghan refugees began to take low-paying jobs away from the local workforce. Weapons smuggled in from the war in Afghanistan or built to order in the workshops of Peshawar, proliferated throughout the country. Political parties became armed militias. Organized criminal gangs soon controlled areas in cities that were carved into semi-independent gangster fiefdoms. Urban instability manifested itself in revolutionary movements. Those in power grew rich from corruption and became more and more ruthless. The word of Islam, and the AK-47, became the icons of the mob.

It was amidst this minefield of hate and murder that Jeff Riner and his family joined a U.S. post that had already endured its fair share of violence and loss. On November 21, 1979, two days after Iranian students seized the U.S. Embassy in Teheran, a mob of some 10,000 Pakistanis rushed from the mosques of Islamabad and, in a vile display of hatred, stormed the formidable U.S. compound. Rumors had swelled through the streets of Islamabad and Rawalpindi, the capital's twin city, that the United States had somehow seized the Grand Mosque in Mecca. And in Pakistan, rumor is as good as truth. The Pakistani police contingent guarding the embassy was lightly armed and ineffectual. A private local security force, trained and paid by DSS, struggled to secure the compound, but the angry protesters, whipped into a frenzy by their religious leaders, were thirsty for blood. The DSS agents on duty and the detachment of fifty-odd marines were no match for the ravening mob of young and not-so-young men, many waving weapons and tearing down the iron gates that surrounded the estatelike property. The mob quickly overran the compound and broke into the embassy buildings. The RSO and his deputies, along with the marines, were powerless against such a flood of humanity. They grabbed their shotguns and donned body armor, but the thousands of jeering men in their white and khaki-colored *shalwar kameez* gowns yelling "Allahu Akbar" as they ripped the embassy's building apart with their bare hands could not be stopped.[5]

The American security forces gathered those in the compound into an airtight safe haven inside the embassy and prayed to God while the mob set everything in sight aflame. A marine standing at his post atop the building's roof was shot in the temple by a sniper. Another diplomat, a consular officer, died of smoke inhalation as he rushed to his apartment to check on a pet. The heat from the flames was so intense that the ceramic tiles buckled and dissolved like cubes of ice melting under the hot desert's sun. If it wasn't for a team of DSS-trained Pakistani investigators and guards, who had made sure that the embassy's water and ventilation system were pumping, the entire American diplomatic community in Islamabad would have been butchered.

A new embassy was built over the charred foundations of the old one. Today, the U.S. embassy in the Ramna Diplomatic Enclave of Islamabad is a seventy-acre fortress that serves as home, office, and place of leisure for the several hundred American diplomats, military attachés, and the U.S. Marine guards who work at the post. The embassy sports a chancery, a consular section, residential apartments, tennis courts, and a swimming pool. It is, without exaggeration, a mini–U.S. city inside a teeming Third World landscape.

On his first full day in Islamabad, Riner, the new assistant RSO on post, was given the nickel tour of the town by one of the embassy guides. Islamabad, as a city, was neatly designed by a Greek city planner—a town meant to serve as the seat of Pakistani government, to segregate power and wealth from the "street" and the masses, and to house the nation's foreign diplomatic representation. Islamabad itself is clean and, for the most part, orderly. Nestled against the Margala Hills, the foothills of the Himalayas in northern Punjab, it is a modern and spacious city of wide, tree-lined streets, large houses, elegant public buildings and well-organized bazaars. Sidewalks are shaded and fairly safe beside rows of flame trees, jacaranda, and hibiscus.

Built in 1958 as a showplace capital, Islamabad is the hub of Pakistan's ruling elite. "Half the marble palaces are owned by government ministers," one DSS agent would comment, "the other half by drug dealers." It has plenty of law and order. The authorities, always fearful of a coup, keep a sizable force of military men in the city, along with police units, plainclothes secret service agents, and the ever-present Pakistani intelligence services.

According to official guidebooks, Islamabad is a city where traffic jams and crowds are rare, and narrow lanes and slums are few and far between. But there is a saying inside the embassy: "You can be inside Islamabad and all is well and good, but if you drive for fifteen minutes in any direction you are in Pakistan." Across town, in Islamabad's sister city of Rawalpindi, the real Pakistan stirred, plotted, and erupted. A mosaic of colors, scents, and squalor, Rawalpindi is a city packed with slums, huts, open-air markets, rotting food, raw sewage, and mosques. It is the true Pakistan. A Pakistan of *katchiabaadis*, temporary houses, built in a dysfunctional style from stones, concrete blocks, corrugated steel, and any other building material that can be found in a junk heap. Water and electricity are luxuries. Pakistan is a nation where honor killings are accepted, where terrorists train, and where the graffiti in the slums of Quetta, Karachi, and Peshawar read "Death to America!" Pakistan is a nuclear power.[6]

BUT DESPITE ALL THE UNKNOWNS IN PAKISTAN AND ALL THE HOSTILE EYES that constantly watched and reconnoitered the embassy in Islamabad preparing for what the security staff knew was the inevitable attack, it was nonetheless a great place for an energetic DSS agent to work. Jeff Riner was fortunate to join a team that was superb. The RSO was a gruff old DSS veteran named Art Maurel, a man who had made a name for himself in South Vietnam working special investigations for the U.S. Air Force. "Art was the kind of guy who didn't take shit from anyone, but he didn't shovel it at you either," commented a DSS veteran of many high-threat posts. "Most importantly," he added, "he knew how to get things done, and in Pakistan that could often be the difference between life and death."[7]

The assistant RSO was a former marine corps lieutenant named Bill Miller, a Georgia bulldog who had actually bid for Pakistan following a four-year stint on the secretary of state's protective detail. Miller had been an infantry officer and was a no-nonsense commander. When the corps downsized in the mid-1980s, Miller sought employment elsewhere. He showed interest in the FBI and a few other agencies located in and around Washington, D.C., but he wanted to travel. He liked the idea of overseas adventure and of dignitary protection. He was a natural for DSS.

Miller relished the opportunity of a Third World high-risk challenge. Three months after he arrived in the Washington field office, Miller was on a plane to Africa for a three-month mission to Botswana. After Africa, and a few other TDYs to other locations around the world, Miller joined the secretary's detail, where he stayed for nearly five years and four secretaries of state. "I came in at the tail end of Shultz, worked all of Baker, all of Eagleburger, and the very beginning of Christopher," Miller remembers. "Even if it was only to be in the airport or the motorcade to the hotel, I traveled to 122 countries during that time. SD was great. We were in places where we saw history being made. I was in there for the Gulf War, for the Madrid peace conference, and got to see all the living presidents. It was great to be where historical events were happening, and to be working in a place where your contribution to safeguarding the principals making that history allowed them to do what they needed to do."[8]

Miller rose up through the ranks of SD—starting out, in his words, as a "hump agent," and eventually becoming a shift leader. In August 1992, when the bid list came out for his eventual posting overseas, he knew he wanted a high-threat location in an Islamic country. Unlike most DSS agents, Bill Miller bid high for Pakistan. "I wanted to work in an Islamic culture and in a high-threat environment. I *wanted* Islamabad."

He learned, during a break from his RSO training class, that the World Trade Center had been bombed. Initial reports were sketchy, and a lot of what his class learned of the attack was what they gleaned from the media. Soon thereafter the connection between the bombers and a mysterious figure named Ramzi Yousef became known, as did the fact that Yousef had escaped to Pakistan. Readying himself for a two-year tour there, Miller had a gut-feeling that he would encounter Yousef in the months to come, or at the least, some of Yousef's comrades.

TOGETHER, THESE THREE SPECIAL AGENTS REPRESENTED "THE LAW" IN THE embassy. They had to rely upon the Pakistani police for security in the streets leading up to the embassy, and on a local DSS-trained and DSS-vetted guard force to protect the embassy's outer perimeter.

Inside, security was strictly an American affair. According to their official job descriptions, the RSO and his staff of DSS agents are assigned to protect the embassy, diplomatic facilities, the American diplomatic community, and overall American interests in-country.

The RSO's office is also in charge of the marine security guard (MSG) garrison at the facility. The mission of the MSGs is to provide internal security to State Department facilities (embassies, consulates, or legations) around the world, to prevent the compromise of classified material, and to provide protection for U.S. citizens and government property. These overseas missions are commonly referred to as "posts," and overall security for the installations is the mandate of DSS. In only the most extreme emergency situations are the marines authorized to perform duties exterior to the buildings, or to provide special protection to the senior diplomatic officers off premises. The MSGs also provide special guard services for U.S. delegation offices at which classified information is kept during regional or international conferences, and assist in guarding the temporary overseas residences of the president, vice president, or secretary of state.

At a diplomatic post, such as the embassy in Islamabad, the marine detachment commander and RSO form the post security team. Their relationship is the key to the security program's success and it is tested very frequently. The RSO's office, together with the detachment commander, conducts what are known in the business as reaction drills, or "REACTs." These exercises are designed to test the detachment's response time, performance, and overall ability to handle emergencies inside the embassy such as fires, bomb threats, intruders, riots, and

demonstrations. The marines on duty, as well as those quickly responding from their living quarters, assemble in the "REACT room" to
receive orders and direction from the detachment commander. This
room provides not only a storage area for weapons, ammunition, and
personal protective equipment, but also a safe and secure position in
which to suit up for the REACT scenario. REACTs were designed to
simulate a terrorist truck bombing of an embassy, or a dedicated effort
by terrorists to assault the compound. Of course, the marines also train
for that much-feared confrontation with a mob of 10,000 screaming
protestors looking to burn the embassy down to the ground.

The RSOs "love their marines," claimed Don Morris, a retired DSS
veteran who has served in nearly half a dozen Middle Eastern posts.
"When the bad guys are climbing over the fence and storming the
gates, the bulldogs [the nickname for the marines] are going to save
your ass every time!"[9]

IN PAKISTAN, THE SPRAWLING EMBASSY COMPOUND WAS, IN MANY WAYS,
like a small American town. Many of the diplomats lived in apartments
on post, because the embassy always filtered its drinking water, maintained round-the-clock generators, and was deemed safer than settling
into the luxurious trappings of a villa in town. There were stores and
swimming pools in the compound, as well as clubs, restaurants, and
athletic fields, including playgrounds for children. And because there
was so little to do in Islamabad, the American embassy enclave became
the focal point for the entire expatriate community, from every nation
outside of Pakistan. Each Thursday, Friday, Saturday, and Sunday night
the embassy's military office would show movies—albeit six to nine
months behind their Hollywood release dates. There were softball
games on the vast property, often attended by hundreds of spectators.
If the compound was like an American town in the midst of the Wild
East, then the three DSS special agents were its sheriffs.

The reach of the RSO's office extended beyond Islamabad. The
State Department maintained regional consulates in Lahore and Peshawar, and the RSO's office in Islamabad was responsible for securing
those facilities with a local guard force. There was also an additional

RSO sitting in the sprawling consulate in Karachi, along with his support staff.

MAINTAINING SECURITY FOR THE EMBASSY AND ITS PERSONNEL WAS A never-ending undertaking. The DSS agents, as well as visiting teams from Washington, frequently conducted series of lessons and lectures to heighten the diplomatic community's awareness of the threats faced in Pakistan. Subjects included surveillance, counterintelligence techniques, and methods to avoid trouble spots.

Mostly, though, the DSS agents labored to drill into their charges that they were "no longer in Kansas," and must be very aware of their surroundings. "You can't walk around here like you would at home." The DSS crew would plead with the embassy personnel to avoid large gatherings of people. "In Pakistan," the agents would teach, "a fender bender has the potential of becoming a full-fledged riot. Two men arguing can soon become a mob, a mob can become a riot, and a riot can envelop you before you have a chance to flee, and then God help you!"[10] Political officers were urged to monitor mass demonstrations from a distance. If there was a disturbance in town, DSS agents would get on an embassy loudspeaker and tell the diplomats to avoid that part of town until the "all clear" was sounded.

But there were always cases where embassy employees, particularly women, simply didn't heed the warnings. In one event, an embassy employee's wife was sure that the "safety awareness" lectures she had listened to did not pertain to her plans to jog every morning around Islamabad wearing spandex shorts and a revealing top. She was mistaken, and taking a wrong turn away from the clean confines of the diplomatic enclave, she loped into town. Soon, she was followed by a small army of men, ranging from boys in their teens to toothless senior citizens waving bamboo canes, chasing her through the streets of the city.

Diplomats themselves often scoffed at the security warnings and ignored the directives. American officials in Pakistan were most vulnerable to the threat of terrorist attack and assassination when they drove about town in their large cars with diplomatic tags. Vehicles were always attractive targets, especially in the gridlock snarls of Islamabad traffic. In countless lectures, the DSS staff stressed the importance of driver awareness to all embassy personnel. "Never bottleneck yourself," the agents would warn the diplomats. "Never position your vehicle in a place where you can be blocked in and become a sitting target. Most importantly, never linger with your vehicle in front of the embassy. The assassins are good and they're smart. They will follow you, watch for an opportunity, and then on foot or on a motorbike, pull up beside you and blow your brains out!" But many did not take the threat of assassination seriously. Embassy workers would regularly block off the fortified entrances and exits to the embassy by leaving their cars where they wished, bottlenecking the narrow roadways leading in and out of the compound and exposing all those waiting to get into the building to a possible terrorist strike.

Some in the Foreign Service actually resented the DSS presence inside the embassy. The agents were cops, after all, and within the embassy they had full powers of arrest. Diplomats suspected of security breaches, selling entry visas to the United States, committing spousal abuse, or worse were all investigated by the RSO's office. In fact, *all* investigations run through the embassy by any agency had to go through the RSO's office.

If someone had a traffic accident in town, the RSO's office received the call. When the burglar alarm would sound inside a diplomat's home, even if it was due to a power outage and the return of service had sparked the signal, the DSS agent on duty was summoned—usually in the middle of the night. When a member of the mission had his pocket picked inside the teeming market, the DSS agent on duty accompanied the angry diplomat to the local police station to file a report. If a diplomat was killed, or met an accidental death, the RSO's office handled the crime scene, the initial investigation, and all liaison with the local authorities.

In one incident, a visiting U.S. Air Force serviceman on an official mission to Pakistan fell out of the fourth-floor window of the Islamabad Marriott Hotel. RSO Maurel, the security officer on duty, secured the scene around the body and maintained it until military investigators could arrive.

The DSS command trio was also burdened with investigating reports of cruelty to animals. There were numerous instances of dogs being poisoned by local Pakistani staff. In one case, a surveillance camera inside a diplomat's home caught on tape a dog being raped by the local gardener. Dogs are not viewed positively in Pakistan; many religious Muslims consider them unclean.

ONE OF THE MOST IMPORTANT TASKS OF THE RSO's OFFICE IN ISLAMABAD was dealing with "walk-ins." A walk-in is the blanket term applied to any foreign national who approaches an embassy's main ceremonial gate, asking to speak to a member of the security staff about an important matter. Sometimes, the Pakistani walk-ins would offer to provide information—for a fee—on the possible location of a wanted terrorist. Others would be hawking whispered secrets about heroin traffickers, money launderers, and counterfeiters. Many walk-ins offered information on allegedly near-perfect counterfeit copies of the copy-proof $100 "super note." It was rumored that Lebanese terrorist groups had perfected the counterfeiting of this new treasury note, but news that there might possibly be printing presses in Peshawar, churning out near-perfect clones of the $100 bill, had serious national security implications.

A report on each and every walk-in was assembled by the DSS staff and sent on to Washington. News of a counterfeit operation in Lahore would be of great interest to the U.S. Secret Service. News of a drug ring with links to the United States was of interest to the DEA. Word on possible nuclear material floating around Pakistan was of immediate concern to the CIA. Yet most of the walk-ins were a waste of time, and some were clearly insane. "The secret police have planted a transmitter in my brain," a rough-and-tumble middle-aged man wearing a soiled *shalwar kameez* once told a guard at the gate. "I need to speak to someone in your intelligence bureau immediately." At the embassy gates, one of the DSS agents would always look the walk-in over and talk to him—his weapon at the ready, and an MSG armed with a shotgun close by.

The RSOs had been trained to be suspicious of any walk-ins, no matter what they looked like and no matter what they had to say. Was the man dressed as a Baluchi farmer for real, or was he an agent from Iran's Ministry of Intelligence and Security, scoping out the security apparatus for a report to be passed on to his associates in Hezbollah? Was the man with impeccable English and Western dress really offering up information of a hashish shipment headed for Newark Airport, or was he an operative for the Pakistani *Jamaat ul-Fuqra*, a fundamentalist Islamic sect whose goal is to purify Islam through violence?

Sometimes, however, the walk-ins offered the real deal—twenty-four karat gold information that was worthy of any fee. "You don't turn away anyone," Riner explained, "because you never know what it is they can offer."

ONE OF THE MOST IMPORTANT FACTORS IN THE RSO'S ABILITY TO WORK in a foreign country, where the language and national complexion is so different, is the DSS practice of hiring Foreign Service national investigators. In Islamabad, the FSNIs were local Pakistanis working for the RSO's office, serving in effect as the eyes and ears of the DSS. Many were military or law-enforcement veterans. They were handsomely paid, well taken care of, and indispensable to bridging the gap between the American security staff and the threats encountered in Pakistan. The FSNIs spoke the myriad of dialects needed to get all sorts of thing done. They knew which tribal chiefs were worthy of a bribe, which roads to take, which police commanders were friendly, and which ones held a deep disdain for the United States. The FSNIs had a roster of contacts that would take any American law-enforcement official a century to foster.

In attempting to fulfill these dangerous and often overwhelming duties, the DSS agents in Pakistan, as well as those serving around the world, faced other hurdles as well. Unlike the relationship between the U.S. Secret Service and the U.S. Department of the Treasury, or that between the U.S. Marshals Service and the U.S. Department of Justice, DSS is *not* an entity separate from the State Department. In the words of one senior agent, "In DSS, we cannot control the way a lot of stuff is done for us, to us, or about us. We don't have that juice. We still

have to answer to everybody and his grandmother at the State Department." There have always been restrictions imposed on how
hands-on agents can function, what they can do, and to what extent
they can do it. But the restrictions, and the limitations in resources
and manpower, created a breed of agents who live by their wits and
get things done by hook or by crook. In Pakistan, that meant dealing
with the local authorities. And contacts with the local authorities, a
true side-by-side working relationship, happened most frequently
when the ambassador, or a visiting delegation, would travel outside the
confines of Islamabad.

Any time the ambassador left Islamabad to visit another city, the
RSO or one of his staff would tag along as his bodyguard. Wherever
any DSS agents traveled, whether it was to the American Club for an
after-hours Budweiser, or to Quetta to hunt down a possible terrorist,
they were armed—their SIG-Sauer P228 9mm pistols, one of the finest
examples of Swiss ballistic genius ever produced, worn in nondescript
fanny packs. Often, however, the DSS agents carried heavier weapons
and enlisted the support of the Pakistani military and its myriad of
intelligence services.

One place in Pakistan that required a heavy security detail, as well
as elaborate planning and preparation, was a trip to Peshawar, in the
lawless North-West Frontier. Once a backwater town at the end of the
famed Khyber Pass, Peshawar has become the tripwire in a global conflict pitting Islamic fundamentalist terrorism against the West. For a
time it was a quaint provincial capital known for colonial-style man-
sions, a relic of the British Empire and the rule of the Raj, until it
devolved into a polluted way station for revolution. Peshawar became
a city where violence and crime were the currency of day-to-day existence. Drugs, primarily heroin and hashish, were cultivated in Afghanistan and routinely shipped and processed in Peshawar before
being sent on to Karachi for points east and west. The DEA always
paid very close attention to this rugged region. Drug lords often
sported gangs of heavily armed fighters and enforcers who were legendary for their ruthlessness.

But the crime lords of Peshawar were no match for the Afghan
resistance groups who turned the city into the front lines of the jihad

against the Soviet Union. During the Afghan War, Peshawar became a forward command post for the CIA personnel assisting the "mooj," the Langley term of affection for the mujahadeen warriors. Fair-skinned Virginia natives milled about the refugees and Pakistani traders as they plotted the campaign against the Soviets, and fueled the pipeline that supplied the war. Craftsmen who once produced necklaces and copper bowls became expert gunsmiths. In parts of Peshawar, weapons production became a mainstay industry. Beautiful copies of the Chinese version of the AK-47 assault rifle could be bought for $200 and a bit of heroin. Russian pistol copies, cheaply made, went for $50. World War II–era British Lee Enfield rifles were lovingly restored and maintained. According to Bill Miller, "You could buy, rent, or barter for just about any weapon known to man in Peshawar, from .50 caliber machine guns to RPGs to 20mm artillery pieces."[11] The staccato sound of gunfire was everywhere The situation was so volatile it could, in Jeff Riner's recollection of motorcading through Peshawar and seeing a hundred Arabs and Afghans brandishing AK-47s, "turn at any moment."[12]

When the war against the Soviets ended, Peshawar did not enjoy the dividends of peace. The city became a polarized hovel of the faithful looking for the next superpower to vanquish. It was a hopeless slum driven by firepower and religious rage.

Peshawar became by the mid-1990s essentially an Afghan city. Peshawar consisted of acrid smoke laced with the indelible scents of gasoline, hashish, and lamb meat on the grill. Trash fires obscured the bright sun with a constant plume of noxious black and gray clouds. Beggars limped through the narrow marketplace, many of them amputees from the Afghan fighting. Afghani prostitutes, preferred by the locals for their fair complexion and discounted rates, prowled the alleyways of the city. Afghan social clubs, restaurants, and financial institutions dominated the skyline.[13]

As the lawless city was overwhelmed by fundamentalists, revolutionaries from around the region—and around the world—began to appear on Peshawar's streets and back alleys. North African, Palestinian, Lebanese, and Yemeni men wearing fatigues and carrying weapons joined the identifiable Pakistani and Afghani faces. Filipinos came to Peshawar, as did Saudis, some very wealthy, moving in and out of Afghanistan in motorcades with heavily armed security details. Bearded rebels from Bosnia, Kosovo, Dagestan, Uzbekistan, and Chechnya appeared in and around the training camps, as did gaunt warriors from Sudan and central Africa. Peshawar became a global clearinghouse for Islamic rage.

Protecting an ambassador on a trip to Peshawar required enormous strategic planning and preparation. The FSNI would make contact with his comrades in the security services and the military, as well as with the local tribal chiefs. There were no bona fide tolls on the highways of Pakistan, though an "honor fee" was expected each time the motorcade of Mitsubishi Pajeros crossed from one disputed stretch of the North-West Territory to another. Each tribal gang was heavily armed; most were ruthless narcotics traffickers. They dealt with those who dishonored their sovereign claim on a stretch of nondescript mountains with violent displays. In many areas of the North-West Territory, even the Pakistani military was loath to enter. "If the bad guys wanted to get you," Jeff Riner recalled, "there was very little one could do. It was a thousand gun barrels against you. You relied on your FSNI's ability to assess the situation, and your contacts with the local authorities. And, of course, you prayed."

Sometimes, the DSS contingent in Pakistan would even have to escort and protect assistant secretaries of state venturing into Afghanistan proper, through the Taliban-controlled stretches of Jalalabad, Kandahar, and Kabul, on fact-finding missions. Every such venture was a potential nightmare.

IF PAKISTAN WAS ANYTHING, IT WASN'T BORING. SECURING AN EMBASSY in a sea of hostility and hate—one that had already been overrun and burned to the ground—was a challenge that could have used the skills and cunning of twenty federal agents, but there were only three in Islamabad. Life and death depended on personal contacts with people who mattered. Those contacts were more valuable than Kevlar body armor and an M4 5.56mm assault rifle. And, no matter how intrepid the DSS agents were, they could achieve nothing in a place like Pakistan without their contacts with the local cops and spies.

In Pakistan, the DSS agents dealt with three levels of Pakistani law enforcement and counterterrorism. The first layer was the Pakistani police. In many ways, this institution was no different from the colonial force that the British had left in place prior to their departure in 1947—certainly their salaries and equipment had not changed. In fact, the overall organization of the police forces remained much the same after partition. Except for centrally administered territories and tribal enclaves in the north and northwest, basic law and order responsibilities have been carried out by the four provincial governments. The Pakistani police were a poorly trained, highly corrupt force that could be very brutal in its dealings with the general public. Bribes could buy one's freedom, or cause a beat cop to turn the other way. Police in Pakistan were generally unarmed. For crowd control, they were trained to use a *lathi*, a five-foot wooden staff that, when wielded properly with the unforgiving speed of a whip, can humble the largest of foes. Some policemen were armed, and those surrounding the U.S. embassy were all equipped with sidearms and submachine guns, though privately the DSS agents wondered how many of the police officers were actually carrying ammunition. "If they didn't sell the bullets, then the ammunition was so antiquated and poor that it would probably misfire," claimed one retired DSS veteran who served as RSO in Islamabad. "If a Pakistani policeman fired over five bullets at the range in a year, he was considered a marksman."[14]

A policeman's pay in Islamabad was poor, but it was better, even if only slightly, than that earned by a factory worker or donkey driver. According to one story, police officers working in the diplomatic enclave around Islamabad were all cops who were being punished for one infraction or another. Inside the enclave, where most of the embassies were situated and most of the foreign diplomats lived, a police officer couldn't simply pull over a car and demand that the motorist pay a bribe. On the other hand, in downtown Islamabad or in Rawalpindi, if an officer needed additional money in order to feed his family, he could shake down pedestrians, motorists, and business owners, and few, if anyone, would bat an eye. Police officers were supposed to have a modest amount of education, though they were paid only the wages of an unskilled laborer—approximately $40 per month. Even an officer with a good head on his shoulders, some talent, and the proper family connections, upon rising up the chain of command to become a head constable would be paid only at the level of a semiskilled worker.

Still, the local cops were a thin blue line of defense insulating the embassy from harm. And even if the RSO's office had concerns about their reliability and skills, the Pakistani police were the only game in town. The cops had to be relied upon to serve as that outer ridge of insulation protecting the embassy from harm.

Maintaining good contacts with the local precinct commander and district boss was essential to the DSS agents in Islamabad. "I teach young agents that we work *with* the local cops, not against them," Jeff Riner told future DSS special agents in advanced training classes. "We don't go in and order people around. We rely on the locals, either here or abroad, to help us do our job. And we turn around and take care of them whenever we can." According to another RSO, based in one of the more volatile posts in the Middle East, "My rule of thumb is never to go to the local commanders when you have a problem. Then it looks like you're there only because you want something. You go and visit the local precinct when everything is OK."[15]

Because the agency has traditionally learned to get by with so little, special agents often survive by their wits and personalities. It is very common for RSOs and their assistant security officers to take the local police commander out to lunch or to bring him a DSS T-shirt, a DSS key chain, or another trinket that the department knows as "throw-downs" to establish a rapport. Building a relationship enables the RSO, in time of need, to get additional forces sent somewhere for added security, or for off-the-record assistance in case a delicate matter comes up. Usually, as RSOs and assistant RSOs rotate out of post, they make a point of introducing their replacements to the local commanders, to continue the personal contact with DSS and its people in-country. "In a country like Pakistan," Jeff Riner reflects, "there isn't a lot of turn-over with the police—especially at a high rank. So a commander might have dealt with seven RSOs over the course of a twenty-year career. He knows our needs and he knows what we need from him."

———

ANOTHER PAKISTANI LAW ENFORCEMENT AGENCY WITH WHICH THE RSO's office in Islamabad had intimate contact was the Federal Investigative Agency, or FIA.

The Federal Investigative Agency, Pakistan's counterterrorist and counterintelligence service, also handles immigration and border control matters. It is a combination of the FBI, Customs Service, Immigration and Naturalization, and Bureau of Alcohol, Tobacco, and Firearms. The FIA is ruthless in the execution of its daily tasks. It fields a force of very cunning agents and handlers who do not have to obtain a warrant or court order in order to extract information. The foot soldiers in this campaign are, of course, informants. Thousands of anonymous eyes and ears roam through the streets of Pakistan and inside the villages and refugee camps around the countryside, providing FIA officials with a true portrait of what is transpiring inside the country. The informants are poor souls, drug dealers, prostitutes, and common thieves who cut a deal by informing on their brothers. The FIA operates in plain clothes. Most of the agents wear nothing more than a gray *shalwar kameez*, but their swagger makes them easy to pick out on the streets and inside the mosques of Pakistan.

A unique character named Rahman Malik headed the FIA. Malik, at one point, commanded Pakistan's countersmuggling and counternarcotics forces and was a rising star inside the country's covert security hierarchy. The three DSS agents assigned to the embassy made a point of meeting with Malik very frequently, and each visit to his office, inside the sprawling FIA complex in Islamabad, was treated with great fanfare. Appearances are everything in Pakistan, and Malik enjoyed the pageantry. He loved to invite the DSS agents to his compound, relishing in waving them through the numerous layers of heavily armed security that surrounded the headquarters.

In his office, Malik made his DSS guests wait for hours—sometimes for an entire day—as they sat on leather sofas in an air-conditioned waiting area, drinking sweet tea under a photo of the FIA director standing side-by-side with FBI Director Louis Freeh. Rahman Malik was something of an FBI buff. He told anyone and everyone invited to his palatial office about his close working relationship with "the Bureau." Malik was a wannabe G-man who had, as one of his most prized possessions, an honorary FBI gold shield that he made sure to show DSS guests each and every time they sat in his ornate office.

The meetings in Malik's office were always cordial. He was a staunch supporter of Pakistani Prime Minister Benazir Bhutto, and he realized that as long as she valued the country's relationship with the United States, it was his mandate to keep the American embassy and diplomatic mission safe from harm. The DSS agents were often wary of requesting anything formally from the FIA. "We knew that if we asked them to *talk* to someone who was of concern to us, they'd generally beat the living shit out of him," a retired DSS agent remembered.[16] Photos of FIA torture victims were often featured in government opposition newspapers reviewed in the RSO's office. The methods were absolutely barbaric and abhorrent to American law enforcement. One rumored torture involved arranging four wooden chairs in two side-by-side pairs back to back and separated by a small distance. The individual being tortured would be laid out on his back, in midair between the pairs of chairs, with one bamboo police staff placed under his knees and the other beneath his shoulder blades. A third bamboo *lathi* would be rammed up the suspect's rectum and then poked deeper and deeper until the confession was blurted out. According to reports from Amnesty International, police torture has become so commonplace that it has slowly lost the capacity to shock and disgust.[17]

THE FIA WAS NOT POPULAR INSIDE PAKISTAN. THE POPULATION FEARED the repressive force, and it was often in competition with the ISI. Inter-Services Intelligence was Pakistan's principal intelligence-gathering agency, founded in 1948 by a British army officer, Major-General R. Cawthome, then deputy chief of staff in Pakistan's army. The ISI's primary mission in the country's first few tumultuous years of independence was to safeguard Pakistani national interests, monitor opposition political groups, and sustain military rule in Pakistan. The intelligence service's mandate also included the collection and dissemination of foreign and domestic intelligence, coordinating the intelligence functions of the three military services, and monitoring all foreigners in Pakistan, as well as members of the national and international media. The ISI also conducted surveillance of politically active segments of Pakistani society, and the diplomats of other countries accredited to Pakistan—especially those serving inside the U.S. embassy in Islamabad.

Over time, however, this powerful intelligence-gathering body became a creature beyond political reigns. The ISI is undoubtedly the most powerful institution inside Pakistan—many powerbrokers in the country believe it is more omnipotent than the military and prime minister's offices combined. Staffed by hundreds of civilian and military officers, plus thousands of other employees, the agency's headquarters is located in Islamabad. The ISI reportedly has a total of about 10,000 officers and staff members, a number that does not include informants and assets. It is reportedly organized into between six and eight divisions, including:

- Joint Intelligence, or JIX, a secretariat coordinating administrative support to other ISI wings.
- Joint Intelligence Bureau, or JIB, responsible for political intelligence.
- Joint Counter Intelligence Bureau, or JCIB, responsible for field surveillance of Pakistani diplomats stationed abroad, as well as for conducting intelligence operations in the Middle East, South Asia, China, Afghanistan, and the former Soviet Union.
- Joint Intelligence/North, or JIN, responsible for covert operations in Jammu and Kashmir.
- Joint Intelligence Miscellaneous, or JIM, tasked with espionage in foreign countries, including offensive intelligence operations.
- Joint Signal Intelligence Bureau, or JSIB, responsible for handling all signal and technological intelligence-gathering methods and operations.[18]

The DSS dealt with the ISI, but here the fine line between friend and foe was less clear than when dealing with the Islamabad police or the FIA. The ISI could not be ignored in Pakistan, but the DSS agents assigned to the embassy realized that the agency was both an ally of the United States and a foe. The ISI's role in the Afghan war offered numerous geopolitical opportunities for its savvy technocrats to play regional chess with the pious pawns of Afghanistan. Between 1983 and 1997, the ISI trained nearly 100,000 mujahadeen in intelligence gathering, special operations, commando techniques, sabotage, and cold killing. Many volunteers inside the ISI training camps were Osama bin Laden's Afghan Arabs. Others, reportedly, belonged to Hamas, Hezbollah, and a dozen more terrorist groups dedicated to striking at America's interests in the region and at the United States itself. But the ISI took its Afghanistan operation one step further: They were the ones who created the Taliban and, covertly, supported al-Qaeda.

Because of the ISI's support of the Taliban as an instrument of Pakistani foreign and domestic policy, it was at odds with the FIA, an agency that waged a violent campaign to undermine the political and military influence of the fundamentalist Islamic organizations in Pakistani politics. In the waning years of the Afghan war, Pakistan intended to become a major player in the postwar political landscape of that country. Pakistan's volatile and porous mountain frontier with Afghanistan demanded that Islamabad have a strong voice in Kabul. The ISI, through the CIA, was allowed to funnel money and arms to mooj factions in Afghanistan. The ISI wanted the dominant Islamic militia in Afghanistan to be one totally subservient to Islamabad's whims. When that group, a mujahadeen formation led by warlord Gulbuddin Hekmatyar, failed to consolidate power inside Afghanistan, or secure Pakistan's North-West Frontier and the land routes to and from the oil-rich former Soviet republics in Central Asia, the ISI created the Taliban.[19]

The Taliban was a Pakistani-produced proxy designed to create a land block of Muslim resistance to Indian dominance of the subcontinent. The ISI of Prime Minister Benazir Bhutto's government provided the Taliban with money, fuel, food, transportation, and weapons. It allowed Islamic students from the *madrassas* to join the Taliban's fight in Afghanistan, and it connected Afghanistan to Pakistan's American- and British-built telephone grid.

But the Taliban became a creature beyond the scope of Islamabad's wildest imagination. They became the champions of Islamic terrorist groups emerging in the Horn of Africa, in the Persian Gulf, in Southeast Asia, and inside Pakistan itself.

In many ways, the ISI and the FIA were at war in the poverty-stricken landscape of Pakistani politics. The ISI used its Islamic guerrillas as deniable foot soldiers to strike at FIA credibility, and according to published accounts, the FIA turned to Israel's Mossad and Shin Bet intelligence services to help track down the fundamentalist terrorists. The exchange of information between the Shin Bet and the FIA was a natural arrangement of necessity. The FIA was very concerned about Hamas and Islamic Jihad commanders spreading their brand of suicidal military operations to the mosques and streets of Pakistan. The Israelis, realizing that Pakistan had become the center of international terrorism, wanted to establish a liaison to the part of the world where many Islamic terrorists trained.

A report of the FIA's work with the Israelis was a source of outrage to the ISI. Israel was a close military friend of India—Israeli arms deals with the Indian military were substantial. Israel's Mossad enjoyed a close working relationship with India's famed Intelligence Bureau (IB), their country's version of the CIA. The ISI waged a campaign of regional chess while the FIA attempted to keep the pin inside the grenade that was Pakistan.

Maurel, Riner, and Miller realized that the friction between the ISI and the FIA's campaign to combat the fundamentalist Muslim elements inside Pakistan had all the trappings of a Third World game of chicken. The classified cable traffic flowing from Islamabad to Washington, D.C., detailed infighting and the potential for anti-American reactions. The DSS agents were determined that the embassy and those in the mission would not be caught in the middle of a violent outburst. Once a week the RSO staff would review a thumbnail translation of the local press, opposition as well as government-controlled, to evaluate the local political mood. It was virtually all anti-American. There were reports of Osama bin Laden in the local media at the time, but his importance was not fully realized. He was just another name on a long list of jihad warriors who were glorified in the Pakistani media as sabers ready to slice the heart out of the Great Satan that was the United States.

The mood throughout the country was palpably anti-American. "Every time you left the embassy, left the compound, you felt it. You felt the eyes staring at the back of your neck," a former DSS special agent commented.[20] The RSO's office never forgot the fact that Pakistan was the crossroads for transnational terrorism. Many people the U.S. government was looking for were in Pakistan. The list of wanted names that Washington sent to the RSO's office was growing. Some of those names were known Pakistani narcotics traffickers who had fled New York or California and were thought to be back at home riding out a storm of federal indictments. Other names belonged to suspected terrorists working for one of a dozen or so of the world's most notorious groups, groups that various intelligence services wanted to know more about. Because of its close relationships with the FIA and the ISI, the RSO's office often had better intelligence-gathering capabilities than did the CIA station chief or his counterpart from the Defense Intelligence Agency. DSS was the clearinghouse for reams of information. These agents were the three-man link that helped make sense of Pakistan to many elements of the federal government in Washington, D.C.

The RSO's office was also hunting for Mir Aimal Kansi. On the morning of January 25, 1993, Kansi ambushed employees making their way to work at a stoplight in front of the Central Intelligence Agency's main headquarters in Langley, Virginia. Without warning, Kansi unleashed a murderous fusillade from an AK-47 assault rifle into the gridlock of parked cars waiting to make a turn into the CIA. The attack occurred during morning rush-hour traffic, and Kansi was able to flee the scene and the United States, avoiding one of the most far-reaching law enforcement dragnets in history.

No one knew who Kansi was. Was he a deranged gunman acting out of rage, or was he a cold-blooded killer on a contract for a terrorist warlord? No one in law enforcement doubted where Kansi went, however. A native of Quetta in Pakistan, a teeming city of squalor, Kansi was back home—a faceless man in a *shalwar kameez* bleeding into the landscape, protected by tribal allegiances.

BUT BY JANUARY 1995 THE ONE NAME THAT TOPPED THE LIST OF WANTED men was Ramzi Ahmed Yousef. Bill Miller had always known that Ramzi Yousef used Pakistan as a transit point for his international operations. That Yousef had escaped to Pakistan following the World Trade Center bombing was far more than coincidence, Miller thought as he stared at the U.S. Department of State's Diplomatic Security Service two-million-dollar reward poster for the elusive bombing mastermind. If ever U.S. law enforcement would be able to get their clutches on Yousef, it would have to be done in Pakistan.

Each time someone from the RSO's office met with the FIA or the ISI, Yousef's name would come up. "Any news?" "Anything?" "If you can just think of something for us to go on we would be very grateful." "*Insh Allah*," or God willing, was the typical FIA or ISI response. "If God wills it, we will be able to find him for you." If Yousef was located, it would probably not be through the auspices of the local, questionably sympathetic officials.

Besides the reward posters for Yousef and Kansi that adorned the RSO's office, a brand-new case of matchbooks produced by the rewards program stood ready to be opened and distributed, having just recently arrived from the States in the diplomatic pouch. Each matchbook featured a photo of Yousef with an offer of the two-million-dollar reward for any news leading to his arrest or capture, printed in Urdu. The matchbooks, as well as other paraphernalia, were to be distributed throughout the Peshawar area. The hope in the RSO's office was that an Afghan refugee, a pickpocket, or *someone* might know where Yousef was or where he might be headed, be tempted by greed and the sum of $2 million, and possess the courage to collect the bounty. "You could buy Pakistan for two million dollars," commented a DSS agent. "It was a lot of cash to dangle in front of an impoverished population."

The Christmas decorations still sparkled brightly inside embassy offices that January. The employees were reluctant to take them down. Many staff members were still returning from visits home to the States, where the wildness and frenetic chaos of Pakistan seemed so many millions of miles away. Winter came with a whimper that January. The harsh brisk winds that usually raced into the city from the Himalayas each winter were light, almost nonexistent. The special agents thought of spring and the realization that summer, and time to be rotated out of Pakistan, was soon approaching.

The RSO's office was on a heightened state of alert, fearing some sort of attack in Pakistan, as were the MSGs and the local guard staff. Countersurveillance teams from the local guard force scanned the areas that ringed the embassy, looking for people watching them in turn. There was an unsettling feeling among the security staff inside the embassy that they were being reconnoitered for some sort of attack. There were no tangible signs of overt surveillance, but cops rely on a gut feeling that sinks to the bottoms of their stomachs and causes the hairs on the back of their heads to rise. January was that kind of time in the American compound in Islamabad.

The rains had yet to come, though dark clouds blanketed the snow-capped Himalayas with a foreboding shade of gray.

Chapter 5

TRUE REWARDS

When DSS special agents arrive in a post like Islamabad, it is not uncommon for them to hang up a countdown book on their walls at home. The calendars start out at "730 days" and then count down day by day until they depart for the United States. The children of these DSS agents are particularly susceptible to the homesick blues. Like military brats, theirs is a life of changing homes, "American schools," fleeting friendships, and the two-year permanence of an embassy apartment. Children are resilient, however. Especially if they do not know the real truth about the threats they face in the countries they are in.

The special agents, especially those serving in hardship—or differential—tours, get through their twenty-four months of service courtesy of the landmarks of time. "You realize that you are in the planet's armpit, but it's only a two-year assignment," a DSS agent with time served in Islamabad and Beirut commented. "You get there in August and right away school starts for your kids. Then, the next thing to look forward to is the Marine Ball in November. And then there's Thanksgiving. After Thanksgiving there's Christmas, New Year's, and spring break. And then you look forward to summer, a new bid list, and R-and-R for you and your family. Possibly even a trip back home. And then you only have one more year to go and, again, you start slicing up the year all over again until it's time to place your worldly possessions inside moving boxes and head out again. In some way, you have to break up time in small parcels of despair and anticipation in order to get through the reality of where you are and the threat that you face."[1]

Landmarks of time aren't always circles on a calendar that one eagerly looks forward to with heartfelt anticipation. Landmarks of time can be those intervals of bone-chilling fear and seconds of heart-pounding action that can define a DSS agent's entire tour of duty in a post so far from America's shores. For Art Maurel, Bill Miller, and Jeff Riner, February 1995 was one of those adrenaline-pumping times. Their years of service in Pakistan were marked and defined by ninety-six remarkable hours when, in a race against time, Islamabad became the center of the universe.

DSS AGENTS ARE LIKE COPS ANYWHERE ELSE IN THE WORLD — THEY YEARN to bring the bad guys to justice. In Islamabad, the DSS crew felt like beat cops, because the list of men wanted by U.S. law enforcement believed to be hiding in Pakistan was a lengthy inventory that grew virtually every day. There were common criminals, arsonists, credit card scammers, and swindlers—Pakistani immigrants to the United States who managed to hop on a flight back home moments before arrest warrants were issued. There were individuals that local sheriff's offices wanted to find for child abuse and insurance crimes. There were also those whose crimes were more serious, such as Haji Ehai Ibrahim, a 300-pound Pakistani wanted for "intent to distribute heroin and importation of a controlled substance" who made the DEA's ten-most-wanted list.[2]

Each man wanted by an American police department was considered important by the RSO's office. DSS, in a far-off outpost like Islamabad, was the U.S. law enforcement liaison with the outside world. Each and every rap sheet faxed or telexed to the RSO's office with a "can you help this department out?" scribbled on the cover sheet received a high priority. Names were run against computer records, and each and every case was brought to the attention of the local police and, in the more serious cases, the FIA. But the DSS agents knew that there was only so much that they could do in a country like Pakistan. Local criminals returned home to avoid jail in America, to be sheltered by their families and villages. Family matters were sensitive in Pakistan, and the local authorities were hesitant to assist in apprehending any felon fleeing U.S. justice. The DSS agents knew that they needed to pool their favors and resources to go after the most important fugitives.

Even the case of Mir Aimal Kansi did not inspire a sense of urgency in the local Pakistani authorities, but the DSS knew that the CIA gunman would not be leaving the country. There were few safe havens for Kansi anywhere outside of Pakistan. With a two-million-dollar bounty on his head, it was only a matter of time before someone in Quetta or in the North-West Frontier found a matchbox or a pamphlet offering a world of money for information leading to his arrest.

Ramzi Yousef was different, however. He wasn't merely a local boy who killed two people in front of the CIA. He was a player—an international operator whose talents for disguise and guile made him a difficult foe to snare. Yousef was smart, arrogant, and visionary. There was nothing ordinary about a man who plotted to murder 250,000 people in lower Manhattan.

There was a feeling inside the RSO's office in Islamabad that if the intelligence reports of Yousef being in Pakistan were genuine, the agents would have only a slim chance to get him. Pakistan was a place where anyone could disappear. Identity papers could be forged and bought, and undocumented refugees from Afghanistan meandered everywhere throughout the country. Even at passport control, inside the arrivals terminal of Karachi or Islamabad international airport, a savvy immigration officer who might pick up on Yousef's true identity might always be offered a wad of cash to look the other way. Law and order in Pakistan often depended on the size of a bribe. A suitcase full of rupees, or an envelope stuffed with dollars, could turn night into day.

By February 1995, especially after the discovery of the Josefa Apartments bomb factory in Manila, the DSS had an inkling that Ramzi Yousef was returning to Pakistan, or had already slipped back into the country. He had traveled to Pakistan immediately following the bombing of the World Trade Center, and it was widely assumed that he could find safe haven inside the country's teeming cities, the crowded refugee camps, or on the lawless frontiers. The trepidation inside the RSO's office in Islamabad wasn't that the elusive Yousef would simply hide out in Pakistan, but that he would use the comforting anonymity of the country's chaos as a convenient cover to target American interests and facilities. Operation Bojinka was designed to compensate for Yousef's earlier failure in New York City. The World Trade Center was to be that one strike against America that, in the minds of Yousef and his masters, evened the score for all the injustices and transgressions that had been perpetrated against Islam. But six dead and 1,000 wounded was a far cry from Yousef's original objectives. And the towers, those symbols of American power and might, still stood tall. The murder of nearly 5,000 people over the Pacific, capped off with an attempted assassination of both Pope John Paul II and President Clinton, would have more than made up for the failure to topple the Twin Towers. If Bojinka proved anything, it was how careful, plotting, and patient Yousef could be. There were nearly two years of thought, preparation, selection, training, and execution in the botched terrorist master play. But, as Murad's interrogation was revealing, Yousef's quest for bloodshed was as much a terrorist mission to please his bosses as it was a matter of ego.

In Islamabad, Maurel, Miller, and Riner could only wonder if Yousef was, in fact, in their midst. Was he watching *them*? Was he targeting the embassy? Was he planning to assassinate embassy personnel? If Yousef did attempt to make up for the failure of Bojinka, they knew one thing—the attack would be massive.

IT WAS AN UNSEASONABLY WARM SATURDAY MORNING IN ISLAMABAD ON February 4, 1995. A cool front was perched over the Himalayas though the local forecast was still springlike, with rain clouds hovering to the north and west. The U.S. embassy ran on Islamabad time, and Saturday, for the embassy, was the second day of a two-day weekend. It was a day off—a quiet time for brunch, a quick set of tennis, or, in Jeff Riner's case, serving as the agent-on-duty inside the chancery. Art Maurel and Bill Miller were sitting over a pot of coffee and a large

DSS Special Agent Tom Gallagher (center foreground), a shift leader assigned to the Secretary's Detail, leads the protective ring surrounding Secretary of State Madeleine Albright during a walk in downtown Sarajevo on June 2, 1997.

(Courtesy: U.S. Embassy/Sarajevo)

DSS Special Agent Tom Gallagher stands his post outside of Yasir Arafat's Ramallah headquarters during a visit by Secretary of State Albright in December 1999.

DSS Special Agent Mark Hipp (foreground) stands at the ready in his Kevlar body armor, awaiting the "wheels down" of PLO Chairman Yasir Arafat's plane at New York's John F. Kennedy International Airport.

The damage inside the bowels of the World Trade Center, February 27, 1993, only a day after the bombing. The lower resolution of this and some of the pictures following reflects their origin in first-generation digital cameras used at the time by field agents conducting counterterrorist investigations.

(Courtesy: Scott Stewart)

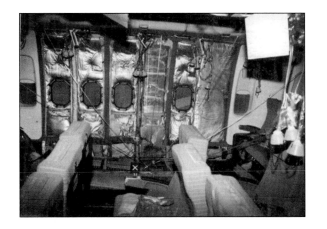

The lethal effects of Ramzi Yousef's "dry run"—the December 10, 1994, bombing of Philippine Airlines Flight 434

(Author's Collection)

The towers that still stood—an aerial view of the Twin Towers of the World Trade Center—as seen from an NYPD helicopter three years after the 1993 blast.

The terrorists who bombed the World Trade Center in New York murdered six innocent people, injured over 1,000 others, and left terrified school children trapped for hours in an elevator. Bombing suspect RAMZI AHMED YOUSEF fled the U.S. and remains at large. As long as YOUSEF is free, more innocent lives could be at risk. The U.S. Department of State is offering a reward of up to $2 million for information leading to

his arrest. If you have information about YOUSEF, contact the U.S. embassy or consulate. In the U.S. contact the F.B.I. or call 1-800-HEROES-1.

HEROES
P.O. Box 96781
Washington, D.C. 20090-6781
U.S.A.

RAMZI AHMED YOUSEF

REWARD

One of the many DSS reward pamphlets circulated around the world seeking clues to the whereabouts of Ramzi Yousef (Courtesy: DSS)

The Su Casa Guesthouse in Islamabad where Pakistani InterServices Intelligence agents, along with DSS Special Agents Jeff Riner and Bill Miller, apprehended Ramzi Yousef (Courtesy: U.S. Embassy/Islamabad)

"What's up, Ramzi?" Moments after Pakistani ISI operatives stormed through Yousef's room at the Su Casa Guesthouse, a DSS special agent snapped this photograph of him. (Courtesy: B. Miller)

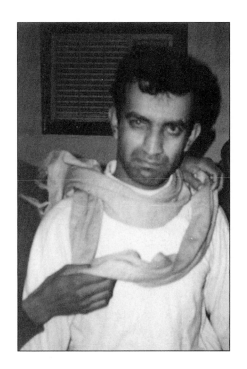

The aftermath of the al-Qaeda bombing of the U.S. Embassy in Nairobi, Kenya, on August 7, 1998 (Courtesy: W. Lee Reed)

The bombed-out shell of the U.S. Embassy in Dar es Salaam, Tanzania, hit by an al-Qaeda suicide truck bomb on August 7, 1998 (Courtesy: John DiCarlo)

The tattered flag sits symbolically on the desk in the ambassador's office—Dar es Salaam, August 7, 1998. (Courtesy: John DiCarlo)

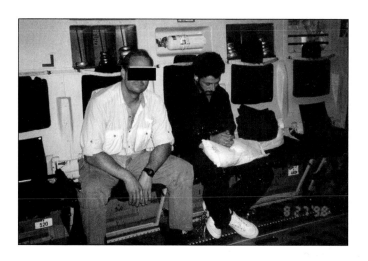

Another of Osama bin Laden's terrorists in DSS custody: DSS Special Agent Fred Piry safeguards Kenya embassy bombing mastermind Mohammed Sadiq Odeh on a U.S. Air Force flight from Kenya to New York. (Courtesy: F. Piry)

During Weapons of Mass Destruction tactical training, a DSS special agent assigned to the Mobile Security Division runs through a live-fire obstacle course.

A DSS MSD all-terrain counter-assault vehicle rushes through a series of explosions during tactical training preceding a deployment to Yemen.

The gold shield of America's Finest—the DSS badge (Courtesy: DSS)

breakfast at the American Club talking shop with Graham Membry, the United Nations security officer for the region, and getting a flavor of what the terrorist situation was like in Afghanistan. What happened in Afghanistan was of great importance to the DSS agents in Islamabad, and the UN security officer was an excellent source of information. The three were also discussing Bill Miller's first choice for his next post—Jerusalem. A series of suicide bombings had rocked Israel for a year, and an attack the week before had left some 30 dead and over 100 wounded. Bill Miller was a DSS special agent who did not succumb to homesickness. He relished the fact that he shouldered the burden of protecting an American diplomatic post and its community. Not many cops had that much responsibility. He felt that it was *his* personal mission, and he took great pride in it.

A FEW MILES FROM THE EMBASSY GROUNDS, A MAN STOOD A NERVOUS watch across the street from a house in the diplomatic enclave where most foreign embassy personnel in Islamabad lived. The house's address had been scribbled on a small sheet of paper by another individual who had watched the house a few days earlier as he made a mental photocopy of the location. Blueprints, even those from memory, were always useful when formulating an assault plan.

The man watching the house that Saturday morning was in his mid-twenties. He attempted to stand calmly behind a parked Toyota sedan as he peered at the villa across the branches of a robust eucalyptus tree. He feared, he would later recall, sparking the suspicion of the neighborhood residents and a call to the police, though he feared the wrath of the man who had sent him more. The Islamabad police patrolled the streets of the enclave with great frequency and were not known to treat locals wandering through the streets of the neighborhood with kindness. To look more Western, the man had shaved his mustache, wore a button-down blouse and trousers, and even had on a baseball cap. He still wore the plastic flip-flop sandals that one could buy in any of the shops inside the market area, and he was highly agitated. His hands trembled and his lips quivered. Beads of sweat covered his forehead, and the rolled up magazine he clutched had become wet from perspiration. The man glanced to his left and right before he crossed the street. There were no police cars on either side of the street and it felt safe to cross and walk toward the house, he remembered in his postincident debriefs. He trembled as he walked under the hibiscus and approached the front door. As he glanced to the west, toward the towering minarets of the Shah Faisal mosque, he wondered if he was betraying his faith. He wondered if he would be able to execute his plans the moment the door opened.[3]

There was a panic-stricken call to the marines' post. One from the distraught wife of an embassy employee. All embassy employees and their families were taught that, in time of crisis, they were to call Post One either on the phone or on a portable radio that each home was issued. "A crazy Pakistani man pounded on my door and forced his way in here," the terrified woman explained to the young MSG manning his post. "Get someone here right away." When the call came through, Jeff Riner was in one of the conference rooms participating in a room-clearing class with DSS special agents from the Mobile Security Division who were in Pakistan to teach advanced tactics to the RSO's office in both Islamabad and Karachi. The room-clearing classes were refreshers, designed to hone the skills needed to kick down a barricaded door and secure a room should an intruder be loose inside the embassy. The class would have to wait. The MSG asked to see Riner immediately. "Sir, we have a problem," the young marine said in a sharply accented South Bronx Hispanic tone, as he tugged on his utility belt. "This woman is scared to death." Riner was immediately patched through to the woman and attempted, as best he could, to calm her down. "You got to get this guy out of here," she pled. "He is so scared and nervous he is scaring me to death. He says he knows something about someone you are looking for."[4]

Within moments, Miller and Riner were en route not knowing whether the disturbance was just an emotional individual preying on an unsuspecting female, or something far more insidious. The worst fear was that the two security officers were heading straight for a possible assassination attempt. Terrorists from Cairo to Athens have ambushed embassy personnel for assassination when they traveled to and from the embassy on official business. Riner had been in-country for only six months that Friday morning; Miller had been there a full year longer. The conversation on the ride to the house was the usual chit-chat that police partners engage in before handling a call. But there was a sense of threat. Both DSS special agents checked the fanny packs holding their SIGs and a pair of plastic flexible handcuffs over and over again as they drove to the enclave.

Miller and Riner entered the immaculate home with marble floors and ornate local weaves hung on the wall, and found a young man who was scared to death. "He was all over the place," Riner recalled. "He was moving around very nervously, and he couldn't stand still for more than a second." As Riner moved into a defensive position behind his partner, ready to respond if the man produced a weapon, Miller moved closer to establish a dialogue and a rapport.

"What's your name?" Miller asked with a shy and soft-spoken Georgian drawl, but the man was having a hard go of it articulating his words.

"You can call me 'Hamid,' "* the man stammered quietly, as he wiped the sweat that was draining down the sides of his olive-skinned face.

"What's going on here?" Miller asked. Miller moved in close to Hamid while he talked to see if there were bulges in his shirt or trousers. Miller patted him gently on the shoulder and on the small of the back to see if he was concealing a knife, a firearm, or even a hand grenade. The man was fearful and intense. He glanced around in a nervous manner, almost as if he felt there was a gun to the back of his head. "I have information on someone you are looking for," he said in a quiet voice through the barrier of quivering lips. He spoke in perfect, virtually unaccented English. He then took a copy of *Newsweek* out of his rear pocket and opened the magazine to the "Up Periscope" section and a brief paragraph showing the face of Ramzi Yousef. "I know him,"

---

*Even though other publications have listed the source's true name, I am honoring the DSS pledge to safeguard the informant's personal information. This is a pseudonym to protect the man's identity.

Hamid stated in a frenetic, overstated manner as if to prove his point through a gesture. "I know where he is."

This was a walk-in and one whose intensity and fear were too real to be insincere. Seeing the terrified man point to the postage-stamp-size photo of Yousef brought out mixed emotions and concerns in the eyes of both DSS special agents. Over the course of their time in Pakistan, both Miller and Riner had dealt with a fair number of walk-ins who were willing to offer up Ramzi on a silver platter. Some were insane, others simply eager for a taste of the huge reward offered for the tip. Every time a walk-in came to the gate of the embassy, the DSS agents would get the basics of the story and then either dismiss the source or bring him into the embassy for a debrief and a case number.

But this walk-in was different. He did not walk up to the embassy's main gate and seek out a security officer in public view. In fact, he did not want to be seen anywhere *near* the embassy. Most walk-ins would not have been able to walk around a block in the diplomatic enclave without attracting the attention of the roving police patrols. Most walk-ins would not have had the wherewithal, or information, to locate the house of a U.S. diplomat—especially since there were no outward signs linking the home to the American embassy. It took some skill to figure out that any vehicle with the diplomatic license plate beginning with "CD-64" belonged to an American, but it showed even greater skill that the walk-in would turn up in the morning. In the evenings, armed guards protected all houses belonging to embassy personnel.

Most walk-ins were cocky, almost arrogant, when they dealt with the DSS agents. This one was scared to death and in a country like Pakistan, where fear was a commodity and panic was worth something. The walk-in was either sincere or a terrific actor.

BILL MILLER, IN PAKISTAN FOR NEARLY EIGHTEEN MONTHS, KNEW THE Ramzi Yousef file like the back of his hand. He had always taken a great interest in the terrorist mastermind who had used Pakistan as a transit point, and he had great interest in Yousef's proposed plan to blow eleven airlines out of the sky. Yousef was something of a hobby for Bill Miller. He had always wondered what type of man could draw up the blueprints for a bombing attack that would kill so many people? Bill Miller wondered what it would be like to slap a pair of cuffs onto those bomb-building hands.

There were many tidbits of information that had been released to the press about Yousef following the attack on the World Trade Center and the discovery of his Manila bomb factory. But there were many items that the FBI, the NYPD, and the Philippine National Police had not released—primarily the fact that the entire blueprint for Operation Bojinka had been seized on a laptop computer. Hookup cables for another laptop had been found in the Josefa Apartments, but that laptop was missing. "Tell us something about Ramzi," Bill Miller asked, hoping to hear a telltale truth that would finally provide proof of Yousef's presence in Pakistan. "He keeps a laptop computer," Hamid offered. "He's let me guard it for him overnight."[5]

Mention of the laptop sent a shiver down Bill Miller's spine. The story was genuine. "What are you doing for the next few hours?" Miller asked Hamid. "How about coming back to the embassy with us for a while?"

The two special agents, realizing that a golden source had possibly fallen into their lap, knew that Hamid would be a difficult informant to work with. He was simply too petrified. As the DSS agents conferred, Hamid suddenly leapt as a car drove by the house and he became highly animated, fearing that he could be spotted from the street. The three men then moved to the backyard of the house, hidden by rows of flowery bushes, to continue their discussions.

Outside the house, Hamid seemed even more startled and fearful of being seen by someone. But he started talking and his lips quivered less. He also began to divulge small tidbits of information that only someone who was in Yousef's inner circle, or who had reviewed the classified file, would know.

It was clear that the two DSS agents had to rush Hamid back to the embassy in as covert a manner as possible. Not only was the man petrified about being seen talking to any embassy employees, let alone setting foot inside the embassy itself, but Miller and Riner knew that almost everywhere they went in Islamabad—and in Pakistan—eyes were upon them. The embassy was under constant watch by ISI agents.

The ISI was an autonomous creature inside Pakistan that followed its own agenda and interests. In regard to its newfound role in supporting transnational terrorist groups inside Afghanistan, the ISI, an intelligence agency that, on paper at least, was an ally of its compatriots in the CIA, was pitted directly against the United States. Miller and Riner knew that the ISI street sweeper who worked in front of the embassy seven days a week, rain or shine, might identify Hamid to his bosses as the three drove into the embassy compound.

Even worse, the sight of a Pakistani man sitting in the backseat of an embassy car, a Suburban used mainly by the security staff, could spark rumors that "American agents" were arresting God-fearing Pakistani men off the streets of Islamabad and start a riot. After all, it had been rumors, nothing but unsubstantiated rumors, of the CIA burning down a mosque that had led to a protest and then to the mob-led assault on the embassy in 1979. "You have to do your best to lay low for the entire two years that you are here, and the last thing that you want to do is something stupid to focus undue attention on you and the embassy," Jeff Riner stated. "Because when the locals would seek revenge, it didn't matter which American it was directed against. Lots of people were going to end up dead."[6]

So, the DSS agents improvised. They hustled Hamid into the back of their Suburban, threw an old dust-encrusted blanket that had been used on those long road trips to Peshawar over him, and drove slowly to the compound. The Suburban's windows weren't tinted, so the DSS agents summoned a pair of MSGs to meet them at a rear gate and to expedite their entrance to the facility. Hamid was disguised wearing Jeff Riner's sunglasses and baseball cap.

THE TWO SPECIAL AGENTS INTERVIEWED HAMID IN A QUIET OFFICE IN THE embassy library, a remote and often unused room in the chancery. Sitting in a comfortable chair underneath framed portraits of President Clinton and Secretary of State Christopher, Hamid grew more at ease. Slowly, over the course of six hours, he talked about Ramzi Yousef and his association with him. Hamid had met Ramzi Yousef while studying at the Islamic University in Islamabad. The university was known throughout the Muslim world as a hotbed for radical Islamic teaching. Students from as far away as Chad, Bosnia, the Palestinian Authority, and Indonesia flocked to study and hear the firebrand sermons of the professors and mullahs. Students attending the university spoke a myriad of languages and represented a mosaic of racial backgrounds, but they all shared an intense hatred for the United States. The evils of the Great Satan were part and parcel of the academic curriculum. American flags were burned almost daily in protests about one thing or another. The students and faculty saw the bombing of the World Trade Center as a great victory for Islam. Sheikh Rahman was revered as a pious spiritual field marshal fighting on enemy territory. Ramzi Yousef was seen as an underground war hero. "He was the Che Guevara of the fundamentalist Muslims," a former senior U.S. intelligence officer with many Near Eastern assignments under his belt would say. "He was a killer afforded rock star status!"

Hamid had been affected by the zealous calls for a holy war inside the mosque and in his classrooms, though he was happy to support the struggle from the sidelines. Yousef, though, searching the university for operatives, recruited Hamid into the fight. Hamid met Yousef casually, at a secluded table inside an Islamabad café over sweet tea and fried honey balls. They were introduced through a go-between, a headhunter of sorts, who roved the Islamic University in search of fair-skinned talents who could appear Western and could travel around the world freely. Yousef was a charismatic and persuasive figure. He also always moved around with wads of Pakistani rupees and American dollars in his pocket. He boasted that he paid for airline tickets in cash—always. His clothes, always Western, were expensive and immaculately pressed. He wore expensive sunglasses and was nearly as concerned about his physical appearance as he was about the global jihad.

Yousef saw great promise in the Pakistani student, even though Hamid was timid, and married with a child. Hamid, in fact, did not volunteer to fight alongside Yousef—he was *volunteered* into the network with little say in the matter. Yousef didn't look for friends to serve in his cells. He sought individuals who were committed and fairly intelligent, but most of all he sought people who were expendable. Results were more important than survivability, and if the cell member was to

be killed while assaulting a target or delivering a bomb, then there
would be one less set of eyes able to pick Yousef out of a police lineup
or identify him under FIA torture. Hamid had already won the job
before the two met. Yousef had an operation in mind for the cowardly
student—an actual operation that would also serve as a test of Hamid's
reliability under pressure.

Yousef's bombs from Manila, the witches' brew of guncotton and
liquid explosives, had worked well on Philippines Air Flight 434. But
as Yousef continued his plans for taking out eleven airliners, he wondered if the sort of bomb that killed the young Japanese traveler, splitting him in half from his crotch to his forehead, would be powerful
and stable enough to detonate as timed. Could it be covertly smuggled
onboard an aircraft without arousing the suspicions of security forces?
In light of the arrests in Manila and the seizure of his laptop, Yousef
knew that security at airports in Southeast Asia would be tighter than
usual. This would be the perfect test for Hamid and his skills and value
as an operator.

Yousef ordered Hamid to secrete one of the aircraft bombs onboard
an American airliner flying out of Bangkok that would connect elsewhere in the Pacific before flying east to the United States. If Hamid
was good, he would disembark the flight in Manila, Taipei, or Narita
International Airport in Tokyo, and then fly back to Pakistan. If Hamid
was unlucky, his body would evaporate in a fireball that nobody would
see somewhere over the darkened Asian sky.

Hamid was told to get a passport. He was then to fly to Bangkok,
through Lahore, where he would meet up with Yousef in a hotel in
the red-light district of the city. Hamid knew little of his mission, other
than that it involved explosives and that he was not to allow the devices
to be confiscated by the authorities. The liquid bomb, the contents of
which were held inside a contact lens solution bottle, was a valuable
piece of coveted fine craftmanship to Yousef and he wanted to protect
it all costs. Yousef flew to the Far East in his typical manner—business
class wearing a neatly tailored suit.

In Bangkok, Hamid rendezvoused with Yousef. In a dark hotel room,
on a floor above a bar and a brothel, the two men carefully assembled
the ingenious explosive devices. Hamid was to walk the bomb onboard

an American aircraft in Bangkok with connecting service to the United States through Japan. He was to plant the device inside the aircraft, and then leave the plane during the layover. By the time the aircraft exploded over the Pacific, Hamid would be on a plane back to Pakistan. "If you see that the Thai Immigration Police are being overly meticulous when checking passports," Yousef told Hamid, "I want you to abort the mission and dispose of the explosive contents."

"Police were out in force the day of the operation in Bangkok," Hamid told Miller and Riner. "I had no choice but to rush to a pay phone, call Yousef at the hotel and tell him that I couldn't go through with the operation." Hamid then went to a men's-room toilet and, after making sure nobody was in any of the stalls, poured the explosive concoction into the plumbing. He washed his hands, threw cold water on his face, and then backtracked out of Terminal One at Bangkok International Airport, past the usual long line of hippies heading back to Europe and Israel, and retreated to his hotel room.

Days later, Hamid attempted to ship a crate with the bomb as cargo aboard an American-flag carrier. The cardboard box, sealed with meticulous care, contained an inexpensive set of cutlery in order to fool any possible X-ray scrutiny. Commercial flights carried cargo, after all, and small packets were often taken onboard regularly scheduled passenger jets with little or no security as long as the shipper paid a surcharge. But Yousef had warned Hamid not to allow anyone to fingerprint him at any cost. After all, Yousef had been linked to the Manila bomb factory as a result of a partial thumbprint left on a bathroom light switch. But here again, Hamid, in way over his head and unable to go through with the assignment, found an out. He told Yousef that Thai Customs officials required that he get an exporter's license before he could ship any goods to the United States, and an export license required a photograph and fingerprints. Hamid traveled back to the hotel, carrying his load of explosives in the trunk of a rickety Fiat cab that made a point of hitting every pothole in town.

Hamid feared Yousef's wrath over not dispatching the explosive witches' brew on an aircraft. Rumors of how the Afghan Arabs dealt with failures—let alone traitors—were common at Islamabad Islamic University. But much to Hamid's surprise, Yousef understood the reasons behind the aborted mission and was even gracious about his student's failure. "We'll try another time and place," Yousef told him. "Don't be bothered by it." The two men emptied the liquid contents of the device into the bathroom sink that night in January 1995. As tourists en route or coming from neighborhood brothels sat in the hotel lobby drinking ice cold Tiger and Singh beers, the two men emptied enough nitroglycerin and TATP explosives to turn the hotel into a crater down a drain into the Bangkok sewer system. Hamid was ordered to return to Islamabad, along with the guncotton. "I'll be back in town in four or five days," Yousef told Hamid, and I'll make contact with you then."[7]

Yousef had managed to stay one step ahead of the clutches of American and Filipino law enforcement by being careful. He never entered a building or a neighborhood, or agreed to a meeting, unless one of his security officers checked out the location first. It delayed spontaneous operations, but spontaneity got people killed. Yousef preferred caution. In Islamabad, Yousef employed an advance agent to set up his meetings and check out security at his safe houses and favorite restaurants. The advance agent had made contact with Hamid the day before he made contact with DSS. "Ramzi will be landing in Islamabad," the advance agent told Hamid, "and he will give you instructions shortly thereafter." The advance agent was never questioned. He was always armed.

MILLER AND RINER SAT IN STOIC SILENCE WHILE THEY LISTENED TO THE details of the aborted bombing run, and Yousef's means of communication. Miller actually felt goosebumps race up and down his arms. Miller's pregnant young wife, en route to Bangkok for a sonogram and prenatal care for their second child, had been on the very same Pakistan International Airlines flight from Islamabad through Lahore to Thailand as Hamid and his bomb. Although the aircraft wasn't the intended target, the fact that his wife and his unborn child had flown on an aircraft holding some ten kilograms of highly flammable guncotton in the cargo hold was a sobering and infuriating fact. It diminished any sympathy that Miller might have felt for the terrified terrorist turned informant. Yousef, not wanting to fly on the same airliner as a load of volatile explosives, had taken a separate flight.

"Are you sure you were supposed to blow up an airliner?" the two men asked time and time again, not believing that Hamid could have been part of a plot to kill over 400 people. "I couldn't go through with it," Hamid told Miller and Riner. "I thought about all the people who would die onboard the aircraft."

Getting back to the technology of Yousef's brand of mass murder, Miller and Riner needed to know more about the type of explosives, detonators, and initiators, Hamid had at his disposal. "Tell us again what you know about bomb building. Where did you learn how to do this?" the DSS agents asked. Finally fed up with the questions, Hamid removed a Casio Databank watch from his left wrist, tossed it on a nearby polished oak table, and chided his interrogators, "Here is the timer. Yousef made a switch through one of the buttons, and this was to be the plug where the wires were going to go in." Photographs of the watch were quickly snapped, and Art Maurel, now sitting in an office next door in order to eavesdrop, began to jot notes down as well.

MILLER AND RINER LEARNED THAT YOUSEF HAD BEEN SHUTTLING BACK and forth between Afghanistan and Peshawar and the Far East. Yousef's brilliant concoction was being mass-produced in Afghanistan and Peshawar. Yousef had been stockpiling his material in the safety of Pakistan and then bringing it out to the Far East when the opportunity arose.

News of Yousef's "shuttle terrorism" outraged the two DSS agents. *What's the fucking use of wanted posters and rewards if this bastard can get on and off flights in some of the most secure airports in the world?* the special agents thought. *What's the use of offering a two-million-dollar reward? He's laughing at us.*

Miller knew that choirboys rarely knew where terrorists were hiding, and that anyone with information on a Yousef, a Kansi, or a heroin merchant wanted by the DEA would be an unsavory character. Hamid, Miller said, "was a nerd who was a wannabe, and when it came to planting bombs onboard airliners, he realized he was in way over his head." Yet he was a field operative in one of Yousef's numerous cells, and he was sent to kill hundreds of people. "He was an unwitting partner of Yousef's who was caught up in the hysteria of the fanatic Islamic Afghan-type cause to do away with the Zionists and the Americans. Even though he had discovered a conscience at just the right time," Miller later reflected, "he was still a dirtbag."[8]

IN THE SIX MONTHS THAT THEY HAD WORKED TOGETHER AS THE FIELD personnel in the RSO's office, Miller and Riner had learned to act like any other police partners teamed together for long hours inside the intimate confines of a patrol car or a squad room. Each knew how the other thought and reacted. Each knew when one was scared or angry. And, during the interview of Hamid, it was apparent to Riner that the hairs on the back of Miller's neck were standing tall and frightened. "Bill had known more about Ramzi Yousef's involvement in the World Trade Center and later Operation Bojinka than anyone else in the office. Bill was the 'Ramzi expert.' He had built an impressive file on Yousef, his crimes, and possible places where he might be," Riner reflected. "He knew intimate details about his modus operandi and his background."[9] So when Hamid sat inside the closed-door sanctuary of the U.S. embassy and spilled, in detail, his full connection to Ramzi Yousef, Bill Miller, the tall red-haired marine from Georgia, turned red in anger. Riner knew, just by looking at Bill Miller's eyes and the way he sat transfixed by the tale, that his partner believed every word. Perhaps the most important element of Hamid's sincerity was the fact that, at the time, he never brought up money and the two-million-dollar bounty on Yousef's head.

The fact that Hamid was a terrorist, regardless of the fact that he was a frightened one, made him somewhat of a confusing character for the DSS tandem to handle. He was a bad guy, the kind of individual these guys were trained to neutralize, capture, or, if they were encountered attacking a motorcade, kill. But Hamid was an in, a possible once-in-a-lifetime opportunity, for the two men to finally grab the elusive fugitive. No matter how unsavory a character Hamid was, no matter how many people he might have conspired to blow up in a plane, he was their partner in a confidential team effort.

For nearly six hours, Hamid was questioned and then grilled again about his relationship with Yousef. "Are you sure you don't know where he is now?" "Think." "A lot depends on what you are telling us." Fear and the draining of adrenaline caused Hamid to slow down his story and his ability to confess. Clearing his conscience was important, and information was important. But Hamid had to be clear of thought and precise if the DSS agents were going to be able to take the confidential information one step further and convince Washington of its veracity. Hamid, however, had reached his limit; his throat was dry, and his brain was overloaded by an odd mixture of fear and relief. Miller and Riner decided to call it a day. Hamid huddled on the floor behind the backseat of the DSS Suburban so that he could be driven out of the embassy. He grabbed the musty blanket and covered himself like an infantryman seeking shelter from a bombardment. "Is anyone following us?" he asked the agents as they pulled out of the embassy compound and headed to a remote stretch of Islamabad. "Just drive," Hamid barked from behind the blanket emerging for brief intervals to guide the two DSS agents through a wild goose chase around the back alleys of Islamabad. "I'll tell you when to stop."

As the sun set over the snow-capped peaks that offer a respite of beauty from the dingy reality of Islamabad and Rawalpindi, the Suburban pulled into an alleyway in a remote section of the Pakistani capital to unload the blanket-wrapped passenger. Miller had given Hamid an embassy cellular phone, and his office number and the extension to his residence. The phone, an old bricklike Motorola, wasn't compact, and it wasn't the sort of gadgetry that Hamid could hide if he was confronted by Yousef or one of his security lieutenants, but a communications link had to be established with the RSO's office. Miller and Riner would meet the man the next day in a remote corner of Islamabad along a nondescript stretch of roadway.

Miller and Riner were concerned that they were being set up for an ambush, but the chance to corner Yousef warranted the risk. The real work of capturing the man had only started, and difficult tasks lay ahead. The two had to configure an operational game plan for headquarters.

From the drop-off point, Hamid headed home, walking in circles, taking cabs on a zigzag journey across town, and boarding buses going nowhere, anything to avoid being followed. He lived in a nondescript apartment in a part of town favored by Afghan fighters. There was a fairly affluent neighborhood around the corner, and across the street from his apartment building was the Su Casa guesthouse, where many of the *Mujahadeen* with money and connections stayed when taking a break from the war in Afghanistan.

After walking through the front door, Hamid bolted it, greeted his young wife, and kissed their small son on the forehead. He ate dinner and then crammed a huge load of guncotton inside a pillowcase so that he could bring the extremely flammable substance to his DSS handlers the next morning.

THE REPORTS AND THE ENTHUSIASM OF HIS TWO YOUNG DEPUTIES IM-pressed Maurel, a veteran of the trenches who, from the streets of Saigon to the Khyber Pass, had seen and done it all. But now they had to convince headquarters and get the wheels in motion. Classified cable traffic is usually reserved for brief, paragraph-length communications that bounce between embassies and departmental heads. The report on Hamid was nearly ten pages long. The cable, coauthored by Miller and Riner, was a highly detailed account of the encounter with the confidential informant. Ten pages of a report earmarked for official top-secret State Department cable traffic was akin to sending a rough draft of *War and Peace* over the busy wires. At the end of the report, one proofread a dozen times to make it perfect, both agents offered their personal assessment of the source's veracity.

There was State Department bureaucracy inside the embassy that had to be attended to as well. Ambassador John C. Monjo had to be informed, as did his deputy, and others inside the embassy's chain of command. "Thank God we had Art Maurel there," Jeff Riner asserted.

"We were going through a cop's rush of interviews and meets and clandestine drop-offs. He was able to step back and look at the big picture." And like any situation involving cops on a big job, Art Maurel was able to act as a buffer between the men in the field and the suits and bureaucrats.

As Miller and Riner retired for the evening, they could only wonder what would happen next. Would the local CIA station take over the operation and the confidential informant? Would the FBI? "The bureau" had a long and sometimes bitter history of flooding a country with an army of shield-waving agents bossing people around, pushing protocol out of the way, and doing what they wanted to do. Both DSS special agents realized that if the FBI did come in force, everyone and his mother in Pakistan would know what was up. Yousef would be a thousand miles away, working at his laptop and selecting new targets, by the time the first bureau agent was checking in at the Islamabad Marriott complaining that the towels were too small or that the reception on the TV was poor.

Islamabad was a DSS beat. It should be their operation.

Both Miller and Riner were good soldiers and exemplary agents. They knew that theirs was a world of rank and procedure and that they would do exactly what they were ordered to do. But this was one case that both men had hoped would not become another bureau fiasco. DSS agents, from the time they leave the Federal Law Enforcement Training Center, are afforded great autonomy and freedom in doing their work. They are told what to do, but don't have to report back to a rigid command structure or bureaucracy for approval. Whatever works, works. It's as simple as that. That autonomy leads to confidence, and confidence allows agents in desolate outposts like Pakistan to do a lot with very little.

Miller and Riner wanted to see that Yousef's arrest was done right. This was their game, their confidential informant, and their operation to run. And, almost remarkably, Washington agreed.

RSO Maurel contacted headquarters for some policy guidance. He telephoned Special Agent Fred Burton, deputy director of the service's Protective Intelligence Investigators (PII)—the office formerly known as the Counterterrorism Division. Burton, who had fifteen years of experience in the most delicate of counterterrorism investigations, advised Maurel to put everything in writing but to direct the cable traffic solely to him.

The response from DSS headquarters could have been any number of noncommittal explanations of protocol, and the trap being laid in Islamabad might have been compromised for good. For both Maurel and Miller, the two agents with the most time in-country, the fear of déjà vu was causing trepidations and anxiety. Both men had been through it once before.

In 1994, a walk-in to the embassy had provided information on Yousef's whereabouts in Pakistan, including detailed information on an Afghani passport Yousef was using inside the country. The RSO's office in Islamabad had followed protocol to the letter, and protocol had compromised everything. According to one former agent, the RSO's office had conveyed the news of Yousef possibly being in Pakistan to a number of offices in Washington, D.C.; news was also shared, prematurely, with the Pakistanis. Inevitably, when the DSS agents and the Pakistani police stormed the suspected safe house where Yousef was hiding, the stove was hot and the kettle was brewing tea, but Yousef was gone—tipped off, it has been alleged, by someone in the Pakistani intelligence service.[10]

Burton knew that the Pakistanis eventually would have to be notified. DSS did not have jurisdiction in Pakistan and could not make any arrests—DSS special agents did not have the authority to arrest anyone outside the United States. They were, however, the U.S. law enforcement representative in an embassy and could, with the help of a host government, supervise an arrest and facilitate the handover of a prisoner. But, Burton feared, notifying the Pakistanis before Yousef had been identified by the DSS special agents would offer Islamabad official deniability in case he was allowed to escape once again. Notifying the authorities in Pakistan once Yousef had been identified—beyond a reasonable doubt—would force Islamabad to cooperate.

As if fate was interceding on behalf of DSS, news of Yousef's possible sighting in Islamabad was wired to Washington, D.C., during one of the worst blizzards on record in the nation's capital. Government offices had been closed, and only those on cross-country skis or all-terrain vehicles managed to survive the slippery conditions on the Beltway. Burton, as luck would have it, had just bought a Jeep and was able to drive in to work, through the snow-covered neighborhoods of suburban Virginia, at the Protective Intelligence Investigations office. Washington, D.C., looked like a Swiss fairy tale that snowy morning. Burton encountered a few hearty joggers on his way to the office that morning, and even one or two hearty souls on skis carrying their attaché cases strapped across their backs.

When Burton came into the office, the only one on the floor, he scanned his cable traffic and felt a sixth sense that the reports from Pakistan might be genuine. Now what to do with the information?

For nearly two years, Burton had sifted through countless Yousef sightings—tips on his possible whereabouts filtered in, first to the Counterterrorism Division, and then to Protective Intelligence Investigations from the four corners of the globe. Some had been far-fetched nonsense from psychos seeking a taste of the two-million-dollar reward. The usual list of suspects, "cooks, crackpots, and criminals," as Fred Burton remembered, routinely sent in a report that Yousef was working in a falafel stand in Tripoli, Lebanon, or that he was driving a cab in downtown Algiers. Other tips had been more credible and required the RSOs in the country of the tip's origin to investigate the matter. In cases when the tip was truly golden, PII would dispatch an agent, most often Fred "Razor" Piry, to investigate the case with added energy.

Burton faced a dilemma sitting on what could perhaps be accurate information on Yousef's whereabouts. "If we let the genie out of the bottle, people all over Washington, D.C., would want their hand in it, and they'd screw it up," Burton recalled. "At this point only a handful of people knew of 'Hamid' and the news that Yousef would be in Islamabad. Considering what had happened earlier the first time, we had to let it just play out."[11]

According to some in the service, morale in DSS at the time had been at an all-time low since the appointment of Ambassador Anthony Cecil Eden Quainton as the assistant secretary of state for diplomatic security. Resentment between State Department bureaucrats and the DSS special agents has always been strong. "The simple fact is that the mandarins at State have never much liked the security people, viewing them as gumshoes and right-wing zealots. The security types have reciprocated, deriding senior diplomats as Black Dragons. In this environment, it has been hard for the two sides to cooperate."[12]

When Ambassador Quainton was appointed assistant secretary of state for diplomatic security in 1992, some believe that this natural tension may have been intensified by a previous encounter between DSS and the ambassador. "Diplomats are career animals," claimed one former special agent assigned to PII, "and they have long memories."

During Operation Desert Storm, Quainton, at the time the U.S. ambassador to Peru, survived an assassination attempt attributed to the indigenous Sendero Luminoso (Shining Path) terrorist group. The terrorists had bombed the ambassador's residence. Quainton escaped injury, but two Peruvian policemen were killed by the blast. The Counterterrorism Division's team that was sent to Lima to investigate the assassination examined every element of the attack—from the forensic clues gathered at the crime scene to the terrorists' ability to gather intelligence on the ambassador's movements and routine. In the opinion of many in the DSS, Quainton never forgave the service, and the Counterterrorism Division in particular, for their postincident examination of the Lima bombing.

Veteran special agents felt that life in the service under Quainton was intolerable. In 1992, in the wake of Iraq's defeat in the Gulf War, Ambassador Quainton took the position that terrorism was dead and that there was no longer a need inside DSS for a Counterterrorism Division and the unit was to be eliminated.[13] "It was as if he was single-handedly trying to chop us down, bit by bit, making us irrelevant," claimed a DSS agent.[14] In an attempt to keep the Counterterrorism Division, along with the Rewards for Justice Program, up and running, DSS managers cleverly changed the name of the office to the innocuous title of Protective Intelligence Investigations.

Burton was determined not to let the Black Dragons compromise a chance to apprehend the world's most wanted terrorist fugitive.

Fred Burton had known Art Maurel for a good many years—the two had worked together on several high-threat terrorist cases in the Far East before. "Art had something of a reputation of being a cowboy," Burton remembered, "but he had been on the job for so long and was so respected, that if he was contacting me with word of a possible 'hit' on Yousef, you had to appreciate its credibility."[15]

Sitting alone in an office building besieged by snow, Burton pondered his next move. Alerting someone in the State Department might have been the course to follow according to the guidebook, but business as usual had, months earlier, allowed Yousef to escape. Business as usual had almost allowed that same man, perhaps one of the most ambitious terrorists ever to emerge, to plot to kill not only the American president and the Pope, but over 4,000 people sitting inside aircraft. Burton knew what he had to do. Illuminated by the flickering fluorescents inside a government office cubbyhole, he typed his top-secret cable back to Islamabad.

As evening fell in Washington, and the nation's capital was draped by a purplish crimson cloud cover over the snow, Burton wondered what the mood was like in Islamabad, knowing that Yousef was close. He wondered what the mood would be like inside the RSO's office once his cable was read.

Later that night, a record time for responses from headquarters, a classified cable was received inside the top-secret confines of the embassy's communications center:

IT HAS BEEN DETERMINED THAT THE RSO'S OFFICE WILL MAINTAIN CONTROL OF THE COOPERATING INDIVIDUAL AND ALL INTERVIEWS WILL BE CONDUCTED BY THE RSO'S OFFICE.[16]

The three DSS agents in Pakistan had been given the thumbs-up to get their man.

SUNDAY, FEBRUARY 5, WAS A CLOUDY BUT WARM DAY IN ISLAMABAD; THE city's dusty complexion was overcast by a dark shade of gray. Miller and Riner left the compound, each carrying a SIG-Sauer P228 with fifteen rounds in the clip, and headed to the rendezvous location to meet Hamid. Fearing an ambush, the two drove with great caution.

They were anxious and they were enthusiastic. Adrenaline fueled the trip. Yet much to their relief, Hamid met them precisely on time at the predetermined location. He was searched for weapons, though he wasn't armed. He was, however, very proud to show off his bag of guncotton. Hamid was calmer and less fearful of surveillance by Yousef's men than he had been the day before. Nevertheless, he was wrapped in the blanket again, got on the floor of the Suburban, and was rushed to the embassy.

Hamid was quite proud of the explosives he brought in for show and tell, though such a large amount of the material caused both Miller and Riner to stand back and grab a fire extinguisher. A small sleeve of the material was taken out back and lit with a fuse. A pagelike piece, when lit, was enough to create a huge fireball. Another smaller sleeve was placed in a clear evidence container to be sent back to Washington for analysis.

For the next six hours, Hamid provided even more information on Yousef and his network. The DSS agents listened intently. Miller, the senior man in Islamabad and the one with the institutional knowledge of Yousef and his operations, was the case agent. Riner, a veteran investigator with an extensive criminal case background, was responsible for taking notes. Hamid developed a unique rapport with Miller. The rock-solid Georgian, with his smooth Southern drawl, offered Hamid a calming presence. Hamid looked at Miller and Riner with relief and gratitude. "The second day that we interviewed him he acted as if there had been a tremendous weight lifted off his shoulders," Riner remembered. "He looked at Bill and myself and felt safe and that we would save his life."

Maurel told his two agents that they needed to fingerprint the suspect for identification purposes, as well as for a possible criminal case. At first, Maurel suggested that the agents offer Hamid a glass of ice water, though the informant politely declined to drink, as it was the feast of Ramadan. Thinking quickly, Art Maurel then slipped a bunch of photographs that they had in the office of a Pakistani local wanted by some local police department in the United States. The photographs were all of the same person, but included a half dozen shots taken at different angles by one of the FSNIs during a surveillance operation. The photos were all placed in clear plastic sleeves inside a black binder.

"Before we go, can you look at the photos and tell me if any of these people look familiar to you?" one of the agents asked. Hamid, eager to help, clutched the plastic sheets with interest as he scanned the faces featured in the fuzzy shots, attempting to placate his hosts.

"I don't know anyone in the photographs," Hamid said, almost embarrassed by not being able to help.

"No problem," said Riner. "We thought that someone in your situation would certainly know some of the people."

As Hamid thumbed through the photos, touching the clear plastic sleeves, Jeff Riner watched and jotted notes. "Right index finger, photo three. Left thumb, photo eleven." The binder was run out of the interview room and rushed upstairs—Jeff Riner was careful to use the palms of his hand to clutch the plastic envelope by the edges. The plastic sheet was placed inside an evidence bag and filed in a box that would soon develop into a storage room full of evidence, interviews, and other materials related to the informant and the attempt to apprehend Ramzi Yousef.

Hamid didn't realize he had been secretly fingerprinted, and had he learned of the ploy it would have shattered the trust he had given to Miller and Riner. Hamid felt so at ease, in fact, that he offered perhaps the most startling bit of information in passing during the second day of interviews, information so daunting that the two DSS special agents listened to it in jaw-dropping silence. Yousef was planning a series of large-scale terrorist attacks that included American targets inside Pakistan.

Concern overtook the two agents. For the first time in twenty-four hours they remembered that they were fathers and husbands. It suddenly appeared that their wives and children were inside the crosshairs of an insidious plot. One of Yousef's targets was the home of the embassy employee where Hamid had made his grand appearance into the world of confidential informants. The other target that Hamid knew of was the home of the Philippine ambassador. Apparently, Yousef had wanted to kidnap one of the ambassador's family members and then hold them hostage in Afghanistan until Filipino police released his comrades seized in the blaze at the Josefa Apartments in Manila.

The urgency to bring Yousef down intensified. He needed to be neutralized before he could potentially unleash his other cells in Pakistan. Miller, attempting to visualize what kind of operations man Yousef actually was, listened intently to Hamid's every word. It appeared to Miller that Yousef, a charming and charismatic man, possessed the rare talent to use his personality to recruit cell members in every country and city he visited. Each cell provided Yousef with safe houses, arms caches, and an endless supply of vehicles and covers. The cells did not know of one another, and there could be as many as five or six cells operating in one city. But the small networks of volunteers, hangers-on, and wannabes were exactly like the motley crew he had assembled in Brooklyn and Jersey City in February 1993.

Yousef demanded results and absolute loyalty from his cells. Hamid said that Yousef constantly threatened his unwilling partner with death. "You are either with me or against me," Yousef chided Hamid. In Bangkok, while Hamid prepared to connect the guncotton and TATP to a Casio Databank, Yousef pulled out a rolled-up copy of *Time* magazine and pointed to an article about the Manila bomb factory being uncovered. "They have my laptop and they know your name," Yousef told Hamid as he stared at the frightened student with his intense black eyes, "and if they find you they will kill you. Of course," Yousef added, "you know what will happen to you if you betray us . . . ?"

Hamid realized that he was at an crossroads. He either had to kill Yousef, turn him in, or die himself, and he didn't have the courage to kill. DSS was his only chance for life.

Back at the embassy, Miller and Riner met with their boss inside a secure room in the chancery. Operational security was of paramount importance, as was the need to present the facts of the opportunity in proper terms, to the proper individuals, in order to obtain assistance, authorization, and support from the DSS hierarchy and the DSS Director. Like field reporters condensing the daylong blow-by-blow of a fierce battle into a three-column article, the agents had to summarize the relevant information and emphasize the opportunity that U.S. law enforcement was now being offered. But Washington, D.C., is a land where bureaucracy, egos, and gridlock dictate the grinding gears of government. There would be a myriad of division heads, SACs, and political appointees in a half dozen federal law enforcement entities, from the FBI to the CIA, who would have a say in what would happen next.

Inside a Washington, D.C., still recovering from the blizzard, Special Agent Burton drove to the Hoover building and FBI headquarters to arrange the possible intricacies of a Yousef capture with John O'Neill, an old friend of his at the Counterterrorism Division of the bureau, and to coordinate matters domestically. Bill Miller had also telephoned the FBI's legal attaché, or LEGAT, in the U.S. embassy in Bangkok. FBI legal representatives were stationed in only a few embassies around the world, and each attaché usually covered a region's worth of embassies and consulates. LEGATs often offered DSS agents a dozen reasons why an operation couldn't happen. Both Miller and Riner hoped that bureau interference would not impede the chance to snare Yousef.

FOR THE NEXT TWENTY-FOUR HOURS THE DSS TRIUMVIRATE PLAYED THE game cops around the world must endure on a daily basis—hurry up and wait. Until Hamid heard from Yousef's advance agent, there was nothing for them to do but wait. For almost two days, Hamid had nothing to report, and the nothing began to make him paranoid.

No matter how much the two hated Hamid for being a terrorist, albeit a repentant one, they had to treat him like one of the team. "Much of what we did was simply baby-sitting the source," Miller remembers. "He was extremely nervous, very agitated, and fearful that he or his family would be made to suffer. So we talked. We talked about bullshit. We treated him like our best buddy. Anything to get his mind off his fears." One topic of conversation that did eventually take the fear off Hamid's mind was money. "Isn't there a reward for information leading to Yousef's arrest?" Hamid asked innocently. "Maybe," one of the DSS agents replied. "We are a long ways away from anyone cashing in on this yet."[17]

ON MONDAY MORNING, FEBRUARY 6, HAMID HEARD A KNOCK ON HIS front door. It was Yousef's advance agent and security chief. "He is in Islamabad," Yousef's security scout boasted. "He will contact you tomorrow. Wait here and don't leave until we call on you."

Miller's cellular phone rang twice before he picked up. Hamid's voice was shaky and dry. He could barely get the first word out of his mouth, and then he blurted out an endless jumble of sentence after sentence. "He's made contact," Hamid blurted out. "What do we do?"

"Do exactly as he instructs," Miller ordered. "We've discussed this over and over again. Just be yourself and don't let on that anything has changed."

Maurel, Miller, and Riner felt the surge of an adrenaline rush, a satisfying high, once Hamid hung up. For three days they had babysat him, spoon-fed him confidence. They were sick and tired of the game. Now, perhaps, they were close to grabbing Yousef and doing something that no other federal agency could do. But still, they would have to wait by the phone for Hamid to call. They waited all day.

On Tuesday evening Hamid called Miller once again. "Yousef made contact again," he said. "He wants to come over tonight and have dinner with me. What should I do?" he said in a frazzled voice choking with fright.

"Relax. You are going to have dinner with him and act like he's your best friend in the world, relieved that you only have to do this for a few more hours. Keep acting!" Miller ordered.

Miller and Riner were law enforcement officials—not intelligence or counterintelligence operatives. They knew the rudimentary basics of surveillance and countersurveillance from the dignitary protection work both men had done back in the States. But they weren't spies and they feared that placing Hamid or Yousef under surveillance would jeopardize the entire operation. "We were only three people in the office," Miller explained. "We didn't have the resources to follow people around or tail them to where they were hiding out."

At the embassy, the three men bided their time as they awaited further word from Hamid. The special agents sat staring at the bank of cell phones placed on a desk, hoping that one would ring. At just after 10:00 P.M. Hamid made contact again. "Ramzi and I are going to fly to Quetta tomorrow morning," he said in a soft voice, hoping not to awaken his wife and son in their small flat. "Will you get him then?"

As FATE WOULD HAVE IT, BILL MILLER AND JEFF RINER WERE SCHEDULED to go to Islamabad International Airport anyway on the morning of February 7. FBI Special Agent Brad Garrett was scheduled to arrive in Islamabad to work on the Kansi investigation, and Miller and Riner were to meet him and help him through the potentially daylong affair of getting through customs. Both DSS agents thought that they would head out to the airport, shmooze with the local cops and their FIA contacts stationed there, pick up Garrett, and arrest Yousef all in one very convenient morning. When either Miller or Riner noticed Hamid and Yousef standing together at the check-in counter, they would summon one of the Pakistani security men and shout, "That's Ramzi Yousef. Arrest him!"

A small airport even by Pakistani standards, Islamabad International serviced a few international routes, primarily to the Far East, as well as a weekly British Airways flight, the favorite of embassy personnel, which flew nonstop to London. The airport was mainly a domestic hub for Pakistan International Airlines flights to Karachi, Lahore, and Quetta, as well as smaller cities throughout the country, such as Peshawar. The airport was clean but without frills. There were a few shops, a few stalls for tea and sweets, and countless police and plainclothed FIA and ISI agents. The airport serviced the capital, so most of those flying in and out of the airport were government workers, the wealthy who chose to live in the relative safety of Islamabad over the crime-ridden hell of Karachi, and foreign diplomats and their families.

Security at Islamabad International Airport was the responsibility of the Airport Security Force, a nationwide federal department with few powers outside their own little domain. The RSO's office in Islamabad maintained excellent relations with the ASF, and each time an embassy employee needed something at the airport, the DSS agents were always sure to precede the request with gifts for the shift commander and throwdowns for the cops. But, like any other police department in Pakistan, the ASF was corrupt. Yousef could slip a hundred-dollar bill inside a passport and be through immigration without even breaking a sweat. After all, Yousef had been in and out of the country on countless occasions since February 1993, and he had almost exclusively used airliners, those with business-class seating, as his primary means of transportation.

Miller and Riner moved about the airport attempting to blend into the morning terminal traffic, but few Westerners raced about departure areas wearing a fanny pack and khakis, while juggling two cellular phones at once. The special agents walked alongside the PIA check-in counters attempting to locate anyone traveling to Quetta. And it was only right for Yousef to attempt to flee to Quetta. "The fruit garden of Pakistan," according to travel brochures, Quetta was the capital of Baluchistan province and the stronghold of the western frontier. American law enforcement had always believed that Yousef, a man without a known country or background, was part Baluchi and part Palestinian. Yousef had a grandmother living in Haifa, in northern Israel, along the Mediterranean coast. Yousef was rumored to have family in Quetta who could shelter him, and Quetta was a convenient transit post for bus traffic heading in and out of Iran.

Miller and Riner realized that if Yousef managed to get to Quetta, he would be virtually impossible to find. Quetta was a town full of military and police commanders who, for a handsome bagful of rupees, would protect anyone on the run—especially someone like Yousef.

As Miller lumbered over the garbage bags of luggage that the passengers were waiting to check in, looking for anyone who resembled Yousef (which, in Pakistan, was every male over the age of eighteen), his cellular phone rang. "He's not going to the airport," Hamid said as he swallowed his words, "and he has changed his travel plans. He wants to take the bus to Peshawar, one that leaves in forty minutes, in order to go to Afghanistan." "Jesus," Miller blurted out in his best Southern pronunciation of the word, and then he bought time with Hamid as he figured out what to do. Both agents entrusted the meet-and-greet with their counterpart from the FBI to an expediter, an FSNI with superb contacts at the airport, and headed toward the parking lot and the trip back into town.

How would they play out the latest news? Miller couldn't very well

drive to the Islamabad bus depot and wait and watch as he looked for
Hamid and Yousef. Embassy personnel were forbidden to take buses
in Pakistan for security reasons. The bus station, a row of asphalt plat-
forms surrounded by crowded rows of stores selling shirts, shoes, and
grilled meats, was not a common spot for tourists in Pakistan—even
backpackers and brave-hearted souls visiting the country on three dollars a day avoided the bus stations. Any white man walking about in
khakis and a fanny pack would certainly be considered "CIA."

Miller contacted Maurel, who was standing by at an embassy command post, to explain the predicament. One of the FSNIs who worked
with the DEA was known to be a truly gifted soul at undercover operations. He was a former cop and a loyal embassy employee, and he
was as sharp as a razor, and as dedicated to his job as any one of the
DSS or DEA agents. Maurel sent the FSNI to the bus station to assist
in a possible apprehension while Miller sat in a Suburban a few blocks
away and awaited the signal that Yousef and Hamid had been spotted.
Maurel had also received authorization to send two DEA agents assigned to the embassy, along with their FSNI, to help out Miller and
Riner with whatever assistance they needed.

Islamabad traffic was fierce that morning, as the two DSS agents
headed to the rendezvous location near the bus station to link up with
the DEA support crew. People didn't drive in Pakistan—they aimed
their vehicles, honked their horns and shouted *Insh Allah!* Miller and
Riner didn't want to get there late. They couldn't be this close only to
miss this golden opportunity because a donkey was blocking an intersection.

And then, as traffic began to inch along, Miller's phone rang again.
"He's changed our plans again," Hamid said in an embarrassed, almost
apologetic voice. "We are going to drive to Peshawar later this afternoon." "Where is Ramzi now?" Miller demanded in a tone used by a
parent when his patience with a misbehaving child reached its envelope. "He is staying in the Su Casa Guesthouse in town," Hamid offered reluctantly. "What room?" Miller quizzed. "Room sixteen. I just
left him now and he is going to take a nap for a few hours before our
trip."

Ramzi Yousef, the world's most wanted terrorist, was sleeping in a

cozy bed in the capital of Pakistan. Any cop worth his salt dreams of
having the chance to kick down the door of a bad guy's house to catch
him in bed. Now, two years after Ramzi Yousef had attempted to topple
one tower of the World Trade Center onto her twin, three DSS special
agents in Pakistan would have just that chance.

THE RSO'S OFFICE HAD BEEN ADAMANT ABOUT KEEPING THE PAKISTANI
government out of the loop for as long as humanly possible, but the
ISI and FIA would have to play some sort of role in Yousef's capture.
The DSS agents needed official support to apprehend Yousef, and they
would need authorization from the prime minister's office to fly him
back to the United States. But what if someone in the FIA or ISI was
sympathetic to Yousef? What if that intelligence agent was on bin
Laden's payroll? Compromising this unique opportunity could not be
risked, and support would have to come from the highest level.

The phone call from Ambassador Monjo to prime minister Bhutto's
office was quick and to the point. A few moments later the ambassador
and Art Maurel were driven in a motorcade toward the prime minister's
residence, where she met the two men along with ISI Director-General
Lieutenant General Javed Nasir and FIA Commander Rahman Malik.
"You have an international terrorist, a fugitive from American justice,
staying at the Su Casa Guesthouse in Islamabad," Art Maurel told the
Pakistani prime minister. "We'd like for you to arrest him. By the way,"
he added, "can we have our people come along?" DSS wanted to act
as eyes-on-target observers and *offer* their assistance.

The Su Casa Guesthouse was an immaculate and nondescript white
villa on the outskirts of town owned by Osama bin Laden as a bed-
and-breakfast for his soldiers to use when in Islamabad. It was a favorite of the Afghan Arabs, though it looked like the majestic home of
a British governor. One could almost imagine British soldiers in red
petticoats protecting the stately manor 100 years earlier as the govern-
ess entertained visitors from London with a lavish outdoor feast. In
February 1995, men in Afghan robes, freshly returned from Peshawar
in muddied Toyota pickup trucks, milled about with rucksacks.

An hour following the ambassador's meeting in the prime minister's office, the ISI was in action. Many Afghans in Islamabad were involved in narcotics and gun-running, and one Pakistani service or another was always monitoring their movements. But the presence at the Su Casa of so many ISI agents, all wearing tan and gray *shalwar kameez* robes, carrying Motorola radios and clutching AK-47 assault rifles, meant that something big was about to happen. Many of the Afghanis dropped their belongings and ran. Others threw their rucksacks and weapons into pickup trucks and sped away.

Miller and Riner discussed the tactical elements of the raid with the ISI field commander, a brigadier general wearing a set of neatly pressed khaki drills, to help coordinate the operation. They wanted Yousef taken alive, and they warned the ISI officer that it was likely that there was a large supply of explosives in his room.

Hamid was still in the guesthouse waiting for Yousef to awaken. As he left the white guesthouse to grab a paper, Hamid saw the massive ISI response force waiting, and he saw his two DSS handlers. It was too late to panic and too late to abandon his betrayal. Using a pre-determined signal that the DSS agents had prepared with him just in case he ever needed to warn his handlers that Yousef was near, Hamid removed the baseball cap from his head and ran his sweaty fingers through his shortly cropped black hair. The gesture was pronounced and overacted. But both DSS agents saw it immediately and did not flinch.

"We have to do this now," Jeff Riner yelled. "Let's move." Bill Miller raced around back to cover the rear while Jeff Riner joined the Pakistani raiding force. Fifteen ISI agents entered the Su Casa and walked up to the front desk with guns at the ready. "Is there anyone in room sixteen?" the ISI commander demanded. The manager, too scared to speak, simply nodded as the barrel from an AK-47 was placed on his temple. The ISI team rushed up the marble stairs and kicked down the door to Yousef's room. Yousef had just dozed off when the ISI agents barreled through his door and yanked him off the bed. Pounding him with blows to the body and head, they threw him up against the window. Three ISI agents forced his hands into the air, while others ransacked the neat room. They threw the sheets off the bed and rifled through a closet. Yousef attempted to turn his head and see what

ISI agents were doing, but they slapped him and told him to freeze. Yousef knew he would be savagely beaten if he disobeyed again.

The ISI was never an agency concerned about lawsuits stemming from unnecessary force. Theirs was a world of brute muscle and cruelty, and Yousef understood it. At first he mumbled something in Urdu about his identification papers, apparently thinking he was being held on an immigration charge. Miller and Riner, both in the room with their SIG-Sauer P228s at the ready, remained silent. They did not utter a word in English until the initial search of the room had been completed. Several ISI agents lit cigarettes, and then Miller and Riner attempted, with overstated hand gestures, to tell the Pakistanis that there might be explosives nearby and that it wasn't a good time to satisfy a nicotine craving.

Yousef had not laid eyes on either Miller or Riner. The two DSS agents, fair skinned and wearing Western khakis, were very much out of context in the small room crammed with a dozen Pakistanis in local garb. As the two special agents put their firearms back in their fanny packs, Miller gestured to the ISI team leader that he wanted him to turn Yousef's head around so that he could be identified. Miller and Riner scrutinized a wanted poster of Yousef they carried with them. The ears looked different, the nose was larger, and he was unshaven. From information that Hamid had provided, they knew that Yousef had injured his eye in a work accident involving explosives in Manila and that he had burned his hand while working on a bomb in Karachi. An acid burn scar was evident under Yousef's left eye, and burns on his right hand were clearly visible.

Hamid had told his two DSS handlers that Yousef was a master of disguises and that he often changed his appearance. He would dye his hair red, cut his hair, trim his beard, or shave his mustache. His face was one that could be molded by the most modest of cosmetic changes. No two wanted posters for Ramzi Yousef looked alike.

Even though three ISI agents were manhandling him, Yousef remained cocky and defiant. He did not shake, nor did he attempt to plead for his freedom. He was silent and stoic, a prisoner of war accepting his fate with an iron will. He must have thought a handsome bribe would secure his release. He didn't appear to be menacing or evil. He was a lanky Middle Eastern man with his face crushed against a window. One almost felt pity for the man.

Riner got a Polaroid camera from his pouch and took a snapshot of Yousef against the wall. The flash startled Yousef, who forced his head free for just a second to look at the source of the blinding light. It was the first time he realized that two Westerners were in the room. Miller, seeing Yousef blinded by the light of the flash, moved up closer to him and smiled. "What's up, Ramzi?" Miller said in an ironic, "you are fucked" drawl. Hearing Miller's definitive Georgian twang hit Yousef like a rocket. His eyes opened wider. His knees buckled. Stoic defiance turned into trembling lips and eyes filling with cascading tears. "The adrenaline rush of knowing he was screwed caused him to shake violently," Bill Miller recalled. "If this was a romance novel, you could have said that he swooned."[18]

Ramzi Ahmed Yousef, one of the most wanted terrorists in the world and a man who had topped the FBI's Most Wanted List, was finally in custody. Yousef's two years on the run came to an end at the hands of a mixed crew of Pakistani intelligence operatives and two intrepid DSS agents.

Sitting on the phone inside the Cone of Silence in Washington, D.C., with an open line to Pakistan, Fred Burton heard the "we got him" live and in person.

YOUSEF WAS FORCIBLY REMOVED BY THE ISI TO A SAFE HOUSE IN ISLAMabad. Miller, the case agent, joined the ISI motorcade for the chance to interview this most elusive and prized catch. Riner remained behind in Room 16 of the Su Casa Guesthouse to help the Pakistanis catalog evidence and handle the explosives. The FBI LEGAT, who had arrived in Islamabad earlier that day, had been wary of using Hamid, and he had questioned the merits of storming the room in the Su Casa. The DSS special agents had explained the importance of what they were doing, but the LEGAT remained unconvinced. Unarmed and searching through legal papers, the LEGAT sat in a car several blocks away during the raid, and learned of Yousef's capture fifteen minutes after the fact. Riner, who had emerged from the Su Casa for a brief moment in order to radio Maurel, grudgingly flashed a thumbs-up to the FBI agent watching the house a hundred feet away.

Riner knew that evidence gathered inside Yousef's room would be needed later, at some point during a trial, and he worked with the DEA agents and their FSNIs to establish a crime scene and to gather evidence. Riner mapped out the room, took drawings, and made measurements in order to pinpoint the location of certain items.

Pakistani explosive ordnance disposal experts had, by this time, rushed to the scene. They cataloged every item that was in the room and photographed it. Yousef's personal items included clothes, several Casio watches, lots of electrical diodes, and a book of international flight schedules for United and American airlines.

For Miller, the new job of baby-sitting was just beginning. He called Hamid and ordered him to meet him on a busy street corner in Islamabad in thirty minutes with his wife and child. "No bags," Miller warned. "Just you and your family." Sitting inside the Suburban en route to the rendezvous, smiles of joy must have been apparent on the faces of the two special agents. Their job was a long way from complete, the two men knew, but they had pulled *it* off.

The special agents found Hamid and his family waiting on a bustling corner in central Islamabad as ordered. Hamid, his wife, and their seventeen-month-old son were hustled into the car. Of course, having disregarded Miller's instructions, Hamid and his family brought with them as much as they could carry. Their bags were abandoned on the street. Miller drove back to the embassy, as Riner sat in the back with an assault rifle ready to respond to any attack on the vehicle. The family was raced through the protective barriers around the compound and rushed to an office inside the embassy. Hamid was no longer a fidgety wreck. Inside the embassy, with his family at his side, he looked peaceful and secure. Special agents from the Mobile Security Division, who were in Karachi teaching defensive skills to consulate employees, were rushed to Islamabad to protect Hamid and his family.

Miller was then instructed to drive FBI Agent Brad Garrett, who

had also arrived in Islamabad, to the ISI safe house to get "up close and personal with Ramzi." It was an opportunity that Miller relished.

THE ISI SAFE HOUSE WAS IN AN UPPER-SCALE SECTION OF ISLAMABAD. PAtrolling the perimeter of the building were a dozen ISI agents, all armed with assault rifles, with shoot-to-kill orders if anyone attempted to crash the gate. Inside the sparsely furnished safe house Miller, Garrett, and an ISI case agent who spoke impeccable English interviewed the elusive fugitive.

Yousef was again arrogant and cocky as he sat handcuffed to a chair, almost as if he was inviting his interrogators to hit him. When an ISI investigator examined Yousef's *shalwar kameez* with his bamboo swagger stick, looking at burns on his ankles, Yousef attempted to leap to his feet and yelled boo! The ISI agent jumped back because of the gesture, and Yousef snickered. Miller and Garrett could not understand Yousef's arrogance.

The ISI agent would have none of it. He grabbed Yousef by the back of the neck in the type of chokehold that only those who have killed before know how to do with one hand. The pain froze Yousef. "They will go home tonight," the ISI agent said in a low-decibel groan used by men of power who never had to raise their voices, "but I will sleep here with you tonight." The threat was unmistakable. Yousef understood that he was in for the torture session of a lifetime if he didn't start cooperating, but he didn't want to talk to either Miller or Garrett.

"Why should I talk with you?" Yousef asked. "You are just going to embarrass me in front of the whole world. You are going to take me to America and tell everyone what an animal I am. Look at me; you are going to embarrass me. I haven't shaven in over a day and I am wearing dirty clothes. You are going to parade me in front of the cameras looking like this."

Yousef was extremely vain. He had several thousand-dollar suits, including an Italian-blend mustard-colored monstrosity—complete with black patent leather shoes—in his room at the Su Casa Guest-

house Apparently this terrorist believed that it was more important to look good than to feel good.

"Let me have my suits and a clock so that I can time my prayers," Yousef demanded, "and then I will tell you what you want to know." Fearing that he might have had guncotton crammed inside the shoulder padding of his suits, they declined to allow him access to his tailor-fitted outfits. Also, knowing Yousef's skill at turning watches into detonators, the two wouldn't give him a timepiece. Looking to establish a dialogue with the vain terrorist, Miller offered a compromise. "Why don't *I* buy you some nice clean clothes? I'll buy you a blazer, a pair of slacks, socks, a shirt, and some ties. We'll get you razors and cosmetics so you'll look good when you arrive in the United States."

With little room to bicker over this gesture, Yousef agreed to cooperate.

"Can we call you Ramzi Ahmed Yousef?" Miller and Garrett asked in a forceful tone.

"Yes I am," a defiant Yousef said softly, in a defiantly subdued voice, as he raised his eyes to meet those of his inquisitor.

"Are you also know as Rasheed Yousef? Kamal Abraham? Muhammud Azan? Rashid Rashid? Kamal Ibrahim? Ramzi Yousef Ahmed? Abraham Kamal? Khurram Khan?" Miller repeated.

"Yes," Yousef replied, "I am also those people."

"Are you Abdul Basit?"

"Yes, you know I am . . ."

"Have you used the American Social Security number of 136-94-3472 when in the United States of America?" Miller continued.

"Yes, that was the Social Security number I used," Yousef answered shortly.

"Did you plan and execute the 1993 bombing of the World Trade Center in New York City?" Miller asked, as he realized that the prisoner was unrepentant.

"Yes I did," Yousef answered. "Yes I did."[19]

Yousef not only told Miller and Garrett where he had purchased the chemicals used to build the bomb, but he even remembered the com-

pany's toll-free number in Jersey City. He recalled where he wanted to park the truck underneath the World Trade Center in order to topple one building into the other and, in Yousef's words, "kill a quarter of a million people."

"Why did you want to perpetrate this type of crime against the United States?" Miller asked.

"Because of American support for the State of Israel," Yousef responded, "both financial and military." What Yousef wouldn't do was implicate any other individuals or corroborate names. The soldier remained loyal even under arrest.

Yousef was a fascinating person to observe in action. He was calm and personable. He had a remarkable ability to read a person and establish a rapport with him. "It was difficult," Bill Miller remembered. "He is speaking to you very calmly and very willingly, almost friendly, and then you remember that this son of a bitch is a terrorist who was trying to kill people."[20] Yousef was confident. He was very proud of his intelligence and knowledge.

FURIOUS HIGH-LEVEL CABLE TRAFFIC RICOCHETED BACK AND FORTH BEtween Islamabad and Washington, D.C., following Yousef's capture. Both President Clinton and Secretary of State Warren Christopher requested of Prime Minister Bhutto that she turn Yousef over to the United States. Wanting to rid Pakistan of the terrorist thorn as quickly as possible, especially before the inevitable bloody protests broke out throughout the country over her collusion with America, Bhutto agreed. After all, the Americans were not requesting custody of Abdul Basit, the loyal son of Pakistani laborers in Kuwait. They were after Ramzi Ahmed Yousef, an Iraqi, and someone who had no right to be in Pakistan in the first place.[21]

There was one caveat, however. Since it was Ramadan, the Pakistanis *demanded* that the American plane that would ferry Yousef back to the United States land and immediately take off *before* sunrise.

At 5:00 A.M. on the morning of February 8, 1995, Ramzi Yousef was shackled and driven to the military section of Islamabad International Airport in a white Toyota sedan. Security was tight at the airport, though scavengers looking for metal scraps were still able to slink past ISI and FIA patrols and checkpoints and come close to the tarmac. The Pakistanis anxiously looked at their watches and were outraged that dawn was emerging over the city. Purple and orange hints of the rising sun had appeared over the airfield, and the plane had yet to appear. ISI commanders were furious, and they made it clear that unless the aircraft landed soon, *they* were not going to release Yousef to the American authorities.

Miller and Riner twitched and turned on the airfield. They feared that a screwup somewhere in Washington or in New York had delayed the military transport, and that four remarkable days of work would be ruined. At shortly after 6:00 A.M. the U.S. Air Force C-141 transport passed over the mountains and landed on a military runway just as the mosques of Islamabad began to summon the morning worshipers to prayer. The ISI agents were outraged that the handoff had not been made before daybreak, but they didn't interfere with the operation.

The aircraft taxied to a full stop, and the C-141's rear cargo ramp was lowered. The ISI motorcade with Yousef drove up to the cargo door and senior FBI officials who had flown from New York met and greeted State Department officials from the embassy along with the ISI operation commander. Paperwork was exchanged and a large force of FBI agents, including some from the bureau's Hostage Rescue Team all dressed in fatigue trousers and T-shirts, quickly formed a human chain around the car holding Yousef. Yousef was led up into the aircraft and fingerprinted—the U.S. attorney general's office did not want the plane lifting off unless Yousef's prints were taken and verified.

THE C-141 TAXIED AND TOOK OFF. THE WORLD'S MOST WANTED TERrorist headed back to New York City in FBI custody to face justice at the scene of his crime.

Ramzi Ahmed Yousef arrived in New York City late at night on Wednesday, February 8, 1995. He had flown from Pakistan to Stewart Air Force Base in upstate New York. Under the tight security usually afforded a visiting head of state, he boarded a Sikorsky S-76 chopper for the thirty-minute flight to New York City. It was a clear and windy night with a 20°F temperature unleashing a wind chill that was well below zero. At 10:00 P.M., a tug from the NYPD's Harbor Unit approached the heliport and fanned the surrounding ice-filled waters with its searchlight. An NYPD Aviation Unit Bell-412 swooped in from the north for one final aerial patrol before Yousef's helicopter landed at the windswept heliport in the glow of the fully illuminated Twin Towers of the World Trade Center. NYPD officers from the Emergency Service Unit, the same unit that rescued so many victims from Yousef's bombing of the Twin Towers two years earlier, stood on guard in full tactical kit armed with Heckler and Koch 9mm submachine guns and Ruger Mini-14 assault rifles. U.S. marshals and FBI agents, some toting Remington shotguns, smiled as the fugitive from Pakistan was tossed into an FBI Crown Vic for the three-minute trip to the International Court House at 26 Federal Plaza for two hours of federal processing.

Yousef was then taken three blocks away to the Manhattan Corrections Center, where he would be just an underground tunnel away from the walk to the federal Courthouse at Foley Square for the morning's arraignment. Outside the courthouse entrance at Duane Street, shotgun-toting FBI guards secured the underground garage. The FBI announced that *they* had arrested Ramzi Yousef in Pakistan.

BACK IN ISLAMABAD, THE DSS TRIUMVIRATE HEADED BACK TO THE OFFICE and to life as normal in Islamabad. There was still a lot of cleanup work to be done around the case. Hamid had by now shown great interest in the DSS Rewards Program and the $2 million he was going to receive. He looked relieved and victorious as he prepared for a European-bound flight, the first leg of a trip to the United States and a lifetime membership in the U.S. Marshals Service Witness Protection Program. Hamid's wife felt a mixture of bewilderment and fury. She was grateful to DSS for their support, attention, and protection. She was enraged by her husband's involvement in a terrorist organization and his association with and initial hero worship of such a vile man.

"I didn't feel any sympathy for Hamid," Miller recalls. "I felt like he got what he had coming to him, but I had to treat him with respect or it would have been apparent that I didn't like him, and then he wouldn't have trusted me. She hadn't a clue why he was always away from home for so long, and now she wishes she hadn't been told the chilling truth."[22]

On a breezy winter's morning, as the mood on the street in Pakistan was rage over Yousef's arrest, Hamid, his young humble wife, and their child were driven to Islamabad International Airport. Wearing U.S. EM-BASSY — ISLAMABAD T-shirts and carrying newly issued documentation, the three departed Pakistan for the last time.

THE CAPTURE OF RAMZI YOUSEF REMAINS A BANNER DAY IN THE HISTORY of the Diplomatic Security Service. In many ways it silenced the Black Dragons who had attempted to cut the service to its bare minimum. Maurel, Miller, and Riner went out of their way not to seek credit personally. "I could care less for credit," one of the special agents involved in Yousef's arrest admitted, "but it bothered me tremendously that the agency did not get credit for Yousef's arrest. It was a chance for the department to show that we don't, as everyone seems to think, spend the majority of our time overseas in these concrete and marble palaces attending cocktail parties and dining at fancy banquets. We protect Americans. We risk our lives on dangerous assignments and we go out and round up people who we are looking for and who have harmed the national security of our country. And, most importantly, we are already there. It doesn't cost the taxpayer another dime!"[23]

DSS did try to promote the fact that its special agents had captured the world's most wanted terrorist fugitive. The Clinton White House, however, decided that it would control all press releases concerning the arrest, and refused DSS pleas to have its role in Yousef's capture highlighted in its statement to the media. A day later, the Justice Department contacted Secretary of State Warren Christopher's chief of staff urging the State Department not to discuss the DSS involvement in Yousef's arrest out of fear that it would jeopardize the case pending against him. The State Department agreed. The FBI soon took credit for Yousef's capture.

For Special Agent Burton, the decision to ensure Yousef's capture rather than adhere to the bureaucratic code had far-reaching implications. An Inspector General investigation was mounted into his handling of the affair and his failure to "communicate the events through the proper channels." State Department outrage over the affair was deep, and their desire to crush his career was strong. "I was morally outraged that the State Department came after me with such a vengeance," Burton reflected, "when the end result was the arrest of a madman terrorist on a relentless campaign. If Yousef had not been grabbed, I am convinced that more Americans would have died."[24] State Department pressure on Burton, and anyone working in his office, was cruel and petty. The witch-hunt only ended when Burton threatened to call Mike Wallace and appear on *60 Minutes*.[25] According to one former special agent in PII, "Ramzi's arrest ruined Fred's career."[26]

IN PAKISTAN, A LAND BESET BY ANGER, THERE WAS LITTLE TIME TO PONDER the question of morale at headquarters in Washington, D.C. Ramzi Yousef was sitting inside a jail cell in New York City, but he still had cells operating in Pakistan. In the week that followed Yousef's arrest, the special agents joined in on a number of FIA raids throughout Islamabad looking for leads and suspects. But most of Yousef's lieutenants were loyal and dedicated to the fight, and they vanished like grains of sand in a dust storm. The FIA tapped into all its sources for tips on Yousef's operational cells in the city, but the informants had nothing to report, and even special attention to prisoners already in custody yielded little more than broken bones.

The silence was disturbing. The DSS agents felt that danger was in the air. Now, in a nation incensed by Benazir Bhutto's treachery in handing over Ramzi Yousef to the Americans, those who had preached jihad now preached vengeance.

Chapter 6

PAYBACK

On a bone-chilling February night, a group of seven men wearing the rags of the Taliban, carrying Soviet-built AK-47 assault rifles, and conveniently *not* carrying identification, walked across the Afghani border into Peshawar along with a group of refugees. A crimson sky covered the mountain town, and the sparks from the cooking and heating fires all around the city cascaded skyward in a show of light. The group did not speak and they did not mix with the other refugees. FIA agents in Peshawar immediately noticed something odd about the group. They were dressed like Afghans, but they didn't look Afghani. In fact, they were mostly Arabs. Only two weeks following Ramzi Yousef's sendoff to New York, the FIA, in no mood for infiltrators entering Pakistan's borders, quickly swept the gang into custody.

News of the Arabs quickly made it to Islamabad and the RSO's office. Arabs armed with guns with travel plans beyond Peshawar were of great interest to the DSS crew in Islamabad. Some sort of revenge was expected for Yousef's apprehension. Were the Arabs part of some plot to avenge Yousef, or to seek his release?

Rahman Malik had the suspects brought to Islamabad to save his American colleagues from having to travel north to Peshawar, and afforded them full access. Working with an FBI agent who remained in Islamabad to clean up loose ends in the Yousef case, Miller headed toward an FIA interrogation center in the middle of town. The build-

ing was a fortlike structure with armed guards wielding Heckler and
Koch MP5 submachine guns at the gates. Forty-foot-high walls ringed
by razor-sharp concertina wire surrounded the compound. Of course
the concern wasn't that someone would try to break in. Few Pakistanis
voluntarily ventured to the FIA facility. The compound's interior was
typical Near Eastern security service. Light blue walls, probably
painted quickly by prisoners, were illuminated by flickering fluorescent
lights. Iron bars adorned each window. The stench of cigarettes and
perspiration was inescapable. It was the kind of place that induced a
migraine headache.

One by one, the seven "Arab" men were brought down to a working
office where Miller and his colleague from the bureau could look them
over. The seven men looked like a *National Geographic* photomontage
of regional facial characteristics. The group consisted of North Africans, a few Arabs from the Levant, and possibly one or two Iranians.
The FIA case agent knew that the men in their custody were serious
players. These men were silent and they were observant. One, though,
really sparked the interest of Bill Miller. The Arab was nervous enough
being in a FIA facility, but the sight of the red-haired Georgian was
very unsettling. Was he a CIA agent? Or, worse, was he an Israeli?
Ever since the FIA had begun its campaign to hunt down the Islamic
transnational terrorists turning the North-West Frontier into a state-
within-a-state, rumors of Israeli Mossad agents walking about Peshawar had started. The CIA, terrorists knew, could only eavesdrop on
their communications. The Mossad would simply blow them to hell
after they were tortured and emptied of all relevant information.

Miller couldn't help but stare at this one Arab male, wearing his
mujahadeen robes. The Georgia native's eyes were focused on the
Arab's face like a gun's laser sight locked on a target. And then it
dawned upon him. In October 1993, when he was a new assistant RSO
in Islamabad and the first "sightings" of Yousef in Pakistan began to
filter in through the embassy, Bill Miller had seen this man's face before. He ran to his Suburban and then raced through the streets of
Islamabad toward the embassy. It was nearly midnight, and the thoroughfares of the city were fairly empty. Searching his filing cabinets
for the file, Miller found the man's photo in a copy of an Afghan

passport. "That's him!" Miller shouted in the empty office of the darkened embassy. He immediately raced back to FIA headquarters.

It was now the middle of the night. The Arab had been standing for quite a while, and Rahman Malik was in a bad mood. The Arab would, after grueling questioning, offer up tidbits of information, though he was testing Malik's patience in the process. The Arab would grudgingly admit to having known Yousef, but then he would close his mouth and stare at the wall or at the black iron bars on the window. The copy of the Afghan passport in Bill Miller's hand was indisputable. This was the guy that DSS and the FIA had sought before.

Outraged, Rahman Malik stood up, looked the Arab straight in the eye, and slapped him forcefully across the face. "Rahman, we can't do this," Bill Miller explained. "We are U.S. law enforcement officials and we can't be involved in something like this."

Rahman Malik smiled at the DSS and FBI agents and said, "No problem." He summoned one of his deputies, and with a flick of the wrist, ordered that the Arab be taken out to the hallway. Ten minutes later the Arab was brought back to the room. He was forced to sit on the arm of a chair and then asked a series of questions. Looking very uncomfortable, the Arab began to, in Bill Miller's words, "sing like a bird."[1]

But after ten minutes of offering up intimate details concerning his relationship with Yousef, the Arab closed his mouth and stared at the wall. And, then, like a bad slapstick movie, Rahman Malik ordered him out to the hallway. He returned moments later, was propped up on the arm of a chair, and sang again. This went on all night.

By dawn, the Arab offered his most important piece of information. Ramzi Yousef's brother was also in Pakistan, and he was also a player. According to the Arab, Yousef's younger brother lived in Quetta. The investigating agents needed to speak to him soon because he, too, was a player in the al-Qaeda network. The concern was genuine. Was Yousef's brother the heir apparent to al-Qaeda special operations in Islamabad, and would vengeance be sought for Ramzi's capture?

Rahman Malik immediately began to work his special magic. He telephoned Benazir Bhutto and requisitioned a Pakistani Air Force C-130 Hercules transport aircraft. He then called Art Maurel and said that he was sending a team of FIA investigators to Quetta and that DSS was more than welcome to come along for the ride.

Hours later, several heavily armed FIA agents, the Arab, and Bill Miller were flying southwest to the teeming city of Quetta. The weather was bad that morning. Harsh winds and driving rains made flying a nightmare. It took a day and a half for the aircraft to reach a remote airfield at the southern end of the city.

The aircraft was forced to land mid-journey in a backwater town some 200 miles from Quetta, and it made Miller feel most uncomfortable. "I'm the only big white guy around and not feeling real good about this," Miller remembered.[2] He sat with his hand on his pants, always touching the cold, comforting steel of his SIG-Sauer P228, and talking to the FIA investigators—not wanting to sleep in an environment he viewed as potentially high-threat. The FIA case agent for the Arab warmed up to Bill Miller, and the two began to talk. Inquisitively, and remembering how the Arab suddenly volunteered information, Miller asked, "When someone is a real hard person to crack and does not want to tell you what you want to know, what do you do?" Slapping the DSS agent on the knee and inching closer to him, the FIA agent removed a bamboo rod from his kit and said in a deep voice, "This is my favorite technique. This is what I did to this man and this is why we are here today and this is why he talked." As Bill Miller, still holding his gun and clutching his gold DSS shield, listened in attentively, almost too scared to move, the FIA case officer continued. "You take four men . . . four very big men. One man grabs one leg, the other grabs another leg, one man grabs an arm, and the other grabs an arm. Then you pull his pants down. We then spread his buttocks and slap his asshole and slap it again. After a while it begins to split. After that, the person will talk the whole night long." Horrified, he now understood how foreign and repugnant such methods were, and, in a haunting moment, realized how very bloody counterterrorism in the Third World could be.

The raid in Quetta went on in typical FIA fashion. The agents kicked in the doors to the suspected house and rousted the people living there in a furious and unforgiving search for clues. The man that the Arab had talked about had fled.[3] But the fact that known associates of Yousef were inserting themselves into Pakistan was an ominous sign.

The RSO's office was aware that there might be a revenge attack for the Yousef operation in Islamabad and, as a result, it was imperative that they follow up on any possible lead, even those like the raid on Quetta, which ended up being nothing more than a waste of time.

The arrest of Ramzi Yousef had been a big deal in Islamabad, but the day-to-day terror of life in Pakistan continued as normal. Rahman Malik's vision of dividends for FIA support of Yousef's capture came true. In 1995, Congress passed the Brown amendment, which provided for the delivery of $368 million of military equipment purchased but not received by Pakistan before the imposition of Pressler amendment sanctions in 1990. The sanctions, which severely curtailed U.S. military, financial, and counterterrorist assistance to Pakistan, were seen by Islamabad as the sort of scarlet letter of shame imposed on nations like Libya and Iraq. Malik hoped that if he cooperated, if he went that extra mile, it might score some points for Pakistan in Washington's eyes. Malik was particularly interested in renewing the FIA's participation in DSS Anti-Terrorism Assistance program courses in the United States. In ATA, foreign police officers are trained in the United States in a wide assortment of counterterrorist subjects. Since 1984, over 25,000 foreign police officers from 117 countries have participated in this training.[4] The program, designed to help the local authorities enforce the law, preserve the peace, protect life and property, and protect their national leadership, the seat and functions of government, and their resident diplomatic corps, including that of the United States, was sought after by foreign law-enforcement entities. It was a status symbol in many countries. Rahman Malik wanted the FIA invited to ATA training.

The RSO's office appreciated the FIA's efforts to crush potential terrorist attacks against the American embassy and diplomatic community. Maurel, Miller, and Riner were realists, however. They realized that there would be payback for Pakistani complicity in apprehending

Ramzi Yousef, and that the dividends of arrest in the Yousef matter might be bloodshed.

ALTHOUGH ISLAMABAD WAS THE PAKISTANI CAPITAL, KARACHI WAS ITS true seat of power. But if Islamabad was a marble tribute to prefabricated symbols of prime ministerial prestige, Karachi was a cataclysmic monument to everything that had gone wrong in Pakistan following independence. The city of some fourteen million souls, most living in ramshackle huts, was a teeming mosaic of business centers, crowded markets, abhorrent slums, and ongoing violence. If anyone ever bothered to assemble crime statistics, they would soon realize that the port city had a greater murder-per-capita rate than perhaps any other place in the world. Cities in Pakistan like Lahore had always managed to maintain and defend the quaint character of a frontier colonial charm. But not Karachi. . . . The city, a barren sliver of land virtually surrounded by the brilliant blue waters of the Arabian Sea, began as a quaint fishing village in 1725, and was built around the commerce associated with the open water. It was always a melting pot, as the poor and the misplaced of the region's arid and war-stricken regions always found a temporary—though unyielding—refuge in the city that Charles Napier, some 100 years ago, called "Queen of the East." Today, Karachi is a trading center beset by crime, racial strife, and indifference. The sounds of gunfire are heard everywhere in the city, virtually twenty-four hours a day. Police stations are frequently set ablaze by gangs of lawless youths. Mobile phones, a favorite communications tool of Sindhi guerrillas seeking independence from the government in Islamabad, have been banned.

Karachi International Airport has always been a favorite transportation hub for transnational terrorists heading to and from Pakistan. The route from Karachi to Dubai to points west is a favorite for the foot soldiers of Islamic terrorism.

Because of Karachi's importance to Pakistan, the State Department maintained a thriving consulate in the city. The consulate even had its own RSO and marine security guards. The consulate general in Karachi was not a fortress like the embassy in Islamabad, but security around the building was always tight. And, in a place like Karachi, terrorism was fairly low on the list of safety concerns for America's diplomats. Crime was rampant. The gunfire heard every day didn't mean that the mujahadeen were in the streets looking for infidels. Having a wallet or owning a car was enough to get you killed in Karachi. Muggings, if the victim was lucky, involved only a knife. The street thugs who controlled the city rarely gave the hapless soul unfortunate enough to drive a car through the wrong street at the wrong hour of the day the opportunity to surrender his or her vehicle. Two bullets to the head often got the job done without too much difficulty. Life meant fear in the city ruled by chaos. The criminals, after all, were better armed than the terrorists. And, anyway, few terrorists were brave enough to walk through the old city near the port, where the most ruthless crime gangs flourished. According to *official* estimates, over 1,000 people were killed in 1994 in Karachi—*unofficial* murder estimates, however, ran to nearly 4,000.

Traffic was another one of Karachi's many minefields. The never-ending stream of motorscooters, bicycles, rickshawlike motorized jalopies, sedans, and trucks spewed billowing clouds of black smoke into the city's air, which grew less breathable every day. Karachi was one giant serenade of honking horns, always blaring no matter what time of day. Police officers, standing on elevated barricades at key intersections, were supposed to control the flow of gasoline- and pedal-powered transportation, but their hand signals and whistles were just another element of law and order that was ignored. Employees of the U.S. consulate were provided with a shuttle bus that took them home from the colonial diplomatic post. "It was better for the employees to avoid crowds and avoid the local traffic," one embassy employee in Islamabad would comment later.

Karachi traffic was typical on the morning of Wednesday, March 8, 1995, full of the noise of grinding gears, struggling transmissions, and the ever-present brain-numbing slapping of car horns. On the Shahrah-I-Faisal Highway, a main thoroughfare that cut the city in two from east to west, traffic was unusually heavy. The highway was a fast-moving stretch that connected the airport and its surrounding sprawl of housing developments to the city center. The Shahrah-I-

Faisal was known as a place to grab a quick bite out or to go car shopping. New and used car dealerships dotted the landscape, as did Western fast-food franchises and more traditional mom-and-pop stands.

The white Toyota minibus crisscrossed in and out of the left lane as it jockeyed for position, heading west toward the consulate. It was 7:45 A.M., early for many of the employees who worked in the consulate to get to the office, but the three passengers—Jacqueline Keys Van Landingham, a secretary in the Economics Section of the consulate; Gary C. Durell, a communications technician; and Mark McCloy— were punctual at their offices. The driver, Nasim ul-Haq, was known to be reliable. He had driven the short route from the eastern fringes of town to the consulate in the heart of the city several times a day, back and forth, for several years.

At 7:50 A.M., near the highway's third traffic light and by a row of shops called the White House Plaza, the Toyota minivan was waiting for the light to change when a yellow-painted taxicab overtook the consulate car and stopped at a sharp angle in front of it. Two men, both carrying Chinese-made AK-47 7.62mm assault rifles, calmly emerged from the cab, raised their weapons, and unleashed a point-blank, furious fusillade at the minibus and its passengers. One of the gunmen fired into the front of the vehicle, peppering the windshield with nearly twenty 7.62mm holes. The second man, who eyewitnesses reported as bearing down on the sliding door of the minibus in text-book assault position, unleashed a banana-clip magazine's worth of am-munition straight into the van, killing Mrs. Van Landingham and Mr. Durell.

It was the kind of operation the *Mujahadeen* had carried out so many times in Afghanistan, ambushing Soviet officers in Kabul. But the kill-ers had not achieved their ultimate goals. The minibus was usually packed at that hour with ten or eleven consulate employees shuttling to and from work. But a majority of those who used the shuttle every morning had just left Pakistan for a group tour of India.

Once the gunmen believed that the occupants of the van were dead, the gunfire came to a sudden end. With the barrels of their assault rifles still red hot, the two gunmen walked confidently back toward their taxi, unfazed by the fact that there were eyewitnesses. The yellow cab, accelerating in a leap over the main road divider, jumped toward the eastbound lane and sped away from the scene of the crime, some say, toward Karachi International Airport.

A Pakistani policeman, directing traffic a short distance away, did not even radio for help.

The gunmen had been professionally trained, but they were not methodical. Mark McCloy survived the attack, emerging with a badly shot-up ankle. The driver, too, survived. As the two other consulate employees lay dying in pools of their blood glistening with shards of broken windshield glass, McCloy waited for onlookers wishing to help out or the sounds of an ambulance and police. But westbound traffic on the Shahrah-I-Faisal continued to flow, circumventing the shot-up Toyota. Gunfire in rush-hour Karachi, after all, was nothing out of the ordinary.

Realizing they had been left for dead, McCloy ordered ul-Haq to drive the still operational bus east, to Aga Khan Hospital, one of the best in Pakistan, two miles up the road. Gary C. Durell died at the scene. Jacqueline Keys Van Landingham died shortly after reaching the emergency room.

There were no claims of responsibility following the killings, no anonymous calls to the local AP office. None was really necessary. The attacks, one month nearly to the second from the day Ramzi Yousef had departed Pakistan on the U.S. Air Force transport, had been celebrated in typical Pakistani fashion—with a double homicide.

Miller and Riner were having coffee at just after 8:00 A.M. Wednesday, March 8, in the RSO's office in Islamabad. Their boss, Art Maurel, was only a few weeks from retiring from the DSS, and he was actually in a good mood—something out of the ordinary for the seasoned and well-traveled veteran of thirty-plus years of State Department wars and battles. Art Maurel had been in the trenches long before many of the young agents working for DSS at the time were even born. He looked forward to settling down and retiring. Miller and Riner thought how wonderful it must be to retire after a coup like Yousef. Capturing the world's most hunted fugitive was an achievement any federal agent would chomp at the bit for. To score such a victory only a short time before putting in one's papers was storybook.

Miller and Riner were laughing with their secretary when the phone rang. The two assistant RSOs couldn't see her face, but she rushed the call straight through to Maurel. Within seconds, a raspy "Oh shit!" was heard from his office. "Two of our people were killed in Karachi," Maurel said. "Let's get to work!" Maurel and Miller took the first flight they could grab a seat on to Karachi to assist the overwhelmed staff at the consulate.

Riner was left behind in Islamabad to deal with an American diplomatic community obviously very scared that they might suffer a similar attack in Islamabad. Riner worked to calm the fears of embassy employees and American businessmen who were learning of the killings in Karachi. "Don't be conspicuous," Riner told the assembled groups he addressed. "Alter your travel plans and itineraries. Don't do anything that you normally do at the normal time you would do it."[5]

Maurel and Miller arrived in a city unfazed by the political assassinations. Police activity at the airport was no different. The intersection where the attack was executed was not cordoned off or even marked by tape or chalk.

One of the DSS agents in the city, a site security manager in-country on a TDY, had the foresight to take the shot-up Toyota minibus from the hospital receiving lot and drive it quickly to the consul general's residence, where it could be locked up and preserved for the investigation.

PRESIDENT CLINTON WAS OUTRAGED BY THE COLD-BLOODED KILLINGS and claimed that the murders "enraged all Americans." He then added, "I have instructed relevant U.S. government agencies to work with the government of Pakistan to apprehend the perpetrators of this cowardly act."[6]

Special Agent Fred Piry had been happy to leave Pakistan in mid-February, after he helped Miller and Riner investigate the bits and trails of evidence that had been left by Yousef in the Su Casa flat. Razor was an old hand in the Third World, but Pakistan wasn't his favorite place to work. With Yousef back in New York City and the extra Mobile Security Division personnel helping the RSO's office in securing the embassy, Razor had returned to Manila for a few additional days of checking out the Bojinka investigation, and then left for Hawaii to check with the FBI investigation team and to coordinate the Islamabad angle of the investigation with evidence in the Josefa flats. It was winter in Washington, and it had been too long since Razor had seen his wife and children.

There is a saying in DSS that a special agent should never be far from a phone, a packed suitcase, and a ride to Dulles. Razor had driven that route so many times, he was more than certain that he could make the trip with his eyes closed. Because of his familiarity with Pakistan, and the fact that he had been there only a week before, he was the natural candidate to be volunteered for a return visit. Razor wasn't the kind of special agent to complain, however. He liked the action and he liked the threat-level environment, even if it meant that he would be far from home and his family.

Razor flew to Karachi on a numbing flight from Dulles through London, along with Special Agent Mike Hudspeth. They arrived in Karachi to find chaos, confusion, and disarray. "It was a nightmare," Razor recalled. "Everyone was scared because the two consulate employees got whacked, and instead of getting down to business to try and find the killers, we began to get into a battle with the FBI over why we were there to begin with."[7]

"Flashing your badge, or wearing your FBI raid jacket, didn't work in a country like Pakistan," a former DSS agent commented. "You had to blend in and rely on the competence and resolve of your guys in the police station, or in secret police headquarters." The FBI sent a small army to Pakistan. Specialists who rushed to Karachi onboard U.S. Air Force transports included forensic scientists, latent print technicians, and sketch artists. DSS would have to use all the resources at its disposal in both Islamabad and Karachi, as well as the MSD contingent in-country, not only to do their work and liaise with the Pakistani security services investigating the crime, but also to *protect* the FBI agents from being attacked and gunned down.

The DSS agents and the FBI contingent did all they could to start an investigatory trail in the one-in-a-million chance of locating the assassins. DSS issued a reward of $2 million or 60 million rupees, for information leading to an arrest. But the investigation was doomed from the start. Pakistani police found the stolen yellow taxi near the airport a short time after the killing. The vehicle should have contained a treasure trove of forensic clues that might have provided federal agents with fingerprints and even, possibly, DNA evidence linking someone to the killings. But Pakistani investigators violated the crime scene. "They sat inside the car, touched everything from the vinyl seats to the steering wheel, and they even smoked in the damn car," claimed one of the DSS special agents rushed to Karachi. "It was almost as if they *didn't* want us to find any clues."[8]

Razor and Hudspeth, along with special agents from MSD, conducted the investigation *their* way. They cultivated leads, worked at night in some of the more dangerous neighborhoods in the port city, and used their hotel in Karachi, the Marriott, located right next door to the consulate on Abdullah Haroon Road, as a place where they could debrief confidential informants. The reward offer for information that DSS had put out through the consulate attracted an assortment of cutthroats, heroin sellers, scoundrels, and pimps. Information was a bankable commodity in Karachi, and there were many city residents who had word on someone who had pulled a trigger in his or her lifetime. The consulate received dozens of phone calls from murky characters claiming to know who the killers were and who had sent them.

There was no way for the agents operating in Karachi to blend into the local landscape. Inside the lobby of the Marriott, on the streets outside the hotel, and anywhere the agents traveled throughout the city, they were watched by eyes monitoring their every move. Would the agents be next on an assassin's list? The confidential informants that the DSS agents managed to get their hands on, killers who for a price would give up their friends and even family, were a treacherous bunch. Working the alleyways and slums of Karachi was dangerous business for a Pakistani cop, let alone a U.S. federal agent armed with nothing more than a sidearm and a diplomatic passport.

More often than not, the confidential tipsters that Razor and his partners interviewed knew nothing anyway. The debriefing of these informants was time-consuming and wasteful. Their leads, even the hints of leads, were all dead ends. And, of course, there was so little to go on. The killers had disappeared into Karachi traffic, abandoning their taxi and escaping on foot or in a waiting getaway car. Few even thought that the assassins were still in Pakistan. The killers had, in all probability, boarded flights to Peshawar, Sudan, or Cairo even before the U.S. consulate learned that two of its employees had been gunned down execution style. Perhaps they had simply disappeared into the gangland anonymity of Karachi.

For the RSO's office in Islamabad, which oversaw much of the investigation into the Karachi killings, the murders sparked outrage. To them, the arrival of a large team of FBI agents attempting to conduct an investigation in Karachi as if they were investigating a bank robbery in Kansas, was maddening. It also meant that much of the DSS effort in Karachi revolved around protection for the FBI contingent sent in to collect evidence and narrow the long list of possible suspects.

But there was a scheduled event on the calendar that the White House refused to cancel. It was, in the anonymous words of one of the special agents sent to Pakistan, "just plain fucking stupid!"[9] The First Lady of the United States, Hillary Rodham Clinton, was scheduled to make a two-day visit to Pakistan, starting on March 26, as part of a ten-day, five-nation tour of southern Asia. The RSO's office would be responsible for dozens of U.S. Secret Service agents arriving in-country, requiring full-time cooperation. The DSS special agents had to do everything from meet-and-greet introductions with their counterparts in Pakistani security, to making sure that they were checked in with nice rooms at the Islamabad Marriott. The bedlam only increased as the hours of the First Lady's arrival neared.

Hillary Clinton's goodwill trip to Pakistan went off without a hitch, but it had been a rough few months for the DSS team in-country. Bill Miller, who had been inside the morgue at the Aga Khan Hospital to look at the shot-up bodies of the two Foreign Service veterans, felt the

deaths hammered home the absolute importance of security and vigi-
lance. And, he vowed, in the posts he would travel to next, he would
not allow anyone to be hurt on *his* watch.

MANY NEWSPAPER AND MAGAZINE REPORTS MADE THE OBVIOUS CONNEC-
tion between the Karachi killings and Ramzi Ahmed Yousef. But Yousef
was under heavy guard in the maximum-security wing of the Manhattan Corrections Center awaiting trial. He had virtually no connection
to the outside world, and none with any link that could connect his
desires, or plans for vengeance, to a phone in Pakistan or Afghanistan.
Interestingly enough, the name Osama bin Laden was never associated
with the Karachi killings, nor had he been linked, by anything other
than circumstantial means, with the bombing of the World Trade Center, the bombing of Philippines Air Line Flight 434 over Okinawa, or
the mind-boggling ambitions of Operation Bojinka. Osama bin Laden
was still, in 1995, a mysterious, seemingly inconsequential player, in a
series of plots that came back almost exclusively to Ramzi Yousef. But
with Yousef, the field lieutenant, in custody and out of commission,
the attention began to focus on the paymaster and the self-proclaimed
leader of the global jihad.

At any border post connecting Pakistan to Afghanistan, any mujahadeen training camp on either side of the Khyber Pass, or even the
cramped classrooms of any Islamic school in Lahore, Islamabad, or
Quetta, Osama bin Laden was known by everyone as a great military
leader and a hero of Islam. But bin Laden was far from the violence
of the North-West Frontier and the storybook existence of an heir to
a fortune become cave-dwelling guerrilla leader. As Ramzi Yousef was
crisscrossing Asia, traveling between Pakistan, the Philippines, and
Thailand, Osama bin Laden was living a fairly luxurious existence in
the Sudanese capital of Khartoum, one of the three sister cities all built
at the convergence of the Blue and White Nile. Khartoum, the second-
largest city of Muslim North Africa, offered bin Laden a far cry from
the opulence of the family homes he had abandoned throughout the
Saudi kingdom, but it wasn't as rugged as the caves of Afghanistan.
The city—and the nation—provided bin Laden with a well-situated

base of operations protected by the one true fundamentalist Islamic regime operating outside of Iran. Iran, in fact, played a large role in shaping Sudan as the terrorist staging ground for attacks against Egypt and U.S. interests in Africa.

Teheran had good reason to see Sudan as a strategic asset. Sudan controls the shipping routes leading from the Red Sea to the Gulf of Eilat and the Suez Canal. And it had an open invitation to exert its influence and power. Jaafer Nimerei, the long-standing dictator of the country, was ousted from power in 1985 in a military coup run by a hardcore cadre of military officers—themselves radicalized Muslims—led by Lieutenant General Omar Hassan al-Bashir. The ruling Revolutionary Command Council junta quietly handed over power to a well-spoken and highly polished lawyer named Hassan al-Turabi, leader of the National Islamic Front, a political group that had grown out of the Muslim Brotherhood.

Shortly after Turabi's ascension to power, a close-knit relationship between Sudan and the Islamic Republic of Iran was forged. The Iranians sent arms and cash to the impoverished African nation, and Sudan reciprocated by supporting Islamic guerrillas throughout the region; many of the top commanders from Hamas and the Islamic Jihad in the Occupied Territories made their way to Sudanese camps run by Iranian instructors. Many of those camps were financed and supported by funds coming from al-Qaeda and Osama bin Laden.

Osama bin Laden found a happy and welcoming home in Sudan. He donated millions of his own dollars to the Sudanese government and got his engineering and construction contacts to build roads throughout the capital. According to State Department reports, when bin Laden was in Sudan he established and financed three terrorist training camps in the north of the country; bought two farms in the east; and paid to transport some 500 Afghan Arabs back and forth from Africa to Pakistan and to other points throughout the Middle East. Al-Qaeda operatives could move freely throughout the country and, sometimes given Sudanese passports, they could move throughout the world. In Sudan, bin Laden had an entire nation at his disposal.

He mixed the dream of a global war with the entrepreneurial spirit.

He established new companies and entered into business ventures with the Sudanese government and, more importantly, with Sudanese ministers who had absolute loyalty to the Saudi zealot who was making them all rich. They turned a blind eye to the dozens of Arabs, soon to be hundreds, who came to Sudan to support his operations there. Some of bin Laden's visitors were hardcore combat instructors touring Sudan to initiate a new cadre of warriors into the global struggle. Others were travel coordinators, document experts, accountants, drivers, and a full-fledged "Help Wanted" section of all the professionals needed to keep a state-within-a-state up and running. The most important managers that Osama bin Laden was seeking to recruit in Sudan were ambassadors—terrorist liaison officers who could link al-Qaeda with Islamic militants around the world.

Sudan was a convenient world headquarters for the bin Laden global vision. Accessible through the desert from the north, south, and west, Sudan was a quick flight from Cairo, Algiers, Morocco, and Chad. To the south, it was a caravan trip from Somalia, Ethiopia, and Kenya. And, with the Khartoum International Airport refurbished in typical Bin Laden Group construction-firm efficiency, the Red Sea and the Persian Gulf were all a quick flight away.

For al-Qaeda, and particularly Osama bin Laden, Sudan was temptingly close to Saudi Arabia—close enough, no doubt, to embarrass the monarchy and, at the same time, force American troops out of the kingdom. First blood was drawn on November 13, 1995, when a car bomb with a payload of 200 pounds exploded in the courtyard of the office of the program manager for the Saudi Arabia National Guard in Riyadh. The explosion killed five American servicemen and injured more than thirty. The bombing shocked many in Washington, D.C., who felt that bin Laden, whose name was emerging in top-secret memos and files marked FOR YOUR EYES ONLY as one of the terrorist superstars, would not strike in his native land. But Riyadh was a probing action. The true test of bin Laden's Saudi power came a year later.

———

FOR SOME OF PILOTS AND SUPPORT STAFF FROM THE U.S. AIR FORCE 58TH
Fighter Squadron, usually based at Eglin Air Force Base in Florida,
the calendar on the wall indicated only two days left. Some elements
of the unit were returning to the United States; others were heading
toward air combat exercises in progress in the region. Airmen were
packing the gear and souvenirs they had purchased at the PX and
during R-and-R trips to Abu Dhabi and Bahrain. The night of June
25, 1996, was a warm one in Saudi. The cooling comfort of the evening
desert had yet to remove the thin veils of sweat that covered the faces
of the airmen cleaning the barracks and Building 131 of the Khobar
Towers complex near Dhahran, and of the Air Force security personnel
manning the barriers at the front of the complex that housed some
3,000 American servicemen, as well as British and French troops based
in the area.

At 9:50 P.M. air force security policemen noticed a sewage truck
entering the base followed by a white sedan. The truck did not look
suspicious, though when the driver parked it near the fence of Building
131, and then fled in the white sedan, the alarm was sounded. The
security police began to evacuate the building as quickly as possible,
but in a blinding flash followed by a deafening roar that literally sucked
the oxygen out of the engulfed building, some thousands of pounds of
explosive ripped through the apartment block. The sewage truck
shaped the explosive charge, and the high clearance between the
ground and the truck gave it the more lethal characteristics of an air-
burst.[10] Building 131 did not collapse, because it was made of prefabricated cubicles bolted together, but the blast blew the walls off the
building and propelled debris and concrete into its battered shell.

The terrorists had selected their target well. They had hoped for
maximum carnage, and by bombing the complex at night, they all but
guaranteed that the building would be full of airmen and soldiers.
Nineteen U.S. airmen were killed in the explosion. Hundreds were
wounded.

DSS, along with the FBI and postblast investigators from the Bureau
of Alcohol, Tobacco, and Firearms, rushed to the blast site in Saudi
Arabia. The carnage and destruction was unlike anything they

had seen since Beirut or, ominously, since Oklahoma City a year earlier.

For men like Piry, who had been to dozens of postblast investigations in his career, the Dhahran bomb was different. "It was a massive device that simply carved out a huge hole in the ground before thrusting all of its energy onto the targeted building," Razor reflected after his return from Saudi Arabia. "The people who built this bomb had access to a lot of material and knew what they were doing."[11]

But unlike other bomb investigations where the host government was eager to allow the Americans to assume the vanguard role in hunting down clues that might lead to the arrest of the perpetrators, the Saudis walked a fine line on noncompliance. Men such as Razor, and the FBI investigative team he worked with, were able to gather forensic evidence and reconstruct the course of events that resulted in the deaths of the nineteen U.S. airmen and the destruction of the Khobar Tower barracks during their weeks of sifting through debris and fragments. But they could do little else.

The Khobar Tower bombings officially put bin Laden on the map in Washington. The Saudis, outraged by the embarrassing reality of an underground Islamic fundamentalist terrorist network operating to oust the caretakers of Mecca and Medina, were quick to hush up the affair, though the lack of arrests made silencing the guilty difficult. According to some intelligence circles, the Saudi al-Istakhbarah al-A'amah, or General Intelligence Service, dispatched hit teams to Khartoum to deal once and for all with the delinquent heir. The Saudi intelligence services, while masterful at quelling internal dissent, were amateur operators outside the safety of the kingdom. It is unknown if the Saudi GIS ever mounted an actual hit on bin Laden, but it was highly unlikely that bin Laden's veil of human armor, the several hundred Egyptian, Palestinian, Yemeni, and Pakistani Afghan Arab commandos who guarded him twenty-four hours a day, could have been penetrated.

Under intense pressure from the United States and Saudi Arabia, Osama bin Laden was forced to leave Sudan. Elements of his operation remained intact in the African nation, but the Saudi militant broke the first rule of terrorist tradecraft—he was becoming a household word. It is believed that bin Laden returned to Afghanistan accompanied by two Sudanese military transport planes carrying some of his wealth, his bodyguard force, and his four wives.

Bin Laden reached the battered Afghani landscape and was received as a returning hero. The government in power in much of the country was a fundamentalist throwback to the fifteenth century, designed and supported by the Pakistani ISI, known as the Taliban. Like bin Laden, the Taliban leader, Mullah Muhammad Omar, had fought in the jihad against the Soviet Union. Mullah Omar provided bin Laden with a safe haven. Osama bin Laden provided the Taliban with enormous infusions of cash and hundreds, soon thousands, of Arab volunteers. Within months of bin Laden's return to Afghanistan, the Taliban raised the green flag of Islam over Jalalabad and Kabul.

Osama bin Laden finally had a country he could call his own.

NEW YORK CITY WAS STILL VERY FAR AWAY FROM AFGHANISTAN AND Saudi Arabia. Nineteen ninety-five had been a year of victory and concern in America's escalating battles against terrorism. Ramzi Yousef was behind bars awaiting trial, and other fugitives, wanted for their role in the bombing of the World Trade Center, were being rounded up as well.

American law enforcement officials knew that Abdul Rahman Yasin, the mysterious figure that the FBI actually had *had* in custody shortly after the bombing, would be the hardest to capture. Intelligence reports all but confirmed that Yasin, an Iraqi citizen, had traveled back to Iraq following the bombing in New York and had found refuge in Baghdad very far from the long arm of the law. Eyad Ismoil was another story.

The young Jordanian student jumped ship on the night of February 26, 1993. He boarded a Royal Jordanian Airlines Airbus 330 out of New York City's John F. Kennedy International Airport and returned to his homeland following a few hours of duty-free window shopping in Amsterdam's Schiphol Airport. Eyad Ismoil, like Mahmoud Abouhalima, like Ramzi Yousef, and like Abdul Yasin, had vanished.

RSO offices around the Middle East were told to check flight manifests leaving New York or Newark on or shortly after February 26, 1993, and to run the names for young men, between the ages of twenty and forty, who might match names and aliases connected to the investigation. In Cairo, Beirut, Damascus, Algiers, Tunis, and Rabat, RSOs faithfully contacted their counterparts in the local police forces and gendarmes, as well as their drinking buddies from the secret police. RSOs were excellent shmoozers when it came to criminal investigations. An RSO in need of a name, a face, or a fingerprint could, with a carton of cigarettes or a U.S. Marine security guard polo shirt, get more done than a mile's worth of red tape.

The RSO in Amman, Jordan, was Special Agent Steve Gleason, a veteran Middle East hand, with tours of duty in Tel Aviv and points beyond. He was also one of the first DSS agents to work in the Counterterrorism Division and crisscross the postblast investigations of the world. Situated at ground zero of the Middle East's regional headaches, Jordan bordered Israel, the West Bank, Syria, Iraq, and Saudi Arabia. Jordan was an ally of the United States, but nearly 60 percent of its population was Palestinian. Groups such as Hamas and the Palestinian Islamic Jihad, embroiled in a bloody suicide-bombing campaign against Israel, had representation and strong support in Amman and elsewhere in the country. Organizations such as Hezbollah had cells in Jordan, as did, unknown at the time, al-Qaeda; in fact, many Jordanians of Chechen descent traveled to the embattled former Soviet province to fight in the holy war for independence.

Although Americans were viewed as friends in Amman, the threat level was considered serious. Gleason knew that if he ever needed any help or support, all he had to do was contact his counterparts in the Public Security Directorate. Whether it was over a cup of sweet tea inside a police commander's office in Wadi Sir, or over a plate of hummus and a Pepsi at the legendary Hashem's, the RSO was able to humbly request almost anything from the local cops.

Jordan, like most countries in the Middle East, requires that its citizens carry identity cards containing their photographs and other pertinent personal information; in Jordan, holders of ID cards are also fingerprinted. Getting information on Ismoil, whose official name was Eyad Mahmoud Ismoil Najim, was easy. Within days of requesting assistance from the Jordanian Public Security Directorate's Criminal Investigative Division (CID), Gleason had a fingerprint file on Eyad that was couriered back to New York City with a TDY agent from the New York field office. The fingerprint sheet matched some, at the time, unknown prints found at the Jersey City bomb factory where Yousef had assembled his lethal package.

Unlike Ramzi Yousef, who moved around parts of Asia with a library of passports and wads of cash, Ismoil had one pseudonym and a student ID card from the University of Jordan. Eyad Ismoil, the man who drove Ramzi Yousef and his bomb to the parking garage under the Vista Hotel, was living an ordinary life in Amman unencumbered by American justice. There was no extradition treaty between the United States and Jordan, and returning a son of the Hashemite Kingdom to New York City to an inevitable life sentence behind bars would have been a politically explosive issue on the streets of Amman. But the Jordanians were embarrassed that several of their native sons were named in the international press in the plot of the century in lower Manhattan. Men such as Mohammed Salameh and Ismoil were black sheep from a nation that had taken a politically painful stance against international terrorism. So, at the highest levels of government, both the United States and Jordan worked on an extradition treaty.

Under the agreement drafted by lawyers representing the two nations, terrorists charged with hostage taking, air hijacking, aircraft sabotage, sabotage, and attacks on internationally protected persons would be covered by the treaty. Treaties, like any other piece of paperwork generated by government bureaucracies, took time, but in a nation like Jordan, with an advanced and highly efficient security apparatus, time was not an issue. Eyad Ismoil was under constant surveillance by plain-clothed agents of Jordan's General Intelligence Department. GID agents were masters at inconspicuously tailing a suspect through the streets of Amman, or anywhere else in Jordan. As long as the GID—and the RSO's office in Amman—knew where Ismoil was, time was not a critical issue in executing his actual arrest.

The 1995 U.S. extradition treaty with Jordan—the first new extradition treaty with an Arab nation in many years—was presented to Congress on April 24, 1995, following pomp, ceremony, and public statements by President Clinton. Treaty 104-3 was ratified by Congress shortly thereafter and then sent to Jordan for King Hussein's signature.

On August 1, 1995, the historic treaty linking U.S. and Jordanian law enforcement was signed into law in a subdued ceremony in Amman. The following morning, GID agents intercepted Ismoil as he left his Amman home for school. A GID agent smoking a cigarette on the corner and concealing his Beretta 9mm pistol in the small of his back, had followed the university student who was more concerned with the books that kept falling from his grip than with the man in the blue polyester shirt walking behind him or with the silver Mercedes with one man behind the wheel and another in the backseat. He was ushered into the backseat of the shiny German sedan and rushed to GID headquarters in Wadi Sir, where he was quickly processed.

The drive to Marqa Airfield, at the outskirts of the city, was a quick one from Wadi Sir; the GID did not like sitting in Amman traffic. Marqa was both a civilian and a military airfield. At one end, in a terminal that was being refurbished to handle the commuter craft that would create an aerial bridge between Israel and Jordan, workers built a small arrivals and departures hall while affluent Jordanians awaited flights to Aqaba, at the southwestern tip of the desert kingdom. On the other side of the tarmac was the military airfield, complete with heavy transport sections, a chopper wing serving the Royal Jordanian Special Forces, and the Royal Squadron used by King Hussein and his family. Security at Marqa was tight—the military airfield frequently used by the king was always ringed by heavily armed troops.

Ismoil must have been terrified entering Marqa and seeing the air force security troops in their neatly pressed grayish-blue uniforms and Heckler and Koch 9mm submachine guns fastened in white canvas holsters, waving the Mercedes through the base's front gate. Driven to the military side of the tarmac, Ismoil must have thought he was going to be interrogated by the GID, or other members of the security services, but instead he was driven to a white cottagelike building adorned with photographs of King Hussein and emblems of the Royal Jordanian Air Force. He could not see the hulking olive and gray U.S. Air Force C-5A Galaxy parked at the edge of the adjacent runway. GID agents handed the worried college student to the smiling custody of a DSS special agent, Steve Gleason's deputy RSO, the last person on earth that Ismoil wanted to see.

Realizing what had happened to him, Ismoil panicked, then promised to confess to everything but knowing that there was a bomb inside Ramzi Yousef's van. With little fuss or resistance, Eyad Mahmoud Ismoil Najim was walked onboard the U.S. Air Force aircraft, met by a dozen FBI agents and several heavily armed U.S. marshals. A doctor had been brought along just to make sure the prisoner was in good health and would not suffer from the long flight back to New York.

It was a brutally hot summer's day in Amman. The temperature hovered at 100°F and the cooling mountain breezes that slapped across the country from the north and west had yet to impact the sun's burning heat. The C-5A Galaxy taxied slowly on the runway, protected by a small legion of Jordanian special forces operators insistent that the transfer of custody proceed smoothly and without incident. Eyad Mahmoud Ismoil Najim lifted off and flew over Amman. In less than twenty-four hours he would be back in New York, at the scene of the crime, to face trial. According to federal agents, Ismoil cried uncontrollably as he was led into court to be arraigned.

The handover of Eyad Mahmoud Ismoil Najim was a political hand grenade in Jordan. The first extradition ever of a Jordanian national accused of a terrorist crime against the United States would also be the last. A week after the extradition of Eyad Mahmoud Ismoil Najim to the United States, the Jordanian Parliament scrapped the treaty.

Ismoil was processed, like Yousef, in lower Manhattan and arraigned in federal court, then remanded to the custody of federal marshals until his trial. One of the largest terrorist trials was soon to open in New York City, and security concerns were high.

MEANWHILE, IN OCTOBER 1995, IN NEW YORK CITY, THE UNITED Nations held a gala celebration of its first fifty years as the international body dedicated to peace and justice. Known as UNGA 50, the festivities involved some 150 heads of state, along with their foreign ministers, traveling to the gridlocked chaos of midtown Manhattan, to attend parties, summits, and black-tie affairs in honor of the United Nations. Operating from a command center inside a five-star midtown

Manhattan hotel, DSS found itself coordinating the protective details
of nearly 200 individuals.

The need for diligence in New York City was absolute. The Diplomatic Security Service and the U.S. Secret Service had learned,
through information passed to them by the FBI from their informant
Emad Salem, that the loose-knit terrorist cells based in Jersey City and
Brooklyn had actually conducted proactive reconnaissance on the Secret Service and DSS protective details of President Hosni Mubarak
and UN Secretary-General Boutros-Boutros Ghali in New York in
1993 with the objective of killing the two Egyptian leaders.

UNGA was a massive dignitary protection operation involving the
U.S. Secret Service, the NYPD, the DEA, the Customs Service, INS,
ATF, the U.S. Marshals Service, the Postal Police, and even special
agents from the Internal Revenue Service. From the front gates of the
United Nations along the East River, to five-star hotels on the West
Side, New York City became a massive gridlock nightmare of crisscrossing motorcades, street closures, and bomb scares. There were over
300 motorcades to contend with, ranging from the mammoth convoy
of vehicles that surrounded President Clinton's limousine to a highway
cop and a follow car for a European foreign minister.

DSS had numerous high-threat details to concern itself with, from
Secretary of State Warren Christopher's package, codenamed "Yoda,"
to the mother of all high-threat protective packages, PLO Chairman
Yasir Arafat. The New York Joint Terrorism Task Force, along with all
city, state, and federal agencies involved in the Herculean protective
operation, were on maximum alert for trouble. One hundred fifty-two
world leaders, including Israeli Prime Minister Yitzhak Rabin, Jordan's
King Hussein, Pakistan's Benazir Bhutto, and Cuba's Fidel Castro, all
gathered one next to the other, were a tempting target for any terrorist
worth his time in a training camp. "Almost every one of those 150 had
some groups of persons who want to assassinate them," Special Agent
in Charge of the DSS New York field office Fred Krug told a local
newspaper. Federal authorities were taking no potential risk for
granted. Interestingly enough, the one world leader not to show up at
UNGA 50 was Egyptian President Hosni Mubarak, perhaps worried

that the al-Qaeda-sponsored groups that had turned Egypt into one giant bloodbath would be gunning for him on the streets of New York City. There was reason for concern. On June 25, 1995, a very well-planned and ambitiously organized assassination attempt was made against Mubarak during a visit to Addis Ababa, Ethiopia, for a summit of the Organization of African Unity. The assassination attempt, carried out by Egyptian militants believed to have been trained in Afghanistan and Sudan, was a calculated and highly professional operation that nearly succeeded.

UNGA 50 passed without incident, allowing the city's attention to focus on the upcoming trial of Yousef in federal court.

JEFF RINER WAS ORDERED TO WAIT BY THE PHONE IN THE SUMMER OF 1996. Ramzi Yousef was on trial in lower Manhattan, charged with the plot to blow up eleven U.S. airliners, and Riner was the star DSS witness to explain to the court just how Yousef was apprehended; Maurel had retired, and Miller was at his new post, in Jerusalem, straddling that dangerous line between Palestinian and Israeli security concerns. Riner was naturally concerned about testifying. The silver-haired special agent was worried about what he would say on the stand, but there were other reasons for apprehension. Ramzi Yousef had decided, in absolute arrogance, to serve as his own defense attorney. "It was absolutely eerie looking at him, in court, as he sat at the defense table, shuffling his papers and looking into his notes," Riner recalled. "I felt a sense of satisfaction that I was doing my bit and doing what I was supposed to. But it was weird. The last time I saw him was in Islamabad under very different circumstances. Here he was in court, looking nice in a dark suit, blue shirt with a white collar. It was all so removed."[12]

"So, Agent Riner, the morning that you arrested Mr. Yousef, were you armed?" Yousef asked, speaking from behind a podium in a classroomlike performance as he cross-examined Special Agent Jeff Riner in open court. Riner answered in the affirmative.

"By what authority did you carry a gun in overseas?" Yousef returned.

"By authority of the secretary of state of the United States through the president of the United States," Riner replied, made wary by prosecutors' instructions to answer all questions directly and decidedly and to refer to Yousef in the third person.[13]

The testimony followed a coached prepared list of questions attempting to question the legality of his arrest, though Yousef seemed to be fishing for anything that would knock holes in the official version of the events in Islamabad. He attempted to convince jurors that his arrest in Pakistan was illegal and that the trial, subsequently, was illegal, as well.

During the four hours of cross-examination, Riner maintained his answers, always thinking in the back of his mind about that day in Islamabad when he came face-to-face with Ramzi Yousef for the first time. *Did he remember who I was?* Riner says he wondered as Yousef cross-examined him. *Did he remember my face from that fateful day?*

On September 5, 1996, Ramzi Yousef was sentenced to 240 years of maximum-security incarceration for his role in the Bojinka plots alongside codefendants Abdul Hakim Murad and Wali Khan Amin Shah. The terrorist turned defense lawyer stood void of emotion or remorse when Judge Kevin Duffy read the sentence. Yousef also knew he would be back in New York City once again occupying center stage in federal criminal court. But Yousef refused to be vanquished by the machinery of U.S. law enforcement. He remained defiant and cocky to the end, even as heavily armed operators from the U.S. Marshals Service Special Operations Group escorted Yousef on his departure from New York City. He did not waver in his arrogant attitude, even after being harnessed in shackles and led toward the chopper that would fly him to a special Marshals Service flight for the trip out West to the supermax prison in Colorado. There was, in hindsight, good reason for Yousef's smug demeanor. He knew that he would not be the last defendant convicted in the Foley Square courthouse for crimes against the United States of America.

In fact, Yousef was back in court a year later to face trial for his role in the bombing of the World Trade Center. Already serving a 240-year sentence for Bojinka, Yousef seemed disinterested in the proceedings charging him in the murder of six people, the wounding of 1,000 more, and the causing of $50 million worth of damage. This time he did not represent himself. Yousef seemed far more involved with the courtroom sketch artist than he was in the details of the trial.

Even when convicted and sentenced, Yousef remained removed and arrogant. In an out-of-character tirade, Yousef unleashed a scathing written diatribe, when offered the chance to address the court.

This case is not about so-called terrorists who planted a bomb for no reason but just to kill innocent people for the fun of it. What this case is about is the outcome of terrorism. . . . You have been supporting Israel throughout all the years in killing and torturing peoples, innocent peoples. . . . You enjoy seeing people having war together. You enjoy sucking blood and shedding blood. . . . You are the first one who introduced this type of terrorism to the history of mankind when you dropped the atomic bomb. . . . And since this is the way you invented it was necessary to use the same means against you because this is the only language you understand.[14]

Judge Duffy would have none of it. He lashed out at the bearded Yousef, always impeccably dressed in his dark suit and polka-dot tie, citing the Koran when calling the Kuwaiti-born terrorist a coward and the "Apostle of Evil." And, in an unprecedented move, Duffy recommended that the Federal Bureau of Prisons keep Yousef in virtual solitary confinement for the rest of his life in order to quarantine him from spreading his terrorist beliefs.

THE DIPLOMATIC SECURITY SERVICE TOOK SPECIAL NOTE OF THE JURY deliberations in lower Manhattan. Regardless of Department of Justice and FBI press releases, Ramzi Ahmed Yousef was captured by DSS. There was pride in the hearts of the men and women of the service that three of their own had managed to locate and secure Yousef. But, many special agents wondered, how many more Yousef's were out there?

Chapter 7

OUTPOSTS

Special Agent Al Bigler had joined State Department security so that he could see the world and, in some of the more desolate zip codes on the planet, make a difference. The chance of travel, exotic locations, and missions in service of his country were what propelled Bigler into the ranks of DSS, and lured him away in 1976 from the U.S. Secret Service, where he served as a range instructor and counter-sniper. Protecting the president of the United States (POTUS) from a sniper's round was exciting work, and teaching new agents how to use their weapons properly at the Secret Service training academy in Beltsville, Maryland, was important—but Al Bigler wanted to travel overseas. There was something about the intrigue of overseas assignments that the ruggedly handsome though soft-spoken Bigler couldn't shake out of his system. When he learned, by chance, of what Security, or SY, did back in 1976, and he learned of the unique job that an RSO has, Bigler was sold. SY had a new agent.

Bigler relished the new job and the massive responsibility thrust upon his shoulders when he left the SY training center equipped with a new badge and a newly issued .357 revolver. He worked a few domestic stints at WFO and at the command center before the chance to go overseas came across his desk. The assignment was the People's Republic of China—long before the United States even had an embassy in Beijing—at the time after Chairman Mao when the Gang of

Four were being persecuted. China offered Bigler the remarkable opportunity to see what life in the Foreign Service was like in a post dominated by a CI (counterintelligence) threat. It was a learning experience with lessons to be devoured on a daily basis about what it was like to operate, perform, and survive in an environment completely alien to Americans. Bigler was determined to remain overseas—after all, if he had wanted to sit in the United States, he could have stayed in the Secret Service—and after Beijing he went on to serve in New Delhi and, shortly thereafter in 1978, on an extended TDY to Afghanistan.

If ever there was a Harvard University for Diplomatic Security Service hands-on training, it was Kabul. Bigler arrived in-country shortly before the Soviet invasion, when coups, violence, murders, and kidnappings were considered routine. On February 14, 1979, Adolph Dubs, the U.S. ambassador to Afghanistan, was killed in an exchange of gunfire between Islamic extremists who had kidnapped him and Afghan security forces. Day-to-day life in Afghanistan became more precarious. Peace Corps workers were evacuated from the country, as were journalists and nonessential embassy personnel. Like a growing number of RSOs serving in other troubled parts of the world, Bigler's sole focus was the survival of his charges and himself. Amid the shelling, all-out gun battles, and other violence being waged in Kabul, the RSO had to maintain constant radio communications with those who worked at the embassy and safeguard their every move. Even Afghanis working at the embassy had to be sheltered and saved from kidnapping and torture. In Kabul, Bigler learned how to survive.

DSS SPECIAL AGENTS SUCH AS BIGLER WHO VOLUNTEERED FOR HARDSHIP posts, tours that required them to be away from home for lengthy stretches without their wives and children, didn't crave adrenaline rushes. There was no thrill to a firefight—only the need to return fire quickly and accurately. There was, however, the satisfaction of being *the* man, the one who everyone depended on for protection and a safe trip home. These special agents embraced responsibility with a passion. They craved the challenge of safeguarding a building and a community from the ravages of shelling, snipers, and suicide bombers. These were, after all, cops. They lived for the job and looked forward to the chance, a year down the road, to sit in a bar somewhere in Brussels or Tokyo while on a detail with the secretary of state, and tell war stories over a pint of ale and a Cuban cigar.

"In a place like Afghanistan," said Bigler, "you become a tight-knit community and you realize that you are responsible for everyone. Most importantly, amid the war, your job is to maintain calm."[1]

There were many posts in the State Department's atlas of strife regarded as high-threat. There were Liberia and Sierra Leone in Africa; and, of course, there were Bogotá and Algiers. But the pinnacle of high-threat was always Beirut. In the 1980s, the Lebanese capital was, block by block, checkpoint by checkpoint, the most dangerous city in the world. There were thirty-odd militias, all praying a different way, wearing different uniforms, and whose fighters—some as young as thirteen—were always searching for that perfect street battle. And Beirut was a smuggler's dream. Cases of scotch, cartons of cigarettes, and the newest video recorders from Japan could all be had for a price. The city was an amazing place for an RSO to work, especially nine years into a civil war that had experienced a full-scale Israeli invasion, the Sabra and Shatilla massacre, the president-elect's assassination, and the omnipresent stationing of U.S. Marines at the edge of the city's airport across the street from Palestinian and Shiite slums.

Bigler had always wanted Beirut, even though it was a hardship tour. A young agent wanting to earn his stripes had to be willing to be where the action was, and Beirut had plenty of action. In August 1983, Bigler touched down at Beirut International Airport. His first impression of the place was one of absolute chaos.

It had already been a bad year for the United States in Lebanon. It was lunchtime on Monday April 18, 1983, on a beautiful spring day in a proud city, once called the Paris of the Middle East, now reduced to rubble. Traffic in front of the U.S. embassy in West Beirut's mostly Moslem Ein Mresisseh neighborhood was typical Levantine—drivers drove with their hands on the horn rather than with their feet on the gas, negotiating the always gridlocked traffic—except, of course, when shells rained down on the city. On the top floor of the embassy's north wing, the CIA station chief was meeting with a group of his agents for "consultations," the term used by the agency when a boss met with his assets in the field.[2] At 1:05 P.M., a truck laden with explosives banked a sharp left turn into the Lebanese Gendarmerie security booth and erupted into a powerful fireball. The roar of the blast rumbled throughout the entire city, and the enormous cloud of acrid black smoke engulfed the bright sunny sky, turning day into night. Sixty-three people were killed in the bombing, the first suicide truck bombing in the city. The attack was at the time the bloodiest assault ever perpetrated against an American diplomatic post.

The embassy had been bombed by a shadowy new group on the Lebanese landscape known then as Islamic Jihad, though the organization's true name was Hezbollah, or the Party of God, an Iranian-backed and Syrian-tolerated Shiite guerrilla movement designed to appeal to Lebanon's poor Shiite underclass as well as to strike out at Teheran's two enemies in the region—Israel, called by the Iranian clerics the "Little Satan," and, of course, the United States, the "Great Satan."

Hezbollah was, indeed, a new force in Lebanon and a matter of great concern for the RSO's office in Beirut. Slowly, Bigler learned the lay of the land, memorizing the seemingly endless roster of militias and private armies that worked alongside the major Sunni, Christian, Druze, Shiite, Palestinian, Syrian, and Israeli forces in the area. Knowing the militias and their leaders would be crucial for Special Agent Bigler to do his job. Militias sometimes owned neighborhoods; often, all they owned was a street corner, and their deed on the property was courtesy of a Soviet-produced 12.7mm machine gun. Bigler would have to become friendly with each militia leader. In Beirut, the militias were the cops, and it was imperative for Bigler to coordinate the ambassador's travels with them, especially the ambassador's daily commute from his home in East Beirut. The interim U.S. embassy at the time was located in Muslim West Beirut, near the American University, in a series of buildings that the U.S. Marines had formerly used, and was protected by 100 marines from an amphibious unit. Other embassy functions were carried out inside the British embassy. Often, Bigler was able to forge such close ties with the local warlords—with the exception of Hezbollah—that they called him and told him about impending battles so that he could pull any Americans out of the fire zone.

But before Bigler had truly immersed himself in the day-to-day realities of Beirut, Hezbollah struck again. On the morning of Sunday October 23, 1983, a powerful truck bomb slammed through the building used as a temporary barracks by the U.S. Marine Corps peacekeeping contingent based at the foot of Beirut International Airport. Over 2,000 pounds of Grade-A explosives were packed into the vehicle, and the destruction was absolute. The bombing killed 241 marines and navy personnel, and injured dozens more. Bigler was at an RSO's conference in Rome when he received word that the barracks had been hit. By the time he returned to the Lebanese capital later that day, efforts at the airport were dedicated solely to the retrieval of the dead and wounded.

At the same time that the barracks were hit, a suicide truck bomber crashed into the barracks of the French paratrooper peacekeepers in the city, killing fifty-eight of the red berets. Suicide bombings had become a trend. So, too, would kidnappings.

Kidnapping had always been one of Lebanon's principal criminal activities, but Hezbollah took it to a new and gruesome level. On the morning of March 16, 1984, William Buckley, the CIA station chief in Beirut, was kidnapped as he drove to work from his home in West Beirut's Fakhani district. Buckley, operating under the cover of "political officer," had been sent to Beirut to replace the previous station chief, Kenneth Haas, killed along with eleven of his key personnel in the bombing of the embassy the previous year. According to reports, a burn bag containing classified material was handcuffed to Buckley's wrist.[3] The kidnapping was the work, once again, of Hezbollah and the opening of an insidious campaign of hostage-taking, torture, and brutality.

Following the bombing of the U.S. Marine barracks at the airport, the State Department moved its embassy into an annex in Christian East Beirut where, officials believed, the diplomatic post would be safer. The annex, near the sea, was located in the middle of the East Beirut neighborhood of Aukar, a quiet residential suburb of hillside homes and luxury apartments built alongside narrow roads.

Security for an embassy had always been a source of contention. Closing off a street to pedestrian and vehicular traffic was difficult to arrange. The U.S. State Department did not own the side streets and crosswalks in foreign cities, and a garrison mentality was not conducive to spreading the good word about the United States. Turning embassies into fortresses was an unthinkable alternative for many ambassadors, who felt that an embassy needed to remain accessible to the local population. Security had always been a source of conflict between the Foreign Service and SY. Ambassadors, and many in the Foreign Service, viewed the world through the rose-colored glasses of diplomacy, and they often clashed with their security officers over what they could and could not do in countries as dangerous as Lebanon. Ambassadors who ignored SY directives were written up in sometimes scathing reviews. SY special agents who were relentless in their attempts to keep members of the embassy staff safe sometimes found themselves on planes back to Washington, permanently exiled from their post.

WHILE A NEW U.S. EMBASSY WAS BEING BUILT IN WEST BEIRUT, TAKING into consideration all the protective barriers that would be required to eliminate the threat of a suicide truck bomber, the embassy annex in Aukar was considered safe. The buildings were part of a compound that straddled homes. A heavily armed Christian guard force had been raised and trained to keep the embassy annex's perimeter safe (a Muslim guard force, consisting of Palestinians, Druze, Sunnis, and Shiites, was being trained for the new embassy in the western half of the city), but a gate—a dozen meters away from the embassy entrance—had yet to be installed.

The sun rose quickly over the Shouf Mountains to the east on the morning of September 20, 1984, indicating that the day would be sultry and humid. Bigler had just returned from leave the day before, hoping that the security systems that had yet to be installed would already be in place. They weren't. Sitting in his office, attending to endless paperwork, Bigler decided to grab a bite to eat in the embassy cafeteria, along with his assistant security officer, to discuss the security arrangements that still needed to be made. In lands far from the shores of the United States, where the spoken languages were those rarely heard by Americans, customs exotic, and foods indigestible, the embassy cafeteria was where the tastes of home could be had for a nominal fee. The cafeteria was an escape. It was where, no matter where you were in the world, you could return to America for a fifteen-minute break. Even in Beirut.

Outside the embassy, several British Royal Military Policemen were standing in the front courtyard of the annex waiting for the British ambassador, David Miers, to conclude a visit with his American counterpart, Reginald Bartholomew. Looking up ahead toward the area where the main gate was going to be installed, one of the Royal MPs noticed an embassy guard arguing with the driver of a van. Then a shot was fired and the van accelerated toward the embassy. Additional guards fired at the speeding van as it got to within thirty meters of the embassy complex. The truck bomb erupted in a blinding orange flash.

"I heard shooting, or I thought I did," Bigler recalled, "but my assistant turned to me and said, 'Al, you are not in West Beirut anymore, that was a jackhammer doing construction work, relax!' " After years in Kabul and Beirut, Bigler knew what gunfire sounded like. He jumped out of his chair and rushed toward the aluminum frame glass door to see what was happening outside.[4]

Bigler, and the door, were blown clear across the embassy cafeteria into the opposite wall by the force of the blast. The hulking RSO had actually been left for dead outside the embassy, placed with other corpses on a pile awaiting the trip to the morgue. But he moved ever so slightly—which even in a place like Beirut indicated life. Al Bigler regained consciousness in a West Beirut hospital emergency room, amid the wailing cries of women weeping over the dead, and a tiled floor turned slippery by the blood flowing from gurneys. Not knowing where he was or what had happened, Bigler found himself lying on a stretcher, his hands restrained, and a surgeon removing glass chunks from his chest. He was soon medevacked out of Lebanon and back to the States.

For the third time in a year, Hezbollah had struck. The powerful suicide truck bomb killed thirty embassy employees and severely damaged the building; most of the dead had heard the shooting and rushed to their windows only to die in a shower of glass from the subsequent powerful explosion.

THE BOMBINGS IN BEIRUT, ESPECIALLY THE ANNEX BOMBING, WHICH WAS the straw that broke the camel's back, were a turning point for security at the State Department. Under presidential directives, Congress authorized retired admiral Bobby Inman to chair a panel that would revamp SY into the present-day Diplomatic Security Service and create the standard by which all U.S. embassies should either be constructed or fortified to be able to withstand the destructive wrath of a suicide truck bomb. Among the recommendations of *The Inman Report of the Secretary of State's Advisory Panel on Overseas Security* was that the embassies and consulates be situated far from streets and busy thoroughfares to avoid contact with traffic; being on the busiest or most fashionable street or corner might have been an asset in earlier days, but in the age of truck bombers, it was a liability. Embassies also had to be constructed in a manner that would enable the building to withstand the initial blast of the most powerful of truck bombs; outer structures had to be fortified and windows had to be shatterproof. Local security force and marine security guard programs also had to be reinforced. American foreign policy would, in most cases, now have to be administered and represented in unattractive fortresslike outposts.

THE BEIRUT EMBASSY BOMBINGS WERE SIGNIFICANT TO BIN LADEN AND the al-Qaeda network as well. Bin Laden and his al-Qaeda operation originally had very little in common with Hezbollah. Like the majority of Muslims around the world, bin Laden was a Sunni, a member of the mainstream sect, but he was a follower of the eighteenth-century cleric Mohammed Wahhab, who preached that the faith should return to the purity of its seventh-century roots.

The Shiites, who differ from the Sunnis in their interpretation of the caliphate, or successive leadership issue following the death of Mohammed and his ascension into heaven, were often at odds with their Sunni brothers. Iran, where the majority of the world's 150 million

Shiites lived, was often at odds with the bin Laden view of the world. The Iranians were far more lenient and progressive in the role women played in society, and they embraced technology and some of the benefits of modernity. Iran, and its primary international terrorist army, Hezbollah, originally had regional interests different from those of bin Laden's al-Qaeda, though they shared one primary common bond: a venomous hatred of the United States of America.

Bin Laden was a keen student of history, and he appreciated Hezbollah's contribution to humiliating the United States in Lebanon during the 1980s. "Hezbollah knew," according to a former Israeli intelligence operative who had worked the bloody alleys and valleys of Lebanon's body-filled landscape, "that if it wanted to get the United States out of Lebanon, all it needed to do is space out the suicide bombings of embassies and soldiers to the point where America loses its patience and resolve."[5]

The man behind much of the Hezbollah carnage was Imad Mughniyah, a former bodyguard of PLO Chairman Yasir Arafat who quickly rose through the ranks as special operations head of the organization in 1982, following the PLO withdrawal from Lebanon. Mughniyah was enigmatic, highly capable, and visionary. He engineered the kidnappings in Beirut, and he was behind the three Hezbollah suicide bombings in Beirut. He also showed a penchant for striking the "enemy" in far-flung outposts where security chiefs felt removed from potential terrorist threats. In 1992, Mughniyah masterminded the truck bombing of the Israeli embassy in Buenos Aires, Argentina, in which twenty-nine people were killed and over 200 were wounded. The embassy attack was followed by a second bombing on July 18, 1994, which destroyed the AIMA building in Buenos Aires, which housed several Argentine Jewish organizations, killing eighty-six people and wounding several hundred.

In 1992, it is believed that Hezbollah and al-Qaeda agents met in Sudan to discuss common interests and objectives. In April 1995, Imad Mughniyah personally traveled to Khartoum to address a conference of international Islamic terrorist chiefs chaired by al-Qaeda. There was a lot bin Laden's organization could learn from the Hezbollah general. The alliance was an ominous harbinger of attacks to come.

AFRICA HAD ALWAYS BEEN A REMOTE OUTPOST OF AMERICAN FOREIGN POL-
icy, but it had been a vital piece of the global jihad puzzle for bin
Laden. In North Africa, his influence had resulted in the deaths of tens
of thousands of civilians caught up in fundamentalist Islamic wars.

In Algeria, al-Qaeda influence was even bloodier. In a nation where
1,000 could die in a week of Islamic-fueled violence, the country's security forces could barely contain the butchery. The message, though,
was unavoidable. Islamic groups were willing to display cold-blooded
barbarity in order to install a puritanical brand of Islam.

To the south, in Sudan and even in Somalia, where bin Laden
claimed his forces had shot down U.S. helicopters and killed eighteen
U.S. Army 1st SFOD-Delta and Ranger Regiment operators, along
with pilots from the 160th Special Operations Aviation Regiment (Airborne), in the October 3, 1993, bloodbath in Mogadishu, the menace
of bin Laden was far-reaching. From Africa's Atlantic coast to the Indian Ocean and south toward Johannesburg, al-Qaeda was spreading
the word of jihad with cash and explosives. The growth of bin Laden's
network in Kenya and Tanzania, two of Africa's more peaceful and
stable nations, was troubling.

Egypt was of particular significance to bin Laden's global vision. His
key lieutenants, Dr. Ayman al-Zawahiri and Mohammed Atef, were
both hardcore al-Jihad operatives vehemently opposed to the regime
of Egyptian President Hosni Mubarak. Both men added a cold-
blooded zeal to bin Laden's vision and global capabilities. For al-Jihad,
and the Islamic Group, the war against Mubarak and his infidel regime
was expressed in a hardcore, blood-curdling manner.

An attack that exemplified this was the November 17, 1997, massacre of sixty-five tourists in cold blood at the 3,400-year-old Queen
Hatshepsut Temple near Luxor in the Valley of Kings. Although the
area was one of the most widely visited tourist sites in the country,
there were no policemen protecting the site, and emergency rescue
personnel were stationed twenty miles away. The tourists killed were
Swiss, Germans, and Japanese who could not evade the fusillade of
AK-47 fire and henchmen swinging hatchets and machetes. "Women

were disemboweled; others were executed by either being shot in the head or having their throats slit," claimed a captain in the Egyptian State Security Investigations Sector, one of the country's domestic counterterrorist agencies coordinating security efforts at the Giza pyramids. "The terrorists shoved notes inside bellies they hacked open that said 'No to Tourists.' "[6] A group claiming to represent the "Omar Abdel Rahman Squadron of Havoc and Destruction" claimed responsibility for the attack.

No terrorists were ever captured or tried for the attack.

KENYA, TOO, WAS AN EASY NATION FOR BIN LADEN'S LEGIONS TO INFILtrate. Bordered by Tanzania to the south, Uganda to the west, Sudan and Ethiopia to the north, and Somalia to the east, Kenya was a potential geopolitical tinderbox trapped by neighbors engulfed by war and famine. Revered by anthropologists as the "cradle of humanity," Kenya is also the heart of African safari country, boasting the most diverse collection of wild animals on the continent. Some thirty million people called Kenya home—including nearly five million Muslims. Kenya was at the crossroads of East Africa and a major transportation hub. Nairobi's Jomo Kenyatta International Airport was the most advanced travel facility in all of East Africa, and a major link for flights to Egypt and Europe. The airport also serviced daily flights to and from Dubai, in the Persian Gulf, which was a hub for air traffic coming in and out of Pakistan and Afghanistan.

DSS SPECIAL AGENT PAUL PETERSON ARRIVED IN NAIROBI ON JULY 19, 1998, along with his wife and children, to take the position as new RSO at the sprawling U.S. embassy in the Kenyan capital. A former Connecticut cop who had served in DSS in numerous posts throughout the world, Peterson had just completed a two-year stint as the assistant special agent in charge of the New York field office, the busiest of all of the twenty-two domestic DSS posts. Together with Fred Krug, the field office's special agent in charge, Peterson and his senior staff had turned NYFO into a hit-the-ground-running academy where young agents were trained and molded. NYFO's criminal program, one of the largest out of the twenty-two DSS national field offices, was impressive. Krug and Peterson realized that young agents couldn't be micromanaged. They required leeway, responsibility, and advice. Their workload was enormous. Young special agents from a myriad of personal and professional backgrounds worked passport and visa fraud cases throughout the tri-state area of New York, New Jersey, and Connecticut, as well as more dignitary-protection details than the sixty men and women working at NYFO could handle.

Life in Nairobi was like life in New York of the mid-1970s. Crime was rampant and clearly out of control. Motorists rarely stopped at red lights out of fear of being carjacked or hacked by a machete-wielding thief. The sounds of gunfire rippled through the city. People were mugged and shot right in front of the embassy. Sometimes, a pickpocket would be caught by a crowd and literally hanged from a tree in the center of town. Homes were sometimes burglarized on a weekly basis.

For Peterson, the true challenge of Nairobi was keeping the people in the mission safe from criminal gangs, rapists, and carjackers. Home invasions were the most dreaded call that Peterson could receive, as a diplomat and his family held hostage by a strung-out gang of teenagers was a far more volatile situation than any terrorist kidnapping. Peterson always traveled with a 12-gauge shotgun in the backseat of his embassy car.

Terrorism wasn't a particular concern for Peterson when he went to work as the DSS sheriff in the Nairobi embassy. "We were geared up for a critical crime factor," Peterson remembered. "This was the major threat to the community inside the embassy. Terrorism really wasn't the primary threat."[7]

Preventing a terrorist attack in Kenya was, first and foremost, the responsibility of the Kenyan police and the Kenyan intelligence services. All embassies relied on the local authorities as their primary line of defense against terrorist attack. The Kenyan police had been invited to ATA training, though Peterson knew security was his responsibility. As the new RSO, Peterson relied on the intelligence briefing reports left behind by his predecessor to fill him in on what the threat environment in Kenya was like. Under optimum circumstances, it usually took an RSO a good two months to make the rounds and meet his counterparts in the local security services. Summer was a bad time, however, for making friends. Officials were on holiday, and even embassy employees, whom Peterson was attempting to get to know, were off on leave. Peterson relied on his two assistant RSOs, John Kane and Bob Simons, as well as one FSNI (a former senior Kenyan police official) for additional background information and support in the always difficult task of understanding the local scene.

From a security point of view, the U.S. embassy was very vulnerable. It had been constructed in early 1980, before the Inman panel standards were established and before terrorists began to blow up diplomatic posts. At the intersection of two of the busiest streets in Nairobi, Moi Avenue and Haile Selassie Avenue, near two mass transit centers, wedged in by office buildings and high-rises, the embassy lacked sufficient setback from the streets and from adjacent buildings. It had been built at a time when it was chic to build embassies on the most coveted piece of real estate in a city, when ambassadors thought of cocktail parties and convenience rather than survival.

To help extend its limited setback from the street, the embassy was surrounded by a ten-foot-high, steel-picket, vertical-bar fence. The building's window frames were not anchored into the core structure, but the windows were covered by 4mm Mylar protective film to prevent the shattering of glass in the event of an explosion.

There was an incident report, as early as 1997, that the embassy had been reconnoitered by unknown individuals. The report, filed a year before Peterson arrived in Nairobi, was not taken seriously. "There was a large Muslim population in the city, there were a lot of Sudanese and Somalis in the city. The Somalis in particular were all heavily armed and heavily involved in the criminal scene, but as far as organized terrorist activity, there was no indication that *anyone* was locked on to anything."[8]

But there were, in fact, several active al-Qaeda cells in the Kenyan capital conducting intensive surveillance operations of the U.S. embassy, and both the CIA and the FBI knew they were there. The CIA station in Nairobi, the agency's largest in Africa, had, since the Mogadishu debacle, carefully tracked activities inside the war-torn countries of East Africa. The CIA knew that bin Laden headhunters had been recruiting Kenyan veterans of the Afghanistan war for operations against the United States and that the country had become a transit stop, almost a transportation terminal, for Iranian and Sudanese intelligence agents working in Africa.[9]

In August 1997, the CIA identified a bin Laden cell entrenched in Nairobi run by one Wadih el Hage, a Lebanese-born naturalized American citizen who had once served as bin Laden's personal secretary. The CIA, and even visiting FBI teams, scoured el Hage's Nairobi home in search of evidence. But the cells in Kenya were highly compartmentalized, and even U.S. intelligence and law enforcement attention did not deter the al-Qaeda operatives.

Even al-Qaeda's methodology was known to authorities. According to an al-Qaeda operational manual, a copy of which was seized by the Greater Manchester Police Special Branch in Great Britain, al-Qaeda operatives were trained to carry out intelligence-gathering sorties on the installations they targeted. Much of the surveillance activity was conducted by operatives in vehicles slowly monitoring activity around a specific target. In order to avoid arrest during a surveillance operation, there were guidelines that al-Qaeda operatives were to follow. Some include:

- Prior to the start of the surveillance mission, making sure that all needs related to the mission, especially money, are met.
- Agreeing on how communications with the cell leader will take place in case the surveillance plan is uncovered (the telephone number of the team leader should be memorized, not written down).
- Agreeing on special signals for exchanging orders and instructions among the surveillance team members while out on an assignment.
- It is not permitted to carry any weapon during the information-gathering process.

Before conducting a surveillance mission in a vehicle, al-Qaeda operatives were instructed to perform the following pre-mission checks:

- Inspect the car's fuel, water, and lights.
- The car should be of a common type so it will not attract people's attention.
- The car should be in good condition and the driver should be experienced.
- It is important to use a false license plate and small numbers in order to prevent anyone from spotting or memorizing it.
- The car's interior lights should be disabled in order to hide the identity of the surveillance team members sitting inside.

News of increased—and suspicious—surveillance activities was relayed to the RSO's office to the U.S. ambassador, Prudence Bushnell. The embassy responded to these reported threats by increasing the number of roving guards around the perimeter of the chancery, closer monitoring of the visa line, and additional vehicular and perimeter searches. The RSO at the time, Special Agent Patricia Kelly, conducted numerous emergency REACT drills (with her MSG contingent) and asked her contacts in the Kenyan government to enhance security around the embassy, especially countersurveillance activities, and met with the Kenyan police to discuss their bomb reaction scenarios.

Ambassador Bushnell, in repeated pleas to the State Department, urged that the embassy be moved and that security be upgraded significantly at the precariously located building. Bushnell understood how vulnerable the site was to terrorist attack. But her appeals fell on deaf ears, and the answer she received was that moving the embassy would be far too expensive for a post not regarded as high-threat.[10] Nairobi was designated as a medium-threat post in the political violence and terrorism category, and the embassy was in compliance with that threat level's physical security standards and procedures as prescribed by the department—except for the lack of a 100-foot setback/standoff zone.

Nairobi, after all, was not Beirut.

Friday August 7, 1998, was the seventh anniversary of the first U.S. soldiers setting foot inside Saudi Arabia to stave off an Iraqi invasion into the kingdom, though few calendars inside the embassy had the day marked. The anniversary wasn't marked off in any calendars in Washington, D.C., either.

The U.S. embassy in Nairobi opened for business bright and early that warm muggy day. The line of people seeking visas was long, and throughout the embassy, staff members were hurrying about their day-to-day tasks, grabbing their notes and one last cup of coffee from the cafeteria before the morning's staff meetings commenced. Paul Peterson was at a "country team meeting" with the acting DCM on the fourth floor of the embassy, in the ambassador's office; Ambassador Bushnell, who usually attended these meetings, was meeting with a Kenyan cabinet minister in the Cooperative House, a towering structure behind the embassy.

The topic of conversation at the team meeting was how depressing the RSO's briefings were regarding the crime situation, and how people were developing a bunker mentality. "Is there anything that you could do to lighten up the briefings?" the DCM asked Peterson. "People are terrified to leave their houses." Before Peterson could respond, his train of thought was interrupted by what sounded like a grenade exploding on the street down below. Electricity in Nairobi was so poor that transformers were frequently blown off their poles by surges of current. Glancing at the clock on the wall, Peterson noticed it was 10:37 A.M. before attempting to explain to the DCM why the post needed to know how dire the threat of criminal activity was to their day-to-day safety. And then the office was hit by a ground-shaking fist of hot air and fire that knocked everyone onto the floor. The windows blew in one mighty punch.

A few moments earlier, Benson Okuku Bwaku, a local embassy guard, was manning a barrier leading into the embassy's underground garage off of Haile Selassie Avenue, making sure that any vehicle that entered the underground garage was not carrying explosives or smug-

gling in unauthorized individuals. The local guard force was tasked
with performing the mundane security tasks outside of the embassy.
They were paid $100 a week, a top salary by Kenyan standards, and
they were unarmed. The guard force was DSS trained and contracted
to keep an eye out for potential signs of surveillance and to man the
barriers preventing vehicles from entering the embassy grounds.

Bwaku had just raised the gate to let in a three-wheeled cart delivering the mail when he noticed a 3.5-ton Mitsubishi Canter truck with
a covered cargo bay turning off of Haile Selassie Avenue and racing
for his position. But the truck, driven by two Arab men, was boxed in
by another vehicle, a sedan leaving the underground parking garage of
the adjacent Cooperative Bank Building. "OPEN THE GATE!" one
of the Arab men yelled at Bwaku, and began shooting at the chancery,
while the other tossed a flash grenade at one of the guards.[11] Bwaku
raced for the busy street, attempting to raise the Marine Post One on
his walkie-talkie. The embassy's single radio frequency was occupied;
the telephone was busy. Seconds later the powerful truck bomb disappeared into a blinding orange fireball.

The sounds of the grenade blast prompted many inside the embassy
to go to their windows to see what the ruckus was about. Those who
did were either killed or seriously injured.

Paul Peterson crawled upon the floor caked with dust and debris for
the emergency exit to make it toward Post One. The ambassador's
office was behind the communications vault, which was protected by
thick slabs of steel and concrete, and Peterson had suffered only minor
cuts and bruises. Embassy employees were streaming out of their offices badly dazed and wounded by the force of the powerful explosion.
"People were heading toward the emergency stairwell missing parts of
their bodies and crying in pain and agony," Peterson recalled. "It was
dark and confusing on the staircase."[12]

For an RSO still alive in an embassy hit by a suicide truck bomber's
blast, the first priority was to assemble the assistant RSOs and the
MSGs, and establish a security perimeter around the embassy to make
sure they weren't going to be "double-tapped" by being hit again. Peterson carried two seriously wounded people down the stairwell out

the front of the embassy, still not knowing what had happened. Blood covered his hands and stained his shirt and tie. Moi Avenue was littered with the dead and wounded. Acrid smoke rushed into his nose and lungs. Dazed, Peterson walked behind the embassy to assess the damage. The scene was of absolute carnage. The Ufundi Cooperative House had been completely demolished by the blast. Hundreds lay dead, charred a crusty and smoldering black, on the street and inside the vehicles they were sitting in hundreds of feet away. The blast decapitated dozens on the street, and wounded over 5,000 people; it shattered all the windows in the twenty-two-story Cooperative Bank House. Buildings as far as ten blocks away were rocked off their foundations, and flames shot through passing crosstown buses, incinerating all onboard. The cries of the wounded, trapped under tons of rubble, were maddening. A triage center was established near the embassy's parking area.

A total of 224 people were killed in the morning attack, of which forty-four were U.S. embassy employees—the dead included twelve Americans and thirty-two Foreign Service National employees. Ten Americans and eleven FSNs were seriously injured. Damage to the embassy was massive, especially internally. Although there was little structural damage to the five-story, reinforced-concrete building, the explosion reduced much of the interior to rubble, destroying windows, window frames, internal office partitions, and other fixtures on the rear side of the building. The secondary fragmentation from flying glass, internal concrete block walls, furniture, and fixtures caused most of the embassy casualties.

Outside the embassy, wearing a Kevlar flak vest taken from the marine room, and cradling a 12-gauge pump-action shotgun, Peterson and his assistant RSOs spread out, attempting to safeguard the embassy until they could be relieved. Peterson had to figure out which of his people were still alive, and then to coordinate them into a defensive holding pattern. As luck would have it, a U.S. military survey team was in-country, and Peterson mobilized the twelve-man force, provided them with weapons from the MSG arsenal, and positioned them inside a perimeter marked by shredded flesh and blood. As the DSS agents and MSGs stood guard, concerned about a second attack and still not comprehending what had hit them, embassy Security Engineering Officer Worley (Lee) Reed led a team charged with the grim task of rescuing those still trapped inside the building and recovering the corpses.

Limiting access to the damaged structure was vital. There was a very real possibility that the building could collapse, and a raging fire was blazing in the rear of the embassy above fuel tanks filled to capacity with 30,000 liters of diesel fuel. There was also serious concern over the classified material—documents and computer hard drives—that were now strewn about a gigantic crime scene. Moments after the blasts, looters, with little regard for their own safety, began combing the remains of the gutted chancery.

Quickly, Peterson, Administration Counselor Steven Nolan, and Acting Deputy Chief Mission Lucien Vandenbrooke established a command center that could funnel communications to the authorities in Nairobi and, most importantly, to Washington, D.C. The center, hastily established on the other side of town at the USAID building, hooked up phone lines and computer links.

Peterson wondered just how sophisticated the terrorists were who had struck the embassy. He wondered when and where a second wave would strike.

Three minutes later, 450 miles to the south in a city named "Abode of Peace" in Arabic, Dar es Salaam, the terrorists displayed just how sophisticated they were.

IF EVER THERE WAS A DSS SPECIAL AGENT DUE FOR A QUIET POST AS AN RSO, it was John DiCarlo. A former MSG who had served in some of the world's most dangerous posts, including Kuwait, DiCarlo was one of those agents who always wanted to be overseas and always wanted to be where the bullets were flying. DiCarlo served as one of the five assistant RSOs in the sprawling U.S. embassy in Cairo (a tour likened to a "freight train out of control") at a time when two of his colleagues, RSO Denny Williams and Assistant Regional Security Officer John Hucke, barely survived an assassination attempt.

After Cairo, DiCarlo served a two-year stint as RSO in Baghdad
from 1988 to 1990. "The threat in Baghdad wasn't really from terrorists," DiCarlo recalled, "it was from Iraqi intelligence operatives. Once
I came home only to find my kitchen chairs placed neatly on top of
my table. It was a gentle reminder from Saddam's spies that they can
get what they want when they want it." The Iraqis, DiCarlo found,
were vicious and petty. They openly followed the DSS security officer,
as well as other members of the American diplomatic community; in
one instance, the wife of an American diplomat was slapped in the face,
because she asked an intelligence official why she was being stopped.
People were taken off aircraft about to taxi for takeoff by the secret
police, so their disappearance would not be reported until the plane
landed at its destination.

DiCarlo was in charge of evacuating the embassy following Iraq's
invasion of Kuwait. It was a frantic and terrifying time for an RSO. If
Saddam Hussein had so wished, the embassy could have been reduced
to rubble. Not knowing if the Iraqis were going to hold him and the
other Americans hostage, or allow them to escape and drive into the
desert only so that his Republic Guard could pick them off one by one
in a turkey shoot as they were doing to others fleeing toward Jordan,
DiCarlo knew that the situation of the post in Baghdad was precarious.
Burning of the classified material inside the embassy commenced a few
hours after Iraq invaded Kuwait and lasted until the middle of August,
when the last American diplomats, including DiCarlo, his family, the
marine MSGs, and other personnel from "various agencies" in Virginia, undertook the precarious twelve-hour drive through the desert
to the Jordanian border.

From Baghdad, DiCarlo headed to the DSS San Francisco field office to recover from the grueling two years, but the calling of overseas
and danger was drawing him toward another high-threat post. DiCarlo
headed to Colombo, Sri Lanka, at the height of the Tamil Tiger war
for independence. Soon afterward, he volunteered to serve in Beirut—
once again unwilling to relinquish the opportunity to serve in a high-
threat post. The tour in Beirut was everything it was advertised to be
and more—365 days of seventy-mile-per-hour motorcades through

East and West Beirut with the ambassador, imminent attack warnings from intelligence services and walk-ins, and the daunting reality that the Lebanese capital was a city where two American embassies had already been hit.

Divorced for a second time—marriages a casualty of the years over-seas—and not wanting to serve in Washington, DiCarlo once again bid on a danger post and a city that had, in the 1990s at least, come to personify man's inhumanity to man—Sarajevo. Bosnia was years of mortar rounds, snipers, and massacres. It was twenty-hour workdays, seven days a week. Beyond Sarajevo, the State Department had also opened offices in Mostar and Banja Luca, and those facilities and the diplomats who served there required extraordinary security and pro-tection. DiCarlo had to worry not only about Serbs, but also about operatives from Hezbollah and bin Laden's al-Qaeda who had made the pilgrimage to the Balkan bloodletting to fight on the side of Islam. It was an exhausting country, and DiCarlo was burned out. He needed—for the first time in his career—a chance to take it easy.

DiCarlo wanted a place to work where he could sit near the ocean, drink coconut milk, and relax for three years. He wanted Dar es Sa-laam. Tanzania was a magical place for anyone in the Foreign Service to work in for a three-year tour. The nation boasts some of the best wildlife-spotting opportunities on the continent, with such famous parks such as the Serengeti and Mount Kilimanjaro, or the wonderful crater of Ngorongoro. For nearly a decade DiCarlo had been racing at top speed, performing in some of the most dangerous places on the planet. When he arrived in Tanzania and had a chance to read the local paper, he knew he had reached the gates of paradise. The front page covered a robbery and a scam regarding automobile insurance. There was no article about a massacre, a suicide bombing, or about jihad.

Even though DiCarlo was rewarded for his years in Baghdad, Beirut, Colombo, and Sarajevo with a low-threat post, he could not shake the realities of his previous tours. In Dar es Salaam he would be the sheriff and he would do things his way.

The first thing that DiCarlo did after arriving in Tanzania was to survey the embassy at night—to see what it looked like to the eyes of a terrorist planner. Instead of sleeping or blowing off some steam at one of the local watering holes his first night in-country, DiCarlo sat at his desk and jotted down ideas on how to fill in the gaping holes in the embassy's security he could see from a few moments outside the building's gate on a moon-filled night. The street out in front of the embassy wasn't cordoned off. Pedestrian and vehicular traffic moved freely in front of the chancery. "Why is the street open?" DiCarlo asked Darlene Hartman, his secretary.

"Because that's the way it has always been," she replied, somewhat concerned over the sudden interest in security.

"This is nuts," DiCarlo fired back. "Even in Baghdad we operated in a sterile environment, with the street closed off to the locals. The only way we were going to be attacked there was if Saddam Hussein wanted us attacked!"[13]

The embassy and annex were surrounded by a perimeter wall that provided a thirty-five-foot setback between the embassy and adjacent streets and properties. The base of the wall was a combination of concrete block and reinforced concrete onto which tubular metal picket fencing alternated with concrete pilasters. Hardened guard booths were located at each of the entryways to the compound. It was a facility that was less vulnerable than the post in Nairobi, but still a far cry from the Inman standards recommended following the Beirut bombings in 1983 and 1984.

Less than a week after he arrived in Tanzania, DiCarlo found himself on the embassy roof supervising some of the local employees installing air-conditioning systems to make sure that they weren't planting any improvised explosive devices—or even eavesdropping bugs—inside the embassy. Wiping his brow from the hot African sun, DiCarlo stood up and scanned the entrance to the embassy compound only to see a blue water truck pulling up to the main gate and the local guard on duty. The unarmed guard smiled at the truck's driver and waved him through without conducting a bomb search on the vehicle. Outraged, DiCarlo raced down from the roof, and in the saltiest language he learned while in the marine corps, "threw up all over the guard." He then brought down the guard force supervisor, and chewed him out in front of everyone. "The next time *you* see a truck pulling into the embassy," DiCarlo scolded the embarrassed guard, "I want you to check it thoroughly for explosives."[14]

The next time a truck did, indeed, pull up into the embassy, it was Friday, August 7.

It was a simmering day in Dar es Salaam—almost too hot for embassy employees to undergo their weekly Friday alarm drill. There were three drills in all: an alarm for a fire, one for a bomb threat, and another for a full-blown terrorist assault. Embassy staff hoped that they wouldn't have to do anything physical related to the drill that hot morning; two months earlier, those with offices on the top floor had donned an emergency descent device to drop to the ground during a fire drill. The ear-splitting chirp of the alarm was audible to the guard force manning the gate that Friday. A water truck pulled up to the main entrance on Laibon Road in the diplomatic quarter, followed by another large refrigerated truck driven by two Arab men. The refrigerated truck, painted bright blue, was crammed with homemade explosives and gas and oxygen cylinders built identically to the truck that had just taken out the embassy in Nairobi, and similar to the design that Ramzi Yousef had used in lower Manhattan five years earlier.

The water deliveryman was a regular, but wary of the wrath from the RSO, the guard administered a thorough examination of the vehicle, careful to scan underneath the chassis with a mirror attached to a pole. The security scrutiny alarmed the second driver, who honked his horn for the water truck to move. As the guards approached his vehicle, the individual in the front seat became skittish and hit the panic switch on his bomb, blowing the truck up and punching a hole through the main gate. The force of the explosion was so powerful that it flung the water truck into the air like a football kicked nearly 100 feet away. Concrete walls were blasted into the building, and computers were thrown off their desks and workstations. The force of the explosion sprayed the battered embassy with a hot cloud of dust and debris as rubble and glass shards were blown everywhere. Marine Post One, the most fortified spot in the embassy, shifted by three inches.[15] The blast produced a fireball that shot 200 feet into the air, and painted a wave of death and destruction over an area 1,000 meters wide. Cars were turned over like toys, and the air filled with the biting stench of smoldering flesh and burnt metal.

John DiCarlo's office was in the front of the embassy overlooking the main street. He was in his office at 10:38 A.M. One of the young MSGs knocked on his door and respectfully asked a favor. "Sir," the young marine asked, almost embarrassed, in a Southern drawl, "the detachment commander isn't in yet, and I was wondering if you could sit by Post One while I run to the bathroom and rush to the finance office to cash a check?" DiCarlo walked to Post One and checked where all the emergency buttons were and where he could find the shotgun.

Suddenly, the blast-resistant windows of Post One breathed in, a special-effects type of bowing indicating that they had been pushed in by a tremendous force. The force of the explosion picked DiCarlo up and threw him across to the opposite wall, knocking the watch off of his wrist. As he attempted to get up on one knee, the room filled with a billowing haze of black smoke. The thick window that had breathed in a few seconds before spiderwebbed into the macabre pattern of fortified glass pushed to the limit of its endurance.

People throughout the embassy were screaming; some had gashes across their faces and hands that were bleeding profusely. Grabbing his shotgun, DiCarlo handed Post One to an MSG and rushed to check out the embassy's staff and physical condition. A second-floor wall had been blown out and flames, billowing high in a mighty orange burst, baked the white building in an intolerable heat. Offices, adorned by oak paneling, personal mementos, and computer terminals, were sliced in two by crumbling concrete. Embassy personnel were trapped under their desks and underneath support columns and slabs of concrete and plaster.

DiCarlo feared a second hit on the embassy and quickly returned to the REACT Room, where the marines kept their tactical equipment and weaponry. The MSG contingent had also raced to the REACT room upon hearing the blast, grabbing their Kevlar body armor and helmets, along with their M16A2 5.56mm assault rifles, and rushed to the demolished Post One. Standing in a row abreast of each other, in a human wall of body armor and camouflage, the MSGs, some covered in a film of dust and debris, asked DiCarlo, "RSO, what do we do?"[16]

"Clear the embassy from top to bottom, and then from bottom to top, and clear everyone out that you find," DiCarlo ordered. "Do it again," he told the young marines, some already serving in their fifth post, "and do it methodically, and turn everything over to make sure that nobody is covered by rubble."

Checking the embassy grounds, DiCarlo and his marines saw the devastation and scanned the roadways for a possible second attack. One of the guards at the front gate was sliced in two, as if he had been hacked in half by a meat cleaver, still at his post near where the bomb went off.

The powerful truck bomb that exploded thirty-five feet from the outer wall of the chancery killed twelve people and seriously injured eighty-five more. No Americans were among the fatalities, though many were injured. The chancery suffered major structural damage and was rendered unusable, but did not collapse. The ambassador's residence, a thousand yards distant and vacant at the time, suffered roof damage and collapsed ceilings. Bones, limbs, and sandblasted chunks of flesh were found in the neighborhood around the embassy weeks after the bombing.

The residents of Dar es Salaam rushed to the embassy to volunteer and help. Men, women, and children rushed to the battered gates to comfort the wounded and help move rubble from piles that might be concealing a victim. "It was so unlike Nairobi," DiCarlo stated, "where looters were literally plucking wedding rings off the hands of the dead. Here, in fitting with the serene character of the Tanzanians, the people just wanted to help!"[17]

Days after the blast, John E. Lange, the deputy chief of mission, took his RSO to the side and said, "You know, John, if you had not made an incident of the truck business the week before, the truck with the bomb onboard would have entered the gate and hit the building, and you and I might not be standing here. And if the bomb had gone off inside the building, you and I would both be selling shoes for a living now!"[18]

———

SECRETARY OF STATE MADELEINE ALBRIGHT LEARNED OF THE ATTACKS IN Rome. The hard-talking and fast-thinking divorced mother of three, who, appropriately enough, was nicknamed "Fireball" by her protective detail, had been viewed as something of a saving grace inside the ranks of the Diplomatic Security Service. Unlike many ambassadors, and unlike most secretaries of state, Madeleine Albright developed a rapport with the men and women following her all over the world wearing their business suits and talking into the Motorola microphones in their sleeves. She became a hands-on admirer of her protectors. On numerous occasions, on diplomatic missions to the Balkans, Albright shocked Foreign Service curmudgeons in Foggy Bottom when she was photographed wearing a DSS baseball cap flanked by DSS special agents carrying assault rifles and Uzi submachine guns.

Albright had traveled to the Italian capital on a commercial flight, along with her protective detail and her staff, in order to attend the wedding of her spokesman, Jamie Rubin, to CNN war correspondent Christiane Amanpour. The wedding was to be a star-studded event in a villa outside Florence, and the secretary of state was going to be the guest of honor.

Special Agent Thomas Gallagher was about to settle into his room at the Excelsior Hotel, removing his suit from the worn garment bag and preparing for a few hours off in Rome, when the knock on the door signaled that there had been an "incident." "Two embassies in Africa were hit," Gallagher was told, as he quickly grabbed his shield and his SIG-Sauer P228, to meet Special Agent Larry Hartnett, the detail's SAC, at the hotel command post. Within an hour, Albright was at the U.S. embassy in Rome coordinating a response with the White House.

The mood at the embassy was somber. Were the attacks in Africa isolated incidents, or were terrorists around the world poised to strike out at other U.S. diplomatic posts? Scores of Carabinieri and Italian counterterrorist NOC operators escorted the secretary of state to a military airfield outside of the city, where she boarded a small private jet, along with Hartnett, Gallagher, and Special Agent Kurt Olsson, for the three-hour flight to Shannon in Ireland, where a U.S. Air Force jet was standing by for the flight to Andrews Air Force Base outside Washington, D.C.

DSS, along with the U.S. military and the FBI, had years of practice in responding to embassies and barracks being decimated by suicide truck bombers. Within hours of the attacks in East Africa, the U.S. government mobilized resources to dispatch to Nairobi. A Federal Emergency Support Team, consisting of FBI agents, DSS teams, and military personnel, departed within about six hours. Unfortunately, the aircraft broke down in Rota, Spain, creating a fifteen-hour delay before a backup plane could arrive and be loaded.

For Paul Peterson and his crew of exhausted security guards protecting the smoldering perimeter, backup couldn't have come fast enough. In fact, it came forty-six hours after the building was reduced to rubble. Peterson's team did not have emergency equipment, they didn't have protective masks, and they were alone, refusing to relinquish their positions, until help came from Washington. The FEST contingent arrived in Nairobi as a welcomed relief to the embassy, helping the ambassador and her staff restore embassy functions, and assisting with communications, with the rescue, and with other emergency relief efforts.

Much to Peterson's chagrin, the local Kenyan authorities were anything but helpful, not offering assistance or even support in those first chaotic hours. A few hours after the blast, Peterson met with one of the senior officers of the Kenyan police, pleading for help. "Mr. Peterson," he confidently proclaimed, "have no fear." That was the last time the RSO saw the commander for nearly a week. When Peterson requested that the Kenyan authorities provide security to the interim embassy and command center being set up at the USAID building, a government official pledged to send a platoon of troops from the Kenyan Rifles as long as the Americans figured out how to transport the soldiers. When a truck was found and the transportation arrangements made, the Kenyan soldiers arrived at the building only to leave a half hour later. They had forgotten to bring their rifles.[19]

A contingent of marine security guards from the U.S. embassy in Pretoria was flown to Nairobi to assist in the security efforts, but the scene outside the embassy was deteriorating. To bolster security efforts, the U.S. Marine Corps dispatched a Fleet Antiterrorist Security Team to the perimeter around the embassy in Nairobi from Bahrain. The FAST teams were on-call special operations units that could respond rapidly to terrorist incidents involving American installations and targets overseas.

The FAST team was needed. Reports filtered back to the security staff around the embassy that the battered remnants of the embassy were *still* under surveillance. Looters were everywhere, picking through the debris and the corpses for anything of value. Securing—and monitoring—the emergency rescue teams that were filtering into the country was also of paramount importance. Teams from Israel and from as far away as Fairfax County, Virginia, had rushed to Nairobi to help in the search for survivors. Classified material was everywhere. It had to be accounted for and secured.

DSS sent a large contingent of special agents to Nairobi, including Patricia Kelly, the former RSO. They provided a large protective detail to Ambassador Bushnell, who was wounded in the bombing, to keep her safe from any assassination operation. Other DSS agents were dispatched to the functioning embassy to assist in security; still others, including a sizable contingent of tactical specialists from the Mobile Security Division, assisted in safeguarding the perimeter surrounding the bombed-out embassy as well as in cataloging and retrieving classified information blown all over the city by the bomb's thunderous blast.

On the FEST flight from Andrews Air Force Base to Nairobi was Fred Piry. When the bombs exploded in Nairobi and Dar es Salaam, Piry was asleep in his suburban D.C. home; he was working at ATA and was about to join the ranks of Secretary of State Albright's protective detail as the handpicked assistant special agent in charge. As Piry drove to the office, he came across DSS Director Peter Bergin and other top organization officials running to Main State. "Well, this is the first time that I am not involved with this shit," Razor said with a smile. "I'm removed from this."[20]

But within a few hours, following a call from the director, Piry found himself reviewing his personal kit at Andrews Air Force Base awaiting the flight to Nairobi—a veteran of four years as an MSD team leader and lead agent on the Karachi killings, Razor was no stranger to crisis. He took his tropical garb, with a kit bag full of Power Bars, medicine, water purifying tablets, his laptop, Level III Kevlar body armor, and, most importantly, his Heckler and Koch MP5 9mm submachine gun. Unlike in his previous postincident investigations, Razor was not interested in simply supervising the sifting of evidence, or hearing reports from the local police commanders. Special Agent Piry wanted to apprehend those responsible for the cold-blooded killings.

Joining the investigation to seek out and find any of the embassy terrorists, Piry and the FBI team went to work in Nairobi. The FBI began searching for clues; DSS and PII needed to start with page one. Piry and his team first looked for photographs of the embassy before the bombing, so that they could, in their minds, reconstruct the damage. "The FBI was more concerned with collecting evidence that would be used in an eventual court proceeding against those involved with the bombing," Piry stated, "but we in PII needed to know how the terrorists operated, how they selected their targets and how they constructed their devices. In order to prevent an attack, you need to know how your adversary does business."[21]

Knowing how the Nairobi cell operated was crucial, especially since the Islamic Army for the Liberation of the Holy Shrines, one of the al-Qaeda front names, had assumed responsibility for the bombings and had, in a statement published in the Arabic daily *al-Hayat*, "promised to continue shipping more American dead bodies to their unjust government until we humiliate America's arrogance and roll its dignity into the mud of defeat." The al-Qaeda threats were taken seriously. On August 18, 1998, Secretary of State Albright flew into both Tanzania and Kenya to view the devastation at the two American embassies during a whistle-stop ten-hour visit to the continent. Security surrounding the secretary of state was tight, and the fear for her safety was genuine. Advance agents joined PII teams and FBI agents sifting through the evidence and questioning possible leads in the poor slums of Nairobi, where North Africans tended to live, and where the embassy bombers were believed to have received their logistical support.

The investigation was primarily an American operation. "The Kenyans and their secret police," one former federal agent stated, "were very capable of keeping tabs on internal dissent, or torturing a political adversary within an inch of his life, but when it came to foreigners establishing cells in their country, even Somalis and Sudanese selling AK-47s in the markets of Nairobi, they seemed not to give a shit. Even more remarkably, there were sections of Nairobi, primarily the Eastly section, where the Sudanese and Somalis lived, where the cops never entered because they knew they'd be killed!"[22]

The hunt for the terrorists was a massive undertaking, and shortly after the blasts there were already men in custody. The first to be arrested was Mohammed Sadiq Odeh. Odeh, a Palestinian engineer with dual Jordanian and Kenyan citizenship, was detained at Karachi International Airport after arriving on a flight from Nairobi with a bad Yemeni passport. Odeh, who listed his final destination as "Afghanistan," was interrogated by Pakistani FIA officers, who pressured the hapless Jordanian to talk and confess his crimes. Odeh admitted that he was a member of al-Qaeda, and was one of *seven* men in the Nairobi cell involved with the technological, engineering, and logistical aspect of the operation. A week after his arrest, Odeh was flown back to Nairobi, where he was met by FBI agents. He was read his Miranda rights and taken into custody.

The second al-Qaeda operative arrested was Mohammed Rashid Daoud al-Owhali. Owhali, the man sitting in the cabin of the Mitsubishi truck that blew up the embassy in Nairobi, had tossed the diversionary stun grenade at the embassy guard. Like the driver of the truck, he was expected to give up his life in the bombing mission. Instead, he ran at the first hint of trouble and was slightly injured by the blast. Owhali, trained in explosives and surveillance at a bin Laden camp in Afghanistan, had been the cell's intelligence officer and had photographed the embassy weeks before the attack.

The FBI and DSS special agents who had rushed to Nairobi joined their Kenyan counterparts in numerous raids on safe houses and possible bomb factories where the conspirators involved in the attack had stayed or even still might be hiding. Sometimes, the trail would be a slow and roundabout route that led to nowhere. Other times, the information received through intelligence sources was true. On August

19, fifteen FBI and DSS special agents, along with six Kenyan detectives, raided the Hilltop Hotel, where it is believed some of the bombers stayed and built their destructive bomb. The DSS element and their counterparts in the FBI, and the bureau's elite Hostage Rescue Team, stormed the hotel wearing full tactical kit with Heckler and Koch submachine guns at the ready. They searched two rooms where four men implicated in the bombing—two Palestinians, an Egyptian, and a Saudi—had, according to reports, built components of the truck bomb.

Often, the federal agents would be examining files or reading interrogation transcripts and a call would come through their Kenyan intelligence service liaison officer that "they had a hot lead." The agents would suit up, grab their submachine guns and assault rifles, and storm the targeted house or place of business—almost as if they were executing a high-threat arrest warrant in Newark, not Nairobi. Razor, with years of experience operating overseas, knew that the American agents could not operate in-country as if they were working in their backyard. "We don't want to be the only blondes in this land of brunettes," the always outspoken Piry warned his colleagues. "This isn't our country."[23]

In one raid, in the slums of Nairobi where the police refused to go, a Kevlar-clad force of FBI and DSS special agents, all armed to the teeth, stormed a shantytown apartment after receiving a lead concerning a possible suspect in the bombing. As the agents searched the building and gathered boxes of evidence, an army of angry neighborhood residents assembled on the street below. "We were supposed to be there for ten minutes, but instead ended up being there for eight hours," Piry recalled. "We had nearly 4,000 people, all residents of the neighborhood, waiting to get a piece of us. All we had were ten federal agents hoping to hold them back."[24]

After three weeks in Kenya, Piry was assigned to escort Mohammed Sadiq Odeh back to New York, where he would be indicted for murder. The FBI had flown Mohammed Rashid Daoud al-Owhali back to New York two days earlier, but Razor was adamant that there be a DSS representative onboard the aircraft. "These were our buildings which were hit and our people killed," he told one of the FBI supervisors.

The flight from Nairobi to Stewart Air Force Base near Newburgh, New York, with a stop in Cairo, took nearly sixteen hours. Odeh sat silently for much of the flight, eating very little and sleeping on a mattress on the floor of the U.S. Air Force C-17 transport aircraft. Piry's role was pretty much to man a fire watch—and to make sure that the suspect "didn't die in his sleep."

The hulking C-17 landed at the base in the dead of a warm and muggy night. Some 100 FBI agents surrounded the aircraft, including members of the HRT. Odeh was whisked to New York City in a government helicopter for processing and arraignment. Piry, who hadn't slept in four days and hadn't changed his clothes in twice that time, was left alone at the base gate, forced to find his own way back seventy miles to New York City's La Guardia Airport and a shuttle flight to D.C.

IN DAR ES SALAAM, OFFICIAL U.S. GOVERNMENT RELIEF ASSISTANCE CAME late as well, though the effort was again a massive one. Aircraft after aircraft landed at local airfields, bring in medical supplies and additional security teams. FAST teams, combat ready and armed with anti-tank rockets and M60 7.62mm light machine guns, were sent in for sixty-day deployments.

A large deployment of FBI agents also arrived in-country, along with additional DSS special agents. The Tanzanian police officials DiCarlo met after the blast, and the Tanzanian intelligence service contacts he subsequently forged, were shocked that terrorists had managed to shatter the tranquil calm of their nation. Local officials were quick to blame people on the island of Zanzibar, where there had been a strong fundamentalist Muslim movement growing in size for years, but the bombing was an act far too sophisticated for local militants.

When the FBI team and additional DSS agents arrived in Dar es Salaam, DiCarlo arranged a meeting between all the U.S. agents and their Tanzanian counterparts. The objective of the meeting was simple: If the two nations didn't work together, side by side, the perpetrators of the crime would disappear into the landscape and beyond the frontiers. So, asking each federal agent to stand up and introduce himself,

DiCarlo paired each U.S. investigator with a Tanzanian. "EOD guys were put together with Tanzanian bomb techs," DiCarlo recalled. "SWAT guys were teamed with the local SWAT guys."

The investigation into the terrorist cells operating in Dar es Salaam moved slowly, however, much of it hampered by infighting among teams of FBI agents dispatched to Africa to investigate the bombing. Initially, as in many of the major crimes committed against the United States by bin Laden's operation, the New York field office assumed a vanguard role in the investigation. But because the FBI's Washington field office had already opened a case against bin Laden in D.C., they wanted the lead role in the investigation. Washington won. When the FBI New York office turned over all their evidence to their counterparts from Washington, it was in a haphazard, almost spiteful manner.[25] FBI agents from the Washington field office arrived in Africa and started reinterviewing witnesses, further delaying any tangible leads into the investigation. To complicate matters even more, the case against the embassy bombers would be back in New York, in U.S. federal court in lower Manhattan.

The embassy's Emergency Action Plan, the one designed to provide written standard operating procedures for all calamities from natural disasters to terrorist attacks, listed the DCM's residence as the "temporary embassy." Another diplomat's house, one with enough setback to deter the wrath of a truck bomb, was soon volunteered for use as a temporary embassy. DiCarlo, along with his MSGs, built ad hoc road obstacles of rebar and fifty-gallon drums to close off the street and protect the location. A four-man MSD team also traveled to Dar es Salaam to assess other U.S. sites in the capital, as well as to bolster security around the embassy compound. The Tanzanian authorities volunteered a platoon of combat soldiers to assist in the security efforts.

Osama bin Laden never released a videotape interview with al-Jazeera TV claiming credit for the embassy bombings, but most in America's intelligence and law enforcement community were convinced that al-Qaeda had perpetrated the attacks. President Clinton was outraged by the Africa bombings, but the response fell far short of a declaration of war against Osama bin Laden and transnational terrorism. On August 20, 1998, U.S. Navy warships launched some eighty warheads, delivered by Tomahawk III Land Attack cruise missiles at al-Qaeda targets in Afghanistan and Sudan. The targets in Afghanistan were training camps where, according to the confession of Mohammed Rashid Daoud al-Owhali, he had trained to perpetrate hijackings and bombings. The target in Khartoum, the el Shifa Pharmaceutical Industries Co., was a bin Laden–owned facility believed by U.S. intelligence to have been involved in the production of chemical weapons agents, including precursor chemicals for deadly nerve agents.

Military officials—and, indeed, many in law enforcement—viewed the strikes merely as symbolic.

U.S. LAW ENFORCEMENT EVENTUALLY SEIZED THIRTEEN OF THE TWENTY-two men indicted for the Africa embassy bombings. Those indicted included Osama bin Laden, Mohammed Atef, Dr. Ayman al-Zawahiri and Fazul Abdullah Mohammed, the man believed to be the commander responsible for executing the bombings.

Shortly after the embassy bombings and the U.S. retaliatory strikes against the Sudan factory and al-Qaeda training camps in Afghanistan, PII's Rewards for Justice Program unveiled a series of reward posters for the man who was now, undoubtedly, the world's most wanted terrorist fugitive. The poster, which featured the upper torso of Osama bin Laden clutching an AK-74 5.45mm assault rifle, was the subject of much debate inside the upper echelons of the State Department. Was it politically incorrect? Did it focus too much on the Arab garb and not on the man? Ultimately, the poster offered a five-million-dollar reward for bin Laden. The hope inside the workstations at PII was simple: By raising the bounty to $5 million, maybe someone in Afghanistan would be willing to turn in bin Laden.

If the African bombings proved anything to the men and women tasked with investigating the crimes and relentlessly pursuing those responsible, it was that al-Qaeda was far more insidious than the face of one man. It was now a global organization that presented a clear and present danger to the national security of the United States. It was also far more sophisticated—and, ominously, far more visionary—than any other terrorist apparatus ever encountered.

Most DSS agents hoped that Osama bin Laden would follow in the footsteps of his most trusted lieutenant and emissary, Ramzi Yousef, and become too cocky and arrogant for his own good. They hoped that someone clutching a matchbook with bin Laden's face or a pamphlet featuring word about the five-million-dollar reward would simply walk into an embassy in Islamabad, Tashkent, Cairo, or even Beirut, and give up the millionaire turned global terror chieftain.

But DSS agents, especially those who had survived the embassy blasts and had witnessed the carnage on emergency TDYs, were realists. Living in places like Beirut, Baghdad, Cairo, Khartoum, and Karachi, hunkered down on embassy cots, living inside the crosshairs, had that effect on federal agents who were far from home and gone for far too long from their families. While they hoped that the State Department would, indeed, be paying out on its five-million-dollar reward to the person responsible for bringing bin Laden to justice, they realized that it was only a matter of time until his network would strike again.

But where would the attack be? When would it come down? How did an Osama bin Laden outdo the carnage achieved in Africa that warm August morning?

Chapter 8

OUTSIDE THE BOX

The two American embassies bombed in Africa signaled a critical escalation of Osama bin Laden's war against the United States. The subsequent cruise missile attacks, in conjunction with the indictment and Rewards for Justice wanted poster, personalized the conflict. The name Osama bin Laden was used to personify the counterterrorist campaign much in the same way that Saddam Hussein had been personalized as enemy number one during the Gulf War.

The escalation and personalization of the often bloody and always messy campaign against terrorists posed risks, and there were certainly going to be victims—many more victims—in the struggle between bin Laden and the United States. U.S. intelligence agencies, as well as federal law enforcement, were convinced that Osama bin Laden would play this transnational game of chess with bloody glee. And, many feared, the victims would continue to be diplomatic outposts around the world and, possibly, the secretary of state.

The embassy bombings began a new chapter in the history of the Diplomatic Security Service. The service grew from some 900 agents to nearly 1,200. More new agents, some days out of training, found themselves on transatlantic flights, reading Lonely Planet guides to African and Asian hotspots where one was likely to contract such wonderful maladies as schistosomiasis, giardiasis, typhoid, malaria, hepatitis A and B, and the State Department favorite—amoebic dysentery. The workload was exhaustive. Special agents in field offices were pulled off criminal cases to travel all over the world on TDY assignments. Protection details swelled. Much of the additional workload, both inside the United States and overseas, fell into the lap of MSD. The Mobile Security Division was a tactical group trained for combat like Special Forces operators. MSD was tasked with teaching basic survival skills to embassy staff in America's 200-plus diplomatic posts overseas as well as with providing tactical support to high-threat protective details and to embassies overseas faced with potential attack.

Not only did the changing landscape of terrorism require that embassies be transformed into fortresses, but that embassy employees—from cultural attachés to Foreign Service nationals—be trained to withstand and survive terrorist attacks. In 1985, DSS Director Dave Fields assigned Al Bigler, following his injuries in the East Beirut embassy annex bombing, to spearhead this new division within the DSS.

"In those early years," Special Agent Scot Folensbee remembered, "DS was looking for people with military backgrounds and teaching skills for this up-and-coming entity within the service. We went out to embassies around the world and trained the Americans and Foreign Service nationals in everything from personal protection, driving, and shooting to hostage survival and surveillance detection."[1]

The Mobile Security Division is made up of eleven four-man teams. Each month, one MSD team is designated on stand-by status for emergency response within twenty-four hours to any place in the world where specific tactical assistance is required. MSD teams have been deployed on emergency-response assignments in western Africa and the Middle East and, of course, in August 1998, following the bombings of the American embassies in Nairobi and Dar es Salaam. These rotational stand-by teams are also deployed if the secretary of state needs to travel to a high-threat location in pursuit of an immediate diplomatic objective. A second team of MSD agents is also on call to be available for deployment with their weaponry, life-saving equipment, Weapons of Mass Destruction kit, and vehicles, within seventy-two hours.

Whether serving on the protective detail for PLO Chairman Yasir Arafat in New York City, or outside the U.S. embassy in Sierra Leone, special agents assigned to MSD needed to be flexible. "Anyone in MSD," Scot Folensbee reflected, "had to be able to think *outside* the box! If a plan didn't work, you had to be able to come up with one that did!"

But inside the close-knit MSD teams, "outside the box" had another definition. It meant courage and sacrifice; it was the DSS term often associated with going above and beyond the call of duty. It was used to describe agents walking enthusiastically into the killing zone without hesitation. It meant rushing to an embassy under fire in a place like Freetown, in Sierra Leone, where two MSD agents rode shotgun for water truck deliveries supplying the post, past stoned teenagers with AK-47s, and rebels literally cutting out the hearts of their enemies and eating them within view of Post One. Outside the box meant working in a country like Algeria, where entire villages, in one night of orgasmic butchery, would disappear in an orgy of throats slit and wombs removed. The special world of MSD was a cruel and dangerous place. Yemen was at the crossroads of this world. It was certifiably outside the box.

YEMEN, A NATION BLESSED BY ITS PERSIAN GULF GEOGRAPHY YET CURSED by a lack of petroleum resources, was a safe haven for Osama bin Laden and the al-Qaeda movement. Bin Laden's family was originally from the village of al-Rubat, in rugged Hadhrami province, where clan rule was the only law. Tribal affiliations in Yemen, split for years between north and south, were far more important than government edicts from the capital. For bin Laden, the image of a Yemeni mountain man suited his propaganda videos well. He was often seen in traditional Hadhrami dress, the gold *shabariya* curved dagger tucked snugly into the six-foot-three man's waistband. The tribal image evoked tradition. It made the wealthy bin Laden appear like a native Robin Hood—one who could be protected by the Yemeni wasteland version of Sherwood Forest.

The desolate mountains of Yemen, an arid purgatory where a man could be closer to his God, provided an ideal setting for bin Laden to capture the awe of the tribesmen he sought to recruit. In a pinch, the tribesmen also provided him with sanctuary. Tribal leaders in the mountains north of the capital tolerated the surge of Islamic fundamentalism that bootlegged audiocassettes of Sheikh Omar Abdel Rahman ignited and that were fueled and fed by Osama bin Laden's anti-American videotape sermons from the plush villas of Khartoum and later the cave hideouts of Afghanistan. Tribal leaders from rugged Hadhrami province were bound by duty and honor to protect the fugitive terrorist chieftain with their lives.[2]

Yemen bordered bin Laden's Saudi homeland—making it an obvious choice as a base of operations for a terrorist campaign to topple the Saudi monarchy once and for all—and it provided his legions with a safe base of operations from which to launch strikes against American forces still stationed in Saudi Arabia, as well as Americans in Bahrain and other Persian Gulf nations. Following the August 7, 1998, bombings of the U.S. embassies in Nairobi and Dar es Salaam, there were even rumors that bin Laden had left his Taliban-protected sanctuary in Afghanistan, where U.S. cruise missiles had zeroed in on many of his training camps, for the rugged and far less inviting mountains of Yemen.[3]

Yemen was in any case an important transit point for bin Laden's international operations. The port city of Aden was a traditional hub for smugglers, spies, and terrorists, and it was used by al-Qaeda as a major command and control center for bin Laden's contacts with the outside world, a particularly important link between Egypt and Afghanistan. Aden was the transit link for most of the Afghan Arabs going to or returning from the war in Afghanistan. The fighters stayed inside Aden's guesthouses and hostels, bought guns from Aden's legendary gunsmiths, and frequented the city's notorious brothels. Aden, for the Afghan Arabs, was like Bangkok for American soldiers in Vietnam. It was a place for R-and-R, and a place where one boarded a plane or a boat for the next jump of a journey.

The al-Qaeda Egyptians, led by Dr. Ayman al-Zawahiri, recruited the local Yemeni Islamic groups as potential allies and foot soldiers. The Yemenis were not as organized or coordinated in their rage and operations as their Egyptian mentors or their Saudi benefactor. The Yemeni groups were heavily armed but loose-knit gangs just as interested in spreading the fundamentalist message as they were in trafficking in kidnapped foreigners and hashish.

But the fundamentalist groups, primarily the Islah party, or Islamic Reform party, had been spurred into action after the end of the Gulf War, when Aden became a port of call for U.S. warships and a way station for U.S. peacekeepers heading to Somalia to serve in the international missions to the famine-stricken country. The Islamic Reform party, led by the gun-wielding firebrand Sheikh Abdul Mejid a-Zindani, served bin Laden as a recruiter for fighters needed for the Afghan struggle. Over 7,000 of his recruits sailed from Aden to Karachi, for the long bus ride north toward Peshawar and the holy war against the Soviets. Many of those veterans, now bored with their normal lives of extortion and smuggling, were again willing recruits, now to bin Laden's call to arms against the United States.

Another fundamentalist Islamic group active in the Yemeni landscape was the pro–al-Qaeda Army of Aden-Abyan. The group specialized in the kidnapping of Westerners traveling in Yemen, primarily British and Australian tourists. Venomously anti-American and anti-British, it included hundreds of veterans of the Afghan Arabs.

Yemen also served as a safe haven for operatives in bin Laden's global network seeking refuge while on the run, or as a training base before they were dispatched for missions in Africa, the Middle East, and North America. According to several intelligence reports, Chechen and Dagestani militants passed through the mountains of southern Yemen before traveling to Saudi Arabia, Jordan, and points beyond.[4] Algerians, Bosnians, and Kosovo Albanians were also rumored to have used Yemen as a transit camp for travel to and from Afghanistan. Filipino authorities are convinced that Abu Sayyaf Group operatives hung their hats in Yemen, honing their kidnapping skills with the world's most accomplished hostage-takers.

IN 1999, U.S. LAW ENFORCEMENT WAS NOT LOOKING AT YEMEN AS A likely location for Osama bin Laden's next attack against the United States. The millennium celebrations, along with fears of the Y2K computer glitch crippling American and international business and government, prompted the CIA and the FBI to focus their energies on the domestic threat in the United States—fears that were only exacerbated by the arrest of Ahmed Ressam in Port Angeles, Washington, in December 1999 en route to carry out a bombing operation at Los Angeles International Airport (LAX). Ressam's car was full of RDX, a high-grade military explosive, and four Ramzi Yousef–style Casio watches fashioned as home-made detonators. Other Algerians, with connections to Osama bin Laden, were arrested in Canada. The plot to blow up one of the terminals at LAX, an operation that might have killed hundreds, was averted simply—and luckily—by a hardcore terrorist, trained in the bin Laden camps of Afghanistan, losing his nerve at a border checkpoint.

In December 1999, the Jordanian General Intelligence Department and the Public Security Directorate arrested thirteen al-Qaeda operatives plotting to carry out a series of attacks against sites on Jordanian territory frequented by Israeli and American tourists. One of those arrested in Amman, Raed Hijazi, a Palestinian with an American passport, was a taxi driver from Boston.[5]

In January 2000, shortly after the Jordanian millennium plots, al-Qaeda operatives planned to launch a suicide attack against a U.S. Navy warship, the U.S.S. *The Sullivans*, as it was moored in Aden. The al-Qaeda suicide squad was to ram a small boat crammed with explosives into the U.S.S. *The Sullivans* at the waterline, sinking the Arleigh Burke–class guided-missile destroyer to the bottom of the port, and killing most of those onboard. But fate and poor planning intervened. As the U.S. warship took on fuel in the oil-slicked waters of Aden's port, two al-Qaeda operatives set out from a remote pier in their explosive-laden craft. But the terrorists overloaded the small boat with hundreds of pounds of high explosives packed in metal cylinders. The boat quickly sank into the deepwater port, and the two terrorists drowned. Osama bin Laden and his al-Qaeda specialists might have missed their chance to sink the destroyer, but that was of little concern to them.[6] They were patient. In the attempt to shore up his nation's sagging and primitive economy, President Ali Abdullah Saleh had agreed to let U.S. military assets refuel and stage out of Yemen. Al-

Qaeda knew that another warship would soon be entering the warm waters of Aden.

THE EASTERLY WINDS WERE A WELCOME AND SOOTHING RELIEF FOR THOSE on deck of the U.S. Navy's Aegis-Class destroyer the U.S.S. *Cole* that warm morning on October 12, 2000. The *Cole*, a guided-missile destroyer en route to the northern Arabian Gulf to join a 5th Fleet battle group on a maritime interdiction mission, had pulled into Aden, Yemen's one-time Mecca of Arab radicalism and Eastern-bloc espionage, for a brief refueling stint. Aden was not a favorite port of call for 5th Fleet sailors; the ancient port town was considered too dangerous for American sailors on shore leave. Bahrain was the place where sailors got drunk and partied with Filipino and Egyptian hookers—not any port of call in Yemen, whose national industry was kidnapping and extortion. The *Cole* was slated to be in Aden for no more than six hours on the morning of October 12. She was to take on fuel and head back to the open sea. Aden was a bustling port, and ships of every size and description channeled through the oil-stained, shimmering waters either returning from the Horn of Africa or heading out to the Indian Ocean. The small skiff sailing close to the *Cole*, piloted by two Arab men in traditional Yemeni garb, sparked little suspicion from guards posted on deck. It was all so routine, so very much part and parcel of the landscape that was Aden. When the skiff erupted into a fireball alongside the ship, it blew a forty-by-forty-five-foot hole in the *Cole*'s side. Seventeen sailors were killed in the suicide-bombing attack, and scores more were critically wounded. According to eyewitness accounts, the two suicide bombers stood at attention just before they detonated the charge alongside the ship's hull.

The two bombers, allegedly born in Saudi Arabia but with family ties to the Yemeni province of Hadhrami, were veterans of bin Laden's Afghan Arab legion. According to the Yemeni interior minister, one of the bombers had been arrested for plotting a terrorist attack in Yemen in 1999, shortly after he returned from a visit to Afghanistan.

Suicide seaborne attacks were something new in the terrorist repertoire—and of great concern to the U.S. Navy and federal law enforcement investigators. Both Yasir Arafat's Fatah, as well as the Popular Front for the Liberation of Palestine General Command, had toyed with explosive boats, though they were to be remote-controlled devices as opposed to the suicidal craft turned into kamikaze torpedoes. Hezbollah, as well, had designed several fiberglass fishing craft to be used for suicidal attacks, though Israeli Navy ships had managed to repel and destroy these boats before they could strike their targeted missile craft. But the use of these innocuous small boats, of which thousands existed throughout the Persian Gulf and the Middle East, was troubling. Were there other ships that al-Qaeda was targeting?

THE ATTACK WAS INNOVATIVE AND WELL-PLANNED, THOUGH LESS SOPHIS-ticated and less synchronized than the twin strike in East Africa a year before. Yet for those in the know, the FBI investigators, DSS special agents from Protective Intelligence Investigations, and intelligence operatives wearing their unassuming khakis at the crime scene in Aden, the careful planning of the attack and the sheer artistry of the explosive charge pointed away from bin Laden and the caves of Afghanistan and toward other familiar territory. The bomb that tore a hole through the U.S.S. *Cole* was a cone-shaped charge of Semtex that created a high-speed, high-temperature blast wave that exploded in two almost simultaneous stages—the first created a vacuum by forcing all the air out of a target with mighty force, and the second stage rushed air and fire back in with lethal devastation. That type of bomb, a masterpiece of destructive design, was a trademark of Hezbollah, prompting many investigators to fear that a working relationship had at last been forged between al-Qaeda and Hezbollah.

Both the CIA and the FBI came close to capturing Imad Mughniyah, the thirty-eight-year-old commander of Hezbollah's Special Security Apparatus, at the beginning of the Lebanese Party of God's initial contacts with al-Qaeda. On April 7, 1995, U.S. intelligence, law enforcement, and military special operations assets attempted to intercept Mughniyah in Saudi Arabia. Mughniyah had been on a chartered Middle East Airlines flight from Khartoum to Beirut, after attending a conference of international Islamic terrorist chiefs in the Sudanese capital that included a high-level delegation from al-Qaeda. The A-310 Airbus was to stop in Saudi Arabia for a quick refueling before completing the flight to Beirut. The Saudi authorities, worried about potential repercussions stemming from their support of an American counterterrorist operation, refused to assist in Mughniyah's arrest. As American federal agents and CIA agents readied their weapons and body armor for an assault on the aircraft, Saudi air traffic control refused the Middle East Airlines jet permission to land in the kingdom. For the CIA agents on the scene, many of whom were eager to bring to justice the man who had personally tortured Beirut station chief William Buckley, Mughniyah's escape was viewed as a lost chance to bring one of the world's foremost terrorists to justice.

As al-Qaeda's importance and influence expanded throughout the Middle East and Muslim world, Mughniyah displayed an increasing interest in maintaining contacts between Hezbollah and bin Laden. Intelligence reports indicated that Mughniyah had acted as liaison between Iranian intelligence, Hezbollah, and the Chechen rebels, supported by al-Qaeda, who were battling Russian forces. The fact that Mughniyah, a Shiite, would make overtures toward al-Qaeda, a Sunni entity, was not surprising. Years earlier in Lebanon, Mughniyah, a Lebanese national, had endeared himself into the ranks of the PLO and Yasir Arafat's elite Force 17 bodyguard unit.

The strengthened link between Hezbollah, Mughniyah, and al-Qaeda was troubling to many in Washington, D.C.

On October 20, 2000, eight days following the bombing of the U.S.S. *Cole*, Sergeant Ali Mohamed, an Egyptian-born volunteer from the ranks of the U.S. Army's Special Forces, confessed in federal court in Manhattan that he and senior bin Laden operatives met with Mughniyah to discuss operational procedures and joint missions between Hezbollah and al-Qaeda. Sergeant Mohamed pled guilty to participating in the 1998 bombings of the U.S. embassies in Kenya and Tanzania. "This probably means that Iran may be cooperating with bin Laden's network and using Hezbollah as the middleman and operations support staff," offered one Israeli special operations officer who has spent years tracking Mughniyah down. "A merger between bin Laden and Mughniyah is like Coke and Pepsi joining forces."[7]

OFFICIAL WASHINGTON WAS QUICK TO CONDEMN THE LATEST AL-QAEDA attack. In Norfolk, Virginia, six days after the attack, President Clinton addressed a memorial service for the sailors killed that morning in Aden. "To those who attacked them, we say: you will not find a safe harbor," President Clinton warned. "We will find you, and justice will prevail." Unlike the embassy bombings in Africa, however, fusillades of cruise missiles were not launched against Yemen, nor were they fired at targets inside Afghanistan this time.

Under the provisions of the Omnibus Diplomatic Anti-Terrorist Act of 1986, investigating the bombing of the U.S.S. *Cole* was, initially, a DSS operation. The directive authorizes DSS to protect executive branch and other personnel overseas as directed by the secretary of state. Within thirty hours of the attack, Special Agent Steve Gleason, deputy director of Overseas Operations/Near-East Asia, was in Aden with a team of ten other DSS agents. Initially, their role was "All Force Protection." The DSS contingent arrived when the *Cole* was still listing from the damage incurred by the hollow charge; the dead were still being recovered and removed. At a heavily protected pier, surrounded by Yemeni special forces and a force of 150 FAST U.S. Marines in full battle kit, helicopters were ferrying the wounded to medical facilities for emergency care. "That was probably one of the scarier things that I had ever done," Gleason recalled. "We really thought that we were going to get hit again."[8]

The initial DSS postblast mission to Yemen was for thirty days. It would eventually continue for nearly two years. The FBI dispatched some 160 investigators to Yemen to try and seek out those responsible for the attack. Obtaining information in Yemen was, in the politically incorrect words of one federal agent sent there, "fucking impossible." Because there was only two weeks advance notice of the *Cole* refueling in Aden, the bombers had very short notice to plan their attack and infiltrate the harbor at the appropriate time. U.S. investigators were convinced that the attack required the help of local harbor workers, and perhaps even government officials. In public statements, the Yemeni government strongly condemned the attack on the *Cole* and actively engaged in investigative efforts to find the perpetrators, but their cooperation with U.S. law enforcement was distant and very limiting. The bombing was an embarrassment to the Yemeni government, and to the *Muchabarat*, or security service. The Yemenis were adamant about controlling the investigation.

Yemeni security officials also wanted to keep U.S. investigators away from groups like Hamas and the Palestinian Islamic Jihad, groups with legal offices in Sana'a and Aden, because of America's close-knit intelligence alliance with Israel's Mossad.

By December 2000, Yemeni authorities had arrested six primary suspects—all veterans of the Afghan Arab force that had battled the Soviets. The suspects, logistics coordinators to supply the various terrorist cells operating in Aden, were low-level operatives, not the operational planners the U.S. had hoped to apprehend; they had only circumstantial links to Osama bin Laden. But in October 2001, Jamil Qasim Saed Mohammed, a Yemeni microbiology student studying at Karachi University, and alleged to be a serious al-Qaeda asset, was arrested by Pakistan's ISI in connection with the bombing of the *Cole* and handed over, under great secrecy, to U.S. authorities.

THE DSS ROLE IN THE *COLE* INVESTIGATION WAS TWO-SIDED. THE RSO's office, along with special agents serving in PII and the Washington field office, joined their counterparts in the FBI in combing through files, gathering forensic evidence, and, when allowed, interviewing actual informants and suspects. According to the Department of Justice, which controlled the overall operation in Yemen, DSS special agents were in Yemen to protect and assist the FBI in its investigation. On the ground in Sana'a, and in Aden, in the souk and in neighborhoods where little children played with real Russian-built Tokorov pistols, the DSS task was to protect them.

The DSS was in Yemen, in force, because intelligence indicated that another attack in the country against a U.S. target was imminent, and the embassy in Sana'a was an obvious target. Two U.S. embassies had been attacked in Africa two years earlier; two other embassies had been destroyed in Lebanon fifteen years before that. Another possible target in Yemen was U.S. Ambassador Barbara K. Bodine. Ambassador Bodine was an attractive six-foot-tall woman from Missouri representing the United States in a part of the world where women were not permitted to hold positions of power. Ambassador Bodine often towered over the Yemeni government officials she met in the president's office and the foreign ministry, and she was outspoken. A veteran Middle East hand in the Foreign Service, Bodine had served in Iraq, and she was awarded the Secretary of State's Award for Valor for her work in occupied Kuwait.

In June 2001, intelligence reports concerning a possible al-Qaeda operation against the embassy were viewed in Washington, D.C., as evidence of a clear and present danger to the post.[9] The threat was considered imminent following the arrest in Sana'a of fifteen al-Qaeda sympathizers who were in possession of hand grenades, machine guns, bomb-making equipment, and maps of the U.S. embassy and the surrounding buildings.

The Mobile Security Division missions to Yemen were threefold. First and foremost, the special agents, trained by U.S. military special operations units, were to bolster the embassy's already formidable defenses, whether it was to add punch to Ambassador Bodine's motorcade, or to sit atop the embassy after dark with night-vision glasses in case a truck bomb breached the gate and a full-scale assault was mounted. The rotating tours of MSD agents were also summoned to help safeguard the evacuation of the ongoing FBI investigatory team, still piecing together evidence from the *Cole*. Yemen had become too dangerous by June for the federal agents, and they needed to be brought out safely. And one of MSD's missions in Yemen was to teach the Yemeni police to execute search warrants in places where they thought *Cole* suspects might be hiding; shortly after the *Cole* bombing, nearly forty Yemeni special forces commandos were killed in a botched raid against an al-Qaeda hideout east of Sana'a.

The Mobile Security Division's work in Yemen was exhausting, dangerous, and proof of just how hard it was to apprehend terrorist suspects in nations where laws were replaced by tribal mind-sets. MSD had come to Yemen prepared for war, but first blood was never drawn. Was their continuing presence in the summer of 2001 an overt statement of tactical resolve, viewed as deterrence? Was the peace in Sana'a merely a deceptive ruse meant to lull an alerted foe into a false sense of complacency? If Yemen wasn't the target, the special agents wondered nervously to themselves and then to one another, *Where would the next strike take place?*

On the way back to Washington, D.C., at the end of their rotating tour, as the special agents slinked back into their coach-class seats, relieved to be making eye contact with European stewardesses wandering the aisles with beverage trays full of beer, they realized that terrorists could not be defeated, let alone apprehended, in places like Yemen using traditional law enforcement techniques. If terrorism was going to be eradicated, and attacks like the bombing of the U.S.S. *Cole* averted, it would require a massive national effort. It would require a full-fledged war.

Postscript

SAME PRECINCT, NEW WORLD

To the West, and particularly the United States, the term "holy war" was redefined on September 11, 2001. In a meticulously devised operation, involving sleeper cells, trained pilots, and years of intelligence-gathering and intensive planning in a global effort, Osama bin Laden's al-Qaeda network triumphed where it had only marginally succeeded in New York City in 1993—it brought the jihad truly to the heart of the United States. Each element of the operation, the worst terrorist attack in history, was planned avoiding the mistakes of previous al-Qaeda strikes and emphasizing the elements that had worked well before.

Ramzi Yousef had, in several well-planned operations in New York City and Asia, hoped to kill well over a quarter million Americans in calculations designed to determine the maximum yield in carnage. But Yousef, for all his slick charm and murderous intent, failed to realize his vision. Mohammed Atta, the coldhearted Egyptian disciple of al-Qaeda's grand plan, was more successful. In the end, though, thanks to emergency evacuation plans put into practice at the World Trade Center following the 1993 bombing, tens of thousands of lives were saved.

Yousef had failed to appreciate the structural strengths of the buildings when he positioned the Ryder van. Atta had failed to appreciate that the buildings, on the first day of public school and a New York

City primary election to determine the candidates in the mayoral race, would not be filled to capacity by 9:00 A.M. Osama bin Laden, Mohammed Atef, and Dr. Ayman al-Zawahiri could never have imagined the courage of the officers from the New York City Police Department's Emergency Service Unit, the Port Authority Police, and the Fire Department of New York. These emergency personnel, many of whom had worked the first World Trade Center attack, put the safety of innocent civilians before their own, marching, without hesitation, up smoke-filled steps into the eye of an enveloping firestorm to save as many lives as they could, in many cases sacrificing their own.

THE HIGHLY COORDINATED TERRORIST ATTACKS TOOK LAW ENFORCEMENT, especially the federal agencies, completely by surprise. Special agents inside the DSS New York field office in lower Manhattan, only blocks away from ground zero, were preparing for the hectic dignitary-protection details for the opening session of the United Nations General Assembly that September morning. They weren't preparing for war.

In Washington, D.C., Special Agent Bruce Tully, in charge of the sprawling DSS Washington field office, was driving to work at 8:47 A.M. when word of the first aircraft slamming into the north tower of the World Trade Center interrupted the morning drive time radio. Until September 11, Tully, an old-timer by DSS standards, with twenty-six years on the job, thought that he had seen and done everything in the organization—from baby-sitting a KGB officer in New York City when he was a mere forty-eight hours out of training, to serving on the secretary's detail and TDYs to South America and the Middle East. Tully had experienced the pressure and responsibility of overseas assignments while serving as RSO in Jakarta, Indonesia. He'd experienced the tactical edge required to repel terrorist attacks while serving as the deputy chief of the Mobile Security Division, and he'd experienced the need to stay calm in a crisis while serving as Secretary of State Albright's SAC during the bombings of the embassies in East Africa. Tully had intended to use his time as head of the field office to shape the next generation of DSS special agents. The field office, a talent pool for new agents learning the job, was involved in numerous and extensive passport and visa fraud investigations. A few of Tully's new agents were heading overseas for the first time.

Tully went to great lengths to ready his young force of new agents for the dangers of the street. He personally reviewed tactical plans for arrests, signing off only on plans that were safe and sensible. Special agents worked in pairs or in foursomes or more. They always wore bulletproof vests. They carried heavy firepower with them. Local law enforcement was always brought into the mix for backup. *How do I prepare my agents for this?* Tully thought as he pulled into the field office the morning of September 11. *How do I ready my people for war?*[1] He ordered his young special agents to fuel up their G-rides, or government cars, assemble their Kevlar body armor and weaponry, check the batteries on their radios and cell phones, and pack their Ready Alert Action Kits. Most importantly, he told those in the field office to call home. "Tell your parents, your wives, husbands, and children that you are okay," Tully ordered the young special agents scurrying about the office, "and tell them you don't know when you'll be coming home. We don't know how long this will last and what will be asked of us."

For Walt Deering, the special agent in charge of Protective Intelligence Investigations, life had already been on a war footing even before the black smoke billowing from the Pentagon could be seen from his window. PII was gearing up for UNGA-56 and the endless reams of top-secret paperwork and material connected to threats surrounding the 150-plus world leaders and foreign ministers due to arrive in New York City.

Early on the morning of September, 11, 2001, Deering boarded a flight at Washington, D.C.'s Reagan International Airport destined for Chicago. Deering was headed to the Windy City to meet with high-ranking FBI officials to coordinate the assignment of DSS agents to the Chicago Joint Terrorism Task Force. His flight lifted off over the Potomac, straddling the Capitol building, just as the four doomed airliners were about to be hijacked. As Deering's aircraft headed north and then west, the first hijacked aircraft were slicing through a parallel course east, on flight paths toward New York City.

For the next two days, Deering ran PII from mobile phones as he tried to make his way back to Washington, D.C.

Protective Intelligence Investigations assumed a vanguard role in coordinating much of the joint federal investigations seeking evidence on the nineteen hijackers who launched the suicidal attacks, as well as those sleeper agents still out in the cold. Because so much intelligence was coming in from RSOs overseas to the special agents assigned to PII, the office was inundated with leads, and possible connections between known al-Qaeda operatives overseas and their contacts who might possibly be in the United States. And, because PII handled the Rewards for Justice program, the office became a clearinghouse for information and tips, including tens of thousands of possible sightings of Osama bin Laden and the al-Qaeda hierarchy. A twenty-five-million-dollar reward was placed on the head of Osama bin Laden and other al-Qaeda leaders—the largest payment in the history of criminal justice.

PII agents joined President George W. Bush, Attorney General John Ashcroft, and others when the twenty-two most wanted terrorists were named and prices offered for information leading to their arrest or capture. The Diplomatic Security Service was intimate with all of the names on the list. The twenty-two had earned infamy by blowing up U.S. embassies in Beirut, Nairobi, and Dar es Salaam, hijacking airliners and seizing hostages in Lebanon, blowing up airmen and sailors in Yemen and Saudi Arabia, and for the deaths of 3,000 Americans in New York City, Washington, D.C., and Pennsylvania.

ON A COLD AND BLUSTERY NIGHT IN NOVEMBER 1990, THE TELLTALE signs of a dark and tenacious enemy declaring war on the United States were revealed in the muzzle flash of an assassin's gun. Unlike other wars that erupt with a massive surprise attack, or with a formal declaration of hostilities, this one began with a rabbi's murder and the belief that the United States was immune from terrorist attack. The terrorists masqueraded as immigrants and refugees, and attempted to expose America's vulnerability by manipulating its freedoms and religious tolerance. The terrorists had planned to kill scores more than were murdered on September 11. Ramzi Yousef invested careful calculations in the hope that 250,000 people could be slaughtered on the streets of lower Manhattan. Thousands more were to be killed in a technological coup in the air high above the Pacific Ocean. When such grandiose schemes failed, the terrorists resorted to an old strategy. They struck at diverse and desolate American targets around the world—a barracks, a pair of embassies, and a warship—in the attempt to wither away American resolve through a war of homicidal attrition. The strategy failed.

September 11 was a last gasp by the terrorists to wither away a nation's resolve. Again, the strategy failed. The images of the collapsing Twin Towers and of the burning outer shell of the Pentagon mobilized a nation to action, and shocked a complacent world to join in. Afghanistan was the first target in a well-publicized American-led campaign to rid the world of terrorists and those determined to commit acts of mass murder to promote a religious or political agenda. It will not be the last. Terrorists rarely emerge from their bunkers and caves to fight a powerful conventional army head on. Terrorists cower and conceal themselves in desolate safe havens through elaborate disguises. It is the nature of their business.

This war against terrorism will continue to other nations and other regions around the world. It is a war that both the military and law enforcement must fight. It will be a long and bloody struggle.

It is unlikely that terrorism will ever be completely eradicated. Terrorists flourished long before Osama bin Laden became a household name, and they are likely to flourish once al-Qaeda is rendered insignificant. After all, if the bombing of the federal building in Oklahoma City proved anything, it was that one individual, determined to express rage or a political position through a murderous vision, can kill hundreds.

For terrorism to be rendered insignificant, however, those sworn to protect and serve the United States will need to remain vigilant and be given the support and resources they need. Terrorists like Osama bin Laden, El Sayyid Nosair, and Ramzi Yousef have proven that money, passports, and transcontinental flights have turned this planet into one borderless—and vulnerable—target of opportunity.

Special agents like Bill Miller and Jeff Riner—and the men and women of the Diplomatic Security Service—have proven to the terrorists just how very small a place this world can be.

Acknowledgments

All I remembered was how cold it was that night in February. I certainly wasn't dressed for it. Luckily, the Kevlar body armor I was wearing was providing a bit of badly needed warmth as I stood outside 26 Federal Plaza, surrounded by an NYPD Emergency Service Unit counterassault team and FBI agents waving 12-gauge shotguns. The evening wasn't supposed to be so eventful, but as it turned out, it would be a night that would change my life.

It all started innocently enough. I was writing notes and taking photographs for an illustrated book on the NYPD's Emergency Service Unit, and I was ready for pin jobs, perp searches, and rescues. It was a Wednesday afternoon when I began riding with Lieutenant Bob Sobocienski, an NYPD hero and my "rabbi in the department and ESU," and the shift, a four-to-twelve, was promising to be an eventful one. There was a perp search through the rat-infested darkness of an abandoned tenement in Harlem, and there was a narcotics warrant to serve in the Bronx. Then the call came. There would be a division assignment later that night in downtown Manhattan to secure a prisoner, a VIP of sorts, who the feds were bringing back from Pakistan. "Pakistan?" Lieutenant Sobocienski looked at me with a confused stare. "Who is so dangerous that he had to be brought back from Pakistan?"

Like any high-threat operation, there was a field briefing and a tac meeting with senior police and FBI officials to discuss tactical re-

283

sponses to any threats on the motorcade. The discussions were held at the helicopter landing pad on the East River just off the FDR Drive. There was a terrific wind bouncing off the river that night, plummeting the wind-chill temperature to well below zero. The wind hit my face with unforgiving force that night, and as I looked up toward the West Side at the Twin Towers of the World Trade Center shimmering in their glow of yellow and white light, I wondered what the wind must sound like on the 101st floor? As I looked at the buildings, I wondered how amateurish were the bozos who tried to destroy the towers. They looked invulnerable that night, standing defiantly in thirty-mile-per-hour gusts. How naïve was I thinking that those two symbols of New York and of America were indestructible?

No sooner did I glance at the buildings then Lieutenant Sobocienski ran back to his red Chevrolet Caprice, excited and awestruck. The prisoner coming in from Pakistan that night was Ramzi Yousef, the mastermind who had hoped to topple the Twin Towers into an orgy of destruction and death. Lieutenant Sobocienski had worked the bomb scene along with the rest of the Emergency Service Unit and seen the devastation firsthand. Tonight, for ESU at least, this would be sweet justice.

As I fumbled trying to get into my heavy Kevlar assault vest for the brief motorcade that would ferry Yousef from the heliport to the bowels of 26 Federal Plaza, where he would be processed before a night at the Manhattan Corrections Center, I realized that I was the first "civilian" in New York and the United States to know of Yousef's capture. I really hoped to get a glimpse of him.

At about 10:00 P.M., as NYPD choppers circled lower Manhattan searching for snipers, and NYPD Harbor Unit boats scanned the frigid river for any signs of trouble, the S-70 chopper carrying Yousef from an air force base in upstate New York landed. Nearly a dozen ESU officers, ready for a firefight with machine guns and assault rifles, covered the convoy of vehicles that would travel a dozen or so blocks toward the Federal Building. The motorcade moved quickly through the abandoned streets. Would Yousef's cohorts try and kill him before he could spill the beans to the authorities? Would they try and free him?

I stood outside 26 Federal Plaza in the subzero freeze for nearly three hours that night. My legs trembled and my fingers were raw, but I was fueled by adrenaline and pride. This was government at its best, and the FBI agents standing outside the building, fingers caressing the triggers of their 12-gauge shotguns, were proud to proclaim how "the FBI captured Ramzi!"

I had never heard of the Diplomatic Security Service that night in February 1995. I had never heard of the Su Casa Guesthouse, or of UNGA, or of follow cars. All I knew was that I had witnessed history.

ANOTHER NIGHT THAT WOULD CHANGE MY LIFE HAPPENED A YEAR LATER— almost to the day—after Ramzi Yousef was returned to New York City to face justice. I was laboring through a chapter on a second book on the NYPD's Emergency Service Unit, trying to put on paper the remarkable and unbelievable exploits of Truck Two in Harlem, and, especially, a chapter on the midnight tour. As I checked my word count, reviewed my notes, and wondered who would believe what I had witnessed, the phone rang.

"What'y'a'doing?" the voice resonated in a heavy Long Island accent. It was Police Officer Vinny Martinez, who made sure that everyone who knew him addressed him by his nickname of "Termite." "I'm busy writing my chapters on my last few ride alongs with you," I said, hoping that he would relent—just this one time—and get off the phone. "Listen, I'm calling from the Waldorf, and when you are done with the ESU book, you *have* to write one on DS!"

"D-Who?" I asked, not having an idea as to what he was talking about and wondering how long this phone call to nowhere would take. "Why would I want to write a book about the Department of Sanitation?"

"DS as in Diplomatic Security!" he scolded me. "Listen, I am just off a detail, and I met some of them and was talking to the guys. They are amazing. You can't imagine what they do and where they serve. There are hundreds of them here at the Waldorf. I got a contact for you. Call him. Good-bye!"

Vinny wasn't Waldorf kind of people, and I was more interested in some of his other cop stories from the hotel—especially the one about the cops mistaking the potpourri in the lobby for potato chips—than I was about this "State Department outfit." Vinny was a great many things, but most of all he was a great cop who knew where the action was. If Vinny recommended looking into this law enforcement agency, it was wise to follow his advice.

I never knew that the State Department had a legion of armed federal agents in its order of battle, and I never knew that they were based overseas, in embassies around the world, or that they protected dignitaries in this country and conducted criminal investigations into passport and visa fraud. Most importantly, I had no clue that they were the ones who had seized Ramzi Yousef in Pakistan.

I called Vinny's contact, a special agent named Tom Gallagher who, with his Cleveland accent and unique sense of humor, managed to spark my interest about the service with tales of travel, terrorists, and dignitary protection. The phone call lasted two hours; my involvement with DSS will soon surpass six years. Shortly after my conversation with Tom Gallagher, I was on the phone with DSS public affairs director Andy Laine. The rest is history.

In the six years that I have been privileged to work with DSS and see them up close and personal, I have been witness to a great many things. I've sat in motorcades for kings, foreign ministers, secretaries of state, and even, on four occasions, Yasir Arafat. I have been inside the nerve center of the UNGA command post coordinating some fifty protective details at once, and I've been inside the U.S. embassy in Cairo during a REACT drill with the marine security guards. I've traveled with DSS to Europe and the Middle East and seen them in action in New York, Washington, and Los Angeles. I've spoken to special agents who have survived the cannibalistic reality of Sierra Leone and Liberia, as well as those mistaken for dead inside the bombed-out shell of an embassy in Beirut.

I have written a number of articles on the organization that have been translated into nearly a dozen languages. I created two documentaries on DSS for cable television, and even a series of action figures (long story . . .). This book, I hope, is not a culmination of my time with the service but a stepping stone for another six years' worth of projects. The years covering DSS have been great and truly rewarding. They are the greatest group of men and women to be found anywhere in law enforcement and beyond.

THERE ARE MANY DRAWBACKS TO WRITING PROFESSIONALLY — ESPECIALLY writing freelance. It is one hell of a way to earn a living, and there are always headaches. There are high-strung editors to deal with, ulcer-inducing TV producers to placate, and magazine accountants always swearing that the check "is *really* in the mail." But doing what I do for a living puts me in the position to see things that most people only see in a James Bond film, and to meet people who make James Bond seem like a nerd. Knowing these great men and women is the true reward of what I do for a living.

This book would have never happened without the friendship, guidance, good laughs, and support of Tom Gallagher. One of the best special agents DSS will ever boast, Tommy is a dedicated and incredibly intense professional who gets the job done. I wouldn't want anyone else protecting my life, and I wouldn't want anyone else bursting through the door of some Third World hellhole if I was in trouble. Tommy provided me with my first glimpse into the world of the Diplomatic Security Service, and the journey is still racing along at full speed. He is one of those lucky souls who works for an organization he loves—even with its bureaucracy and occasional bullshit—and is proud to represent.

And speaking of unique characters who have inspired me to write this book, Special Agent Craig "Curly" Siebert is a mountain among men—literally. You have never really experienced life until you have had Guinness, on tap, in a bar in Jerusalem with Curly. You have never laughed so hard in your life until you have heard Curly's motorcade stories about the secretary of state, or of his jungle adventures in Ethiopia, tribal dress and all. And you have never truly learned about balls and dedication until you hear about Curly protecting an ambassador in the mortar-shell thunderstorms of war-torn Sarajevo.

Finally, I would like to offer a very special thanks to Don Morris, DSS retired. There isn't enough that can be said about Don, or that hasn't been said already. If Tom Gallagher was my first glimpse into the world that is DSS, Don Morris was my first earful. I had the great fortune to sit next to then Special Agent Don Morris in a follow car protecting the Cuban foreign minister during a mini-UNGA in New York City some four years ago—it was one of the most memorable experiences I ever had and one of the most educational. Listening to Don Morris spin his tales of DSS travel and service, from Europe to Asia to Africa and the Middle East (a lot of stories about Israel . . .), I felt honored to be invited into a world that I never knew existed. Don was a great teacher about DSS, and one of the best agents they'll ever have.

Very special thanks also go to "Razor." Special Agent Fred Piry was, at first, reluctant to open up to this stranger with a camera who was asking too many questions—in Razor's neck of the woods, *he* asked the questions. But Razor has been to more trouble spots around the world than a legion of UN relief workers, and he has defined sacrifice, dedication, and courage.

I would like also to offer special thanks to Special Agent Walt Deering. Walt, a veteran of some of the most difficult posts in the Middle East and one of the busiest field offices in the United States, was kind enough to take me under his wing very early on in my writing on DSS, and he was generous with his time and friendship in showing me the ropes.

I am lucky to have gotten to know and to see in action several hundred of the 1,200 special agents who currently sport the gold shield and diplomatic passport. They have treated me remarkably well. I would like to thank Assistant Secretary of State for Diplomatic Security David Carpenter for his kind assistance and support, and I would especially like offer my gratitude to DSS Director Peter Bergin. Director Bergin was most kind and helpful in cutting through the sometimes inescapable red tape, and he never minded the endless faxes and e-mails brought to his attention concerning "more" proposals involving DSS. I would also like to thank Special Agent Bob Franks, Special Agent Stan Joseph, Special Agent Larry Hartnett, Special Agent Fred Krug, Special Agent Bernard Johnson, and especially Special Agent Bruce Tully.

I would, of course, like to thank the DSS special agents who were
kind enough to speak with me, entertain me with their tales, and look
after me in embassies around the world and in more follow cars than
I can remember. I would like to offer special thanks to Special Agents
Jeff Riner and Bill Miller, two heroes who are as humble and suppor-
tive as they come. I would also like to thank Special Agent Mark Hipp
for his serving as guide into the world of MSD, Special Agent Dale
"Chip" McElhattan for looking after me in a part of the world where
people need looking after, Special Agent Scott Gallo for looking after
me in Cairo, and Special Agent Liz McAleen—one terrific cop, and a
calming influence inside a follow car filled with "characters." I would
also like to thank Pat O'Hanlon, Special Agents Al Bigler, John
DiCarlo, Paul Peterson, Scot Folensbee, Pat Donovon, Dave Schnor-
bus, Mike Valle, Ryan Christenson, Mike Evanoff, Nelson Yang, Jeff
Breed, and, of course, Tony Diebler. You really have never experienced
life unless you've been on an Arafat detail with Tony . . .

I would also like to offer my special thanks to Fred Burton and Scott
Stewart.

I would like to offer my true gratitude to DSS spokesman Andy
Laine for his assistance throughout the many and varied projects. And
I would like to thank Darlene Kirk, in DSS public affairs, for her
assistance and invaluable help.

Last but not least on the "federal side," I would like to thank Special
Agent Vincent O. Martinez III. After seeing what DSS was all about,
Police Officer Vincent O. Martinez, one of New York's Finest from
Emergency Service Unit Truck Two, left the five boroughs of the Big
Apple for the global stage. The world hasn't been the same since . . .

I WOULD ALSO LIKE TO THANK MY AGENT, AL ZUCKERMAN FROM WRITER'S
House, for his support, diplomatic skills (worthy of the most accomplished Foreign Service negotiators), vision, and friendship. I would
also like to offer a special thanks to Steve Hartov, one of the most
talented espionage fiction writers I know, and a great friend who can
always be counted on to watch my back during the many angst-ridden
crises in publishing. I would also like to thank my close friend Deputy

Inspector (Ret.) Ralph Pascullo for his expertise, advice, and friendship. Ralph is one of the most decorated Housing cops in that department's history, and he rose through the ranks from walking a vertical beat in some of the toughest projects of New York City to serving as executive officer of the NYPD's Special Operations Division, writing policy for counterterrorism responses, and protecting popes and presidents. Ralph is a great teacher about what it is to be a cop, and what it is to be a true friend and role model. I would also like to thank Lieutenant Robert Dwyer and Police Officer Mike McCormack, Jersey City Police Department Emergency Service Unit, for their expertise and assistance. I would also like to thank my friend former NYPD Commissioner Bernard B. Kerik, his chief of staff, John Picciano, Jr., and his deputy commissioner for public information, Tom Antenen.

Of course, with any book of this nature, there are a great many people who should be thanked, but because of what they do and where they serve, will have to be shown appreciation anonymously.

FINALLY, AND ALWAYS MOST IMPORTANTLY, I WOULD LIKE TO THANK MY wife, Sigi, for her patience, tolerance, understanding, and love. The pressure that surrounded completing this book on time, on a deadline postmarked by the 9–11 attack on America, was intense. It wasn't easy for my wife or children to live with a nonperson for three months of twenty-hour days, exhaustion, and angst. Most wives would have packed their bags and left. I am sure that the thought crossed Sigi's mind once or twice. But she stood by me and supported me with kindness and love. And, for this and so many happy years together, I will always be grateful.

Notes

Prologue: **SPECIAL AGENTS**
1. Benjamin C. Runner, "DS Officer's Lament," *U.S. Department of State Bureau of Diplomatic Security Update*, November–December 1997, p. 10.

Introduction: **BADGES WITHOUT BORDERS AGAINST AN ENEMY WITHOUT FRONTIERS**
1. Interview, Tom Gallagher, October 28, 2001.
2. Ibid.

Chapter 1: **SIGNPOSTS ALONG THE ROAD**
1. Interview, Pat O'Hanlon, November 5, 2001.
2. Simon Reeve, *The New Jackals: Ramzi Yousef, Osama bin Laden and the Future of Terrorism* (Boston: Northeastern University Press, 1999), p. 142.
3. John Miller, "Greetings, America. My Name Is Osama bin Laden. Now That I Have Your Attention . . . ," *Esquire*, February 1999, p. 101.
4. "Jihad in America." PBS, 1997.
5. Mary Anne Weaver, *A Portrait of Egypt: A Journey Through the World of Militant Islam* (New York: Farrar, Straus and Giroux, 1999), p. 90.

6. Chris Hedges, "Muslim Militants Share Afghan Link," *The New York Times*, March 28, 1993, p. 14.

7. Interview, Jordanian intelligence officer, Zarqa, Jordan, August 25, 2000.

8. Interview, Jersey City police officer, Emergency Service Unit, New York, November 18, 2001.

Chapter 2: **"THE TRAVELER"**

1. Bruce Crumley, "Bolting the Door," *Newsweek*, November 12, 2001, p. 77.

2. Interview, DSS special agent, November 2, 2001.

3. Brian Duffy, "The Long Arm of the Law," *U.S. News & World Report*, February 20, 1995, p. 50.

4. David B. Ottaway, "Retracing the Steps of a Terror Suspect: Accused Bomb Builder Tied to Many Plots," *The Washington Post*, June 5, 1995, p. A1.

5. Simon Reeve, "From a Student Bar in Swansea," *Maxim UK*, April 2000, p. 78.

6. Reeve, *The New Jackals*, p. 120.

7. Interview, NYPD lieutenant, New York City, January 4, 2002.

8. Interview, Scott Stewart, November 2, 2001.

9. Reeve, *The New Jackals*, p. 144.

10. Ibid., p. 146.

11. Greg B. Smith, "Yousef Eyed Gassing WTC, Feds Say," *New York Daily News*, September 9, 1996, p. 16.

12. Interview, Fred Burton, November 2, 2001.

13. Interview, Jordanian intelligence officer, Amman, August 24, 2000.

14. Interview, Scott Stewart, November 2, 2001.

15. Ibid.

16. Interview, Pat O'Hanlon, November 5, 2001.

17. Interview, Amman, August 24, 2000.

18. Susan Schinerette, "On the Trail of Killers," *People*, September 22, 1997, p. 139

Chapter 3: **AMBASSADOR OF THE APOCALYPSE**

1. Cesar A. Majul, "The Iranian Revolution and the Muslims in the Philippines," in John L. Esposito (ed.), *The Iranian Revolution: Its*

Global Impact (Miami: Florida International University Press, 1990), pp. 262–63.

2. Interview, Filipino intelligence officer, November 8, 2001.
3. Ottaway, "Retracing the Steps of a Terror Suspect," p. A1.
4. Ibid.
5. Interview, Israeli intelligence officer, Tel Aviv, November 24, 2001.
6. Doug Struck, Howard Schneider, Karl Vick, and Peter Baker, "Borderless Terror Network," *The Washington Post*, September 22, 2001, p. A3.
7. Interview, Filipino intelligence officer, November 8, 2001.
8. Ottaway, "Retracing the Steps of a Terror Suspect," p. A1.
9. Reeve, *The New Jackals*, p. 79.
10. Ibid.
11. Interview, Colonel (Ret.) Ed Gatumbato, October 20, 2001.
12. Interview, DSS Special Agent, October 21, 2001.
13. Interview, Ed Gatumbato, October 20, 2001.
14. Struck et al., "Borderless Terror Network," p. A3.
15. Ibid.
16. Russell Watson, "Cracking the Conspiracy," *Newsweek*, February 20, 1995, p. 38.
17. Ibid.
18. Interview, DSS Special Agent Dale McElhattan, August 24, 2001.
19. Interview, Filipino airport security officer, November 8, 2001.
20. Ibid.
21. William Branigin, "Manila Reports Threat Timed to Visit: Arrest of Two Terror Suspects Reported on Eve of Pope's Arrival," *The Washington Post*, January 12, 1995, p. A20.
22. Ibid.
23. Interview, DSS Special Agent Fred Piry, Washington, D.C., August 2, 2001.

Chapter 4: **"THE STANS"**
1. Interview, DSS Special Agent Jeff Riner, July 26, 2001.
2. Ibid.
3. Ibid.

4. John McCarrey, "The Promise of Pakistan," *National Geographic*, Vol. 192, No. 4, October 1997, p. 59.

5. Interview, U.S. Marine Corps officer (Ret.), July 31, 2001.

6. Robert D. Kaplan, "The Lawless Frontier," *Atlantic Monthly*, September 2000, p. 75.

7. Interview, DSS Special Agent Bill Miller, September 30, 2001.

8. Ibid.

9. Interview, Don Morris, New York City, January 4, 2002.

10. Interview, Jeff Riner, July 26, 2001.

11. Interview, Bill Miller, September 30, 2001.

12. Interview, Jeff Riner, July 26, 2001.

13. Kaplan, "The Lawless Frontier," p. 73.

14. Interview, DSS special agent (Ret.), New York City, December 20, 2001.

15. Interview, DSS special agent, August 20, 2001.

16. Interview, DSS special agent (Ret.), New York City, December 20, 2001.

17. Kaplan, "The Lawless Frontier," p. 74.

18. B. Raman, "Pakistan's Inter-Services Intelligence," *South Asia Analysis Group*, January 8, 2001, Paper 287, p. 5.

19. Kaplan, "The Lawless Frontier," p. 77.

20. Interview, DSS special agent (Ret.), December 20, 2001.

Chapter 5: **TRUE REWARDS**

1. Interview, Jeff Riner, July 27, 2001.

2. Courtesy, *DEA Public Affairs Bulletin*.

3. Interview, Jeff Riner, July 26, 2001.

4. Interview, Jeff Riner, July 27, 2001.

5. Interview, Bill Miller, September 30, 2001.

6. Interview, Jeff Riner, July 29, 2001.

7. Interview, Bill Miller, September 30, 2001.

8. Ibid.

9. Interview, Jeff Riner, July 27, 2001.

10. Interview, Fred Burton November 2, 2001.

11. Ibid.

12. David Ignatius, "Bugged at the State Department," *The Washington Post*, December 22, 1999, p. A33.

13. Interview, DSS Special Agent (Ret.) Scott Stewart, November 2, 2001.

14. Interview, DSS special agent, Washington, D.C., November 3, 2000.

15. Interview, Fred Burton, November 2, 2001.

16. Interview, Jeff Riner, Washington, D.C., August 1, 2001.

17. Interview, Bill Miller, September 30, 2001.

18. Ibid.

19. Ibid.

20. Ibid.

21. Interview, Scott Stewart, November 2, 2001.

22. Interview, Bill Miller, September 30, 2001.

23. Interview, Jeff Riner, July 26, 2001.

24. Interview, Fred Burton, November 2, 2001.

25. Ibid.

26. Interview, DSS special agent (Ret.), November 3, 2001.

Chapter 6: **PAYBACK**

1. Interview, Special Agent Bill Miller, September 30, 2001.

2. Ibid.

3. On December 30, 1995, Filipino police arrested a nine-man al-Qaeda cell in a series of raids that resulted in confiscated weapons and explosives. The men arrested included Iraqis, Saudis, Sudanese, and Pakistanis. One man, however, who intrigued authorities more than the others was Adel Anonn. Anonn, the owner of a tourist-district butcher shop, was known by a confidential informant to have used several aliases as well as a number of Iraqi passports. Most significantly, he was believed to be Ramzi Yousef's twin brother.

4. U.S. Government, *International Crime Control Strategy* (Washington, D.C., 1988), p. 82.

5. Interview, Special Agent Fred Piry, August 2, 2001.

6. "Pakistan Hunts for Gunmen Who Killed 2 Americans," *The New York Times*, March 9, 1995, p. A6.

7. Interview, Fred Piry, August 2, 2001.

8. Interview, Jeff Riner, July 27, 2001.

9. Interview, U.S. federal agent, New York City, November 10, 2001.

10. Rebecca Grant, "Khobar Towers," *Air Force Magazine*, Vol. 81, No. 6., June 1998, p. 32.

11. Interview, Fred Piry, August 1, 2001.

12. Ibid.

13. Ibid.

14. Patricia Hurtado, "Apostle of Evil," *Newsday*, January 9, 1998, p. A3.

Chapter 7: **OUTPOSTS**

1. Interview, Special Agent Al Bigler, November 8, 2001.

2. Robin Wright, *Sacred Rage: The Wrath of Militant Islam* (New York: Touchstone Books, 1986), p. 16.

3. John K. Cooley, *Payback: America's Long War in the Middle East* (McLean, Va.: Brassey's, 1991), p. 111.

4. Interview, Al Bigler, November 8, 2001.

5. Interview, Israeli special operations officer (Ret.), Jerusalem, August 22, 2001.

6. Interview, Egyptian security officer, Cairo, June 23, 2000.

7. Interview, DSS Special Agent Paul Peterson, October 14, 2001.

8. Ibid.

9. Douglas Waller, "Inside the Hunt for Osama," *Time*, December 21, 1998, p. 27.

10. James C. McKinley, Jr., "Security Flaws Left Nairobi Embassy Open to Attack," *The New York Times*, September 9, 1998, p. A5.

11. Ibid.

12. Interview, Paul Peterson, October 14, 2001.

13. Interview, DSS Special Agent John DiCarlo, October 20, 2001.

14. Ibid.

15. John E. Lange, "Dar es Salaam—Confronting the Crisis," *State*, October 1998, p. 21.

16. Interview, John DiCarlo, October 20, 2001.

17. Ibid.

18. Ibid.

19. Interview, Paul Peterson, October 14, 2001.

20. Interview, Fred Piry, August 2, 2001.

21. Ibid.

22. Interview, Paul Peterson, Washington, D.C., October 14, 2001.

23. Interview, Fred Piry, August 2, 2001.

24. Ibid.

25. Interview, John DiCarlo, October 20, 2001.

Chapter 8: **OUTSIDE THE BOX**

1. Interview, DSS Special Agent Scot Folensbee, Washington, D.C., October 23, 2001.

2. John F. Burns, "Remote Yemen May Be Key to Terrorist's Past and Future," *The New York Times*, November 5, 2000, p. A5.

3. *London Al-Quds al-'Arabi*, March 9, 1998—see www.ict.org.il.

4. CNN, October 15, 2000—see www.ict.org.il.

5. Judith Miller, "Dissecting a Terror Plot from Boston to Amman," *The New York Times*, January 15, 2001, p. 15.

6. Judith Miller, "Holy Warriors: Killing for the Glory of God in a Land Far from Home," *The New York Times*, January 16, 2001.

7. Interview, Israel Defense Forces military intelligence officer, Tel Aviv, August 29, 2001.

8. Interview, DSS Special Agent Steve Gleason, December 10, 2001.

9. Audrey Gillan, "Near Miss for US Mission in Yemen," *The Guardian*, June 19, 2001, p. 3.

Postscript: **SAME PRECINCT, DIFFERENT WORLD**

1. Interview, Special Agent Bruce Tully, December 10, 2001.

About the Author

Samuel M. Katz has written more than twenty books and over a hundred articles on Middle East security issues, international terrorism, and police and military special operations. His articles have appeared in *Playboy*, *Esquire*, and *Jane's Intelligence Review*. He is editor in chief of *Special Ops*, a journal dedicated to profiles of military and law enforcement special operations units worldwide, and has created documentaries on this topic for the Discovery Channel, A&E, and The Learning Channel. Samuel M. Katz also lectures law enforcement agencies around the country on tactics, counterterrorism, and the history of terrorism.